The Complete

IDIOT'S

Guide to

Multimedia

by David Haskin

alpha
books

A Division of Macmillan Computer Publishing
201 W. 103rd Street, Indianapolis, Indiana 46290 USA

To my mother-in-law, Gerry Schmit, for her love and support.

©1994 Alpha Books

International Standard Book Number: 1-56761-505-8

Library of Congress Catalog Card Number: 94-71684

96 95 94   8 7 6 5 4 3 2 1

Interpretation of the printing code: the rightmost number of the first series of numbers is the year of the book's printing; the rightmost number of the second series of numbers is the number of the book's printing. For example, a printing code of 94-1 shows that the first printing of the book occurred in 1994.

Printed in the United States of America

Publisher
Marie Butler-Knight

Managing Editor
Elizabeth Keaffaber

Acquisitions Manager
Barry Pruett

Product Development Manager
Faithe Wempen

Development Editor
Kelly Oliver

Production Editor
Michelle Shaw

Copy Editor
San Dee Phillips

Cover Designer
Scott Cook

Designer
Barbara Webster

Indexer
Johnna Van Hoose

Production Team
*Gary Adair, Dan Caparo, Brad Chinn, Kim Cofer, Lisa Daugherty,
Jennifer Eberhardt, Beth Rago, Bobbi Satterfield, Carol Stamile,
Karen Walsh, Robert Wolf*

*Special thanks to Wayne Blankenbeckler for ensuring
the technical accuracy of this book.*

Contents at a Glance

This page unintentionally left blank.

Contents

ZEN TEXT

Introduction

I love bicycles and in my mind, there's a direct line from bicycles to multimedia. About twelve years ago, I bought my first "good" bike for the then-princely sum of $400. I used my new bike for longer rides and kept my old bike for bombing around town.

Unfortunately, riding two bicycles meant repairing two bicycles and when it came to bicycle repair, I felt like an idiot. Yet, I simply couldn't continue to afford paying others to maintain two heavily used bikes. Finally, during one long winter I made this leap of logic: People create bicycles. I was a person. Ergo, I could learn to repair bicycles.

So I bought a few bicycle repair books and over the course of the winter completely disassembled and, amazingly enough, reassembled both my bikes. Of course, I made some mistakes (ball bearings lost that winter still show up in the corners of the basement), but even so, I realized I didn't have to feel like an idiot about bicycle repair if I didn't want to.

By coincidence, this also was the dawn of the PC age. Emboldened by my success at bike repair, I turned my attention to computers—and promptly felt like an idiot again. I continued to feel like an idiot until I employed my own special version of Idiot's Liberation, like I had done with bicycle repair.

Using computers often makes many people feel like idiots. This is particularly true when we are bombarded with buzzwords, such as *multimedia*, but we don't quite know what those words mean.

That's where this book comes in. You know you're not an idiot, and I know you're not an idiot. However, let's face it, we've both felt like idiots, whether the subject is bicycles or multimedia.

This book is meant to help you understand multimedia. It will help you get your PC ready for multimedia and discuss why (and whether) you need multimedia. It also teaches multimedia basics, such as navigating through multimedia applications, and even some of the basics about creating your own simple multimedia applications.

All things considered, I think this Idiot's Liberation Movement is growing. And that's a good thing.

Who Should Read This Book?

Other books about multimedia assume you are a computer expert. This book assumes that you have other things to do with your life—such as riding your bicycle—than learning how to use computers and multimedia.

About all this book assumes is that you already know how to start your PC and how to start and navigate Windows. Beyond that, you don't have to know anything else about computers to read this book.

How Do I Use This Book?

While undoubtedly a great work of literature, this book isn't a novel, so you don't have to start at the beginning and keep reading until the end. Instead, this book is designed so you can find what you need quickly, and then get on with your life.

When you have a question about something, look it up in the table of contents or the index, go to the referenced pages, and learn what you need to know.

I'll try to make descriptions and instructions clear. I'll also provide special types of information that you can find by looking for visual clues. Those special types of information are:

Provides more detailed descriptions of technical issues, should you want to learn them.

Simple definitions of computer jargon so, if you want, you can show off at parties.

Tips that streamline how to do specific tasks.

Warnings about what can
go wrong and help getting
yourself out of it when it
does go wrong.

The Least You Need To Know

Sums up all the main points in each chapter. If you read only
this section at the end of each chapter, you will know
enough to show others you're a computer geek.

Acknowledgments

As always, this book simply would not be possible without the love,
support, and patience of my wife, Mary, and the still-at-home kids, Sam
and Elisabeth.

Many thanks to the superb crew at Alpha. They proved to me again that
professionalism and having a good time are not mutually exclusive. And
extra special thanks to Robert Waring, John Barillo, and Barry Pruett for
spending long hours putting together the CD-ROM in the back of the book.

Trademarks

All trademarks are the property of their respective owners. If you owned a
trademark, you (and especially your attorneys) would want that fact
acknowledged, right? All terms mentioned in this book that are known to
be or are suspected of being trademarks or service marks have been appropriately capitalized. Alpha Books cannot attest to the accuracy of this
information, however.

**What are you looking at this page
for? Can't you see it's blank?**

Part I
Getting Down to Multimedia Basics

It happens all the time: You hear about something exciting and you just have to have it. You have to have it so bad it hurts. The problem is, you don't know what "it" is.

For many people, multimedia is one of those things. But before you go off half-cocked, you should know what you're getting into. That's what Part I does: it describes multimedia and what you can use it for.

Chapter 1

The Top Ten Things You Need to Know About Multimedia

If you're the type of person who says things like, "Bottom line me, baby!" this chapter is for you. This chapter's also for you if you'd like to say things like that but are too embarrassed. Here's the bottom line: the top ten things you need to know about multimedia before you dive in.

1. **Have no fear!** You already know more about multimedia than you realize. In the simplest sense, multimedia is merely the mixing together of more than one medium. (A medium is a method of transmitting information.) That being the case, you've used multimedia your entire life. Newspapers and magazines have text and pictures; that's multimedia. If you've used the on-line help system in virtually any Windows application, like your word processor, that's a simple form of electronic multimedia.

    Multimedia is a buzzword, and like all buzzwords, it can scare the uninitiated. The truth is, you've been initiated into this world and you didn't even know it! So there's no reason to be scared.

2. **Multimedia is addictive.** Once you get into using multimedia applications, you won't want to switch back to old-fashioned applications, particularly for learning and some forms of entertainment. That's because multimedia (or at least well-designed multimedia) not only is instructive, but it also involves the user and should be intuitively easy to use. That combination spoils you quickly for less engaging methods of transmitting information.

3. **You (and your kids) learn better when you're entertained.** We all have memories of struggling to stay awake while a teacher bludgeoned us to death with facts. Here's a simple fact about many multimedia applications: You learn better when you are involved and entertained. This holds true for more than just *educational* multimedia applications, such as encyclopedias. It also holds true for most other types of multimedia, including multimedia business presentations. With multimedia, we soak in more information with less effort. Multimedia often enables you to choose what you learn and the pace at which you learn, so that you have more control over the learning process.

4. **You can find multimedia for virtually every type of need.** There are thousands of commercial multimedia titles currently available and more titles become available every day. The titles cover all conceivable subjects ranging from early learning for children to learning new languages, sales presentations, and even, um, adult topics. At this writing, there are hundreds of small companies creating commercial multimedia applications and even the huge companies, such as Microsoft, are into it in a big way. Also, you can create your own simple multimedia presentations.

5. **There are some things that multimedia doesn't do well.** Multimedia isn't a replacement medium for familiar things, such as books. It's a different medium. That means it does many things well, but it doesn't do *everything* well. A well-designed multimedia educational, reference, or entertainment disc is more compelling and easier to use than more traditional counterparts. A multimedia encyclopedia, for example, teaches by showing videos and animations, and playing sounds. However, so far, I haven't seen a multimedia version of a novel that makes me want to give up my wonderfully well-worn position on the sofa where I spend hours entranced with good fiction.

6. **While simple to use, sophisticated multimedia can be difficult to create.** Creating basic multimedia presentations is simple. However, creating large, complex multimedia applications is as much an art as a science. It requires the appropriate use of the right media at the right time and a solid grasp of *human engineering* issues that make using multimedia simple.

7. **You won't enjoy installing multimedia hardware and software.** Getting multimedia to work with PCs requires the installation of a conglomeration of hardware and software that must function smoothly together. That's often not easy. If you can buy a PC already outfitted for multimedia, you'll save yourself a lot of grief and probably won't spend much more money than if you do it yourself. If you can afford to have somebody install multimedia for you, go for it.

8. **Multimedia power is increasing and price is quickly decreasing.** Perhaps we take it for granted, but we live in a golden age of high-tech. Every week, it seems, you can buy more high-tech capabilities for less money. That certainly is true for multimedia hardware and software.

   There is a downside, however. With technology moving forward so quickly, the stuff you buy today—particularly the hardware and software needed to make multimedia function—will be out of date distressingly soon. The cutting edge equipment of today most assuredly won't be cutting edge in a year or two.

   That doesn't mean you should either wait or replace your equipment every year or two. It does mean you should make hardware and software purchases with your eyes open. Sometimes, it pays to spend a bit more (if you can swing it) to buy hardware that can run the more sophisticated applications that will come out in the near future.

9. **Multimedia isn't just a "young-guy thing."** Rather, there's something for everybody in multimedia. It doesn't matter whether you are a man or a woman, young or old, green, gold, or some shade in between. There are many commercially available multimedia titles, such as encyclopedias, health-related titles, and travel titles, that are of interest to a broad range of individuals.

10. **Multimedia may be a paradigm shift, but who cares?** You hear a lot of loose talk about the new age of multimedia and how multimedia is *converging* with the information superhighway. That makes multimedia a focal part of an important *paradigm shift*, or a fundamental shift in the way we operate as a species.

Hey, I like a good paradigm shift as much as the next guy, but for purposes of this book, let's leave those theoretical discussions to others. I do know this, however: Multimedia is quickly becoming a fact of life that can improve our knowledge base and provide great amounts of entertainment. This book is about how to get multimedia into your life and what to do with it.

Chapter 2
Now That You Mention It, What Is Multimedia?

In This Chapter

- ☞ Multimedia defined
- ☞ A description of the parts of multimedia
- ☞ Different types of multimedia applications
- ☞ Interacting with multimedia

Remember "Where's the beef?" How about "Achy Breaky Heart"? We live in a world that adores here-today-gone-tomorrow buzz phrases and public in-jokes. *Multimedia* is another of those buzzwords that flies off everybody's tongues.

Let's be honest: Most of us know just enough about these high-tech buzzwords to respond with a pat, well-rehearsed sentence when the subject comes up at a party. Then we set off to find the guacamole before our ignorance shows.

This chapter describes the elements that make up multimedia. This is an important service because it will help you prevent making a fool of your-self at your next party if you accidentally find one of the few people who actually knows what multimedia is.

Putting the *Multi* in Multimedia

Media   Refers to the method used to deliver information. Media is plural; medium is the singular form. Types of media described in this book include text, video, still images, sound, and animation.

Interactive multimedia Lets you communicate with the application or presentation to get the specific information you want, or to take a specific path through a body of information. A simple example is a multimedia training program that asks you to click your mouse on one of several buttons, each of which takes you to a different topic.

If you're clever, the key to understanding multimedia is right in front of your face. *Multi* means many. *Media* means, well, more than one medium. It is the method of presenting information, like sound or video. Get it?

In its simplest form, multimedia is a computer-based application or presentation that combines two or more of the following items:

- Text
- Recorded sound and music
- Still images
- Video
- Animation

Multimedia can be as simple as adding sound capabilities to your PC to enhance the fun when you play computer games. It can be static, kind of like an on-screen newspaper: You look at it, and that's that. But the best modern multimedia is *interactive*. No, interactive doesn't mean taking a multimedia presentation to a party where it can meet new friends and make small talk.

The result of mixing different media into interactive applications is very powerful. For example, say you use an interactive encyclopedia to learn more about jazz. A good interactive encyclopedia doesn't just describe jazz with words, it also lets you choose whether to hear audio clips of different types of jazz. It also might include buttons that you click on with your mouse that lead to biographies of leading jazz musicians. Sound excellent? It is!

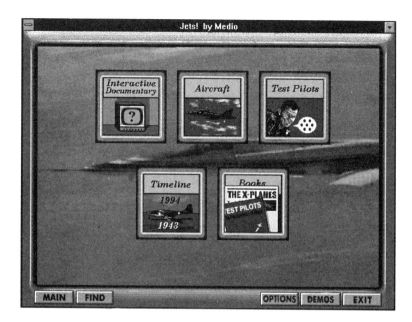

Click on a button to learn more.

Let's take a quick run through the specific elements of multimedia to give you a greater understanding. After finishing the next few sections, you should have enough conversational ammo to send everybody scurrying to the guacamole! Remember, though, we're just beginning. Later chapters tell you more about the elements of multimedia and how they work together.

Say It with Words

You might think that in this high tech age we don't need words anymore. However, written words, also known as *text*, are the glue that holds together many multimedia presentations.

What multimedia has succeeded in doing is reducing our reliance on text. Instead of using a thousand tedious words to describe something, you can use just a few words to introduce a video or still picture showing that item in action. (Hmm— there's a cliché there somewhere, something about what a picture's worth. . . .)

An example is a multimedia training presentation about common life-saving techniques. In the old days, you read a paper document with the token odd illustration or two. With a multimedia training presentation, you might see an on-screen button with accompanying text that says: "Click on this button with your mouse to see a video that teaches you how to save a life with the Heimlich Maneuver."

In this case, the text merely sets up another medium that teaches you more effectively than words alone. The following figure shows a multimedia application in which text is an equal partner to other media, in this case an image.

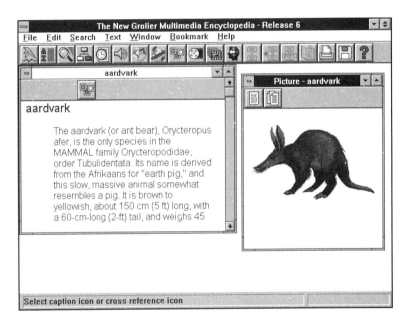

In some multimedia applications like this encyclopedia, text plays a supporting role to other media.

Not all multimedia works this way, of course. Some multimedia applications remain very word-oriented. For example, there are probably many entries in a multimedia encyclopedia that are likely to be text-based, similar to their paper-bound cousins.

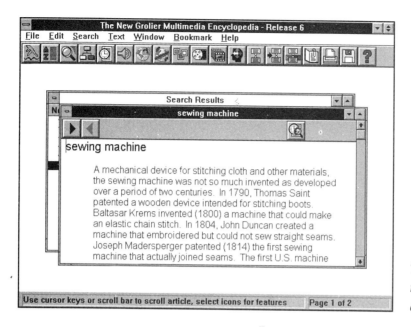

Text still plays a focal role in some multimedia applications.

Whether text is the focus of a multimedia presentation or whether it plays a supporting role, a good presentation should help you find specific text. This is particularly important for reference works. This process is often called *text retrieval*.

Image Is (Almost) Everything

Here's where we get to the part about images and a thousand words. As with text, images can either take center stage or serve to illustrate other media, such as text.

These days, most computers can display on-screen full color photographs, not just black-and-white line drawings and other simple illustrations. Chapter 6 describes the kind of video hardware you need to display photos.

Text retrieval   A way to find specific instances of text in the application. This is particularly useful in multimedia reference works because, like an index, it speeds the process of homing in on the precise information you want.

Image   Image refers to a nonmoving picture. In multimedia, that picture can be anything from a full-color photograph to diagrams, or even stick figures and line drawings.

While almost as old-fashioned as text, well-used images can be instructive and even inspiring. For example, I have a CD-ROM about the natural wonders of Argentina. While the disc includes many videos, the most amazing part is an album of still photos showing some of the awesome beauty of that country.

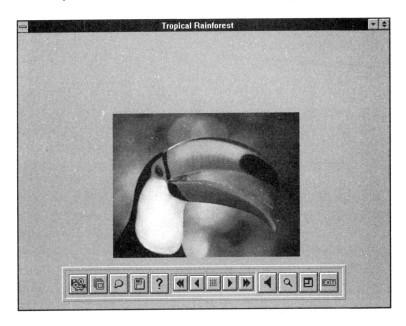

Still images can show rather than tell.

Of course, there are more types of still images than just full-color photos. A multimedia guide to bicycle repair, for example, may show a blow-apart technical diagram of how all those bearings work together to help your wheel turn. Unfortunately, even multimedia can't prevent all those bearings from spilling on the floor and rolling away when you are repairing a wheel hub, but that's another story.

There are many different computerized formats for images that you may want to know about if you are creating multimedia. We'll talk about those in Chapter 24.

TECHNO NERD TEACHES...

Remember the media guru Marshall McLuhan? He coined one of the buzz phrases of the sixties: "The medium is the message." McLuhan referred to media such as text and still images as "hot" media because they involved our minds by making us fill in the blanks, like creating an eyelid movie in our imagination. "Cold" media (the movies or television), are primarily passive activities and don't encourage us to use our imagination as much.

These principles hold with modern multimedia. Interestingly, though, using two "hot" media together, like pictures and text, may create a "cold" experience. That's why creating effective multimedia is as much an art as it is a science.

Lights! Camera! Video Action!

If a picture is worth a thousand words, how many words is a video worth? Bazillions, at least. Well, if they're like some of the videos on MTV, maybe dozens—or less. But wisely used, video can make multimedia snap, crackle, and pop with excitement.

Video, in this context, is the conversion of familiar media (television or film) into a form that your computer can play back. Multimedia video is "live," that is, moving images captured with some sort of camera.

As with any medium, video can vastly improve the multimedia experience or it can be, well, boring. I've seen many multimedia discs chock full of less-than-exciting videos, such as somebody sitting behind a desk explaining something. Why bother?

SPEAK LIKE A GEEK

Video Video refers to live-moving images captured by a video camera. It shows real-life situations, while animation shows, in simple terms, drawings in motion.

On the other hand, a narrated video of a shark stalking its prey on a reef near Hawaii recently grabbed my attention. The combination of taut narration, well-selected sound, and vivid video was powerful and educational.

To be honest, though, at this writing the quality of PC-based video often isn't that great, although it is improving constantly. As discussed in other chapters, computer-based video requires loads of computing horsepower. Even if your PC has the horsepower, you still are likely to see choppy motion or lips and words that are out of synch.

Also, as of now, on-screen displays of video usually are in teeny windows that can be hard to see on your computer monitor, as the next figure shows.

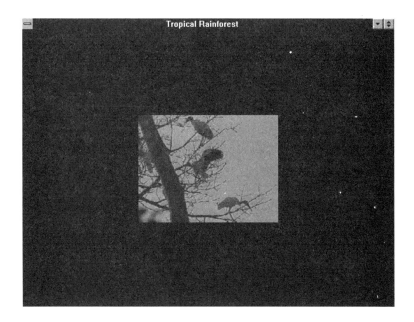

Video normally takes only a small part of your screen.

Before you can play videos, you'll have to do some tweaking. Specifically, you need to install a type of program called a *driver* that enables video to work.

As discussed later in this book, however, this is changing. Someday soon, the technology to provide larger and smoother video (and computers with the power to run this technology) will be commonplace. In the meantime, you might want to get out the old bifocals.

Th-th-th-that's All Folks! Animation in Multimedia

Who among us is bold enough to claim that we didn't like cartoons as kids (or that we still do)? Well, animation is an integral part of multimedia, so it's okay to like it—and admit that we like it.

Driver A program that enables two pieces of computing hardware or software to communicate with each other. For example, a driver enables your word processor to use your printer. Similarly, you need a driver so that your video adapter and monitor can display an image or video stored on a CD-ROM.

Animation in multimedia typically consists of drawings or other nonphotographic still images shown in rapid sequence, such as the flipbooks of old, to create the illusion of motion.

Animation is in some ways similar to video. Both involve a series of still images placed together in rapid sequence to display motion. One primary difference relates more to how they are created than how they work. Video shows things in "real time," that is, it shows them as they happen in the world, such as a person walking down the street or a bicycle race in progress. As such, you would use a video camera to capture videos. Animations begin as drawings or other nonphotographic images and, using a somewhat different process, are stitched together as animations.

Most of the animation used in computer multimedia isn't the awesome kind, such as wily coyotes chasing roadrunners. No, typical multimedia animations are more mundane, like a spinning corporate logo that begins a multimedia sales presentation. Sometimes, being an adult isn't much fun.

And just as you won't get computerized video that rivals what we see on television or at the movies, animations also are relatively crude compared to, say, the coyote and roadrunner. Like videos, however, that's quickly changing as technology improves and computers become more powerful.

Even so, animations can be very instructive. Remember the blown-apart diagram of a bicycle wheel discussed in the section about images? Imagine a multimedia presentation teaching bicycle repair with an animated sequence showing how the parts of a bicycle wheel and hub fit together. The blow-apart diagram is useful, but an animation is more educational still.

As with videos, however, you must install drivers before you can view animations in Windows.

The Sound of Music, and Such

Who doesn't like a catchy tune? A real finger snapper, a real toe tapper. You know, like that $^#@$@ "Achy Breaky Heart." Music often is an intrinsic part of multimedia, as are the spoken word and sound effects.

As you would expect, sound used in multimedia is just that—recorded sound. However, while sound is sound is sound, it is somewhat different for multimedia. That's because sound must be *digitized*. When you digitize something, you convert it to a format that computers can use. For that matter, video and still images also must be digitized so that computers can play them.

Like text, sound frequently plays a supporting role for other media. For example, a presentation about bird watching may show a video of the bird and have an accompanying soundtrack of the bird calling. An entry on the clarinet may include a sound clip of a clarinet.

Sound often serves two other purposes in multimedia: narration and background music. That exciting video of a shark stalking its prey I discussed earlier also had some well-written narration and well-selected background music to heighten the suspense of the video.

Of course, as with video and animation, you'll need to do some fiddling to get good sound on your PC—even your Windows PC. That's because, unlike Macintosh computers, PCs don't have built-in sound capabilities. That means you'll need to install a *sound card* and some drivers in order to play sound. Chapter 11 describes what to look for in a sound card and Chapters 13–15 provide help installing them.

The Least You Need to Know

In this chapter, you learned:

- ☞ A multimedia application can contain any combination of text, images, video, animation, and sound.

- ☞ The best multimedia is interactive, which means you can communicate with the application to learn what you want, or you can navigate through the information.

- ☞ Text is important to multimedia applications, but no longer plays the dominant role it used to.

- ☞ Still images, like text, are an older technology but are critically important to multimedia applications.

- ☞ Video and animation are newer media frequently used in multimedia applications.

- ☞ Sound used in multimedia presentations is *digitized* so that your computer can handle it.

You could fit a lot of haiku on this page.

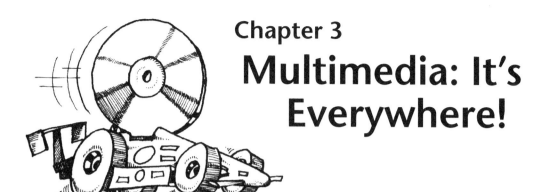

Chapter 3
Multimedia: It's Everywhere!

In This Chapter

- Multimedia you already know
- Introduction to CD-ROMs and drives
- A type of book that doesn't get dusty

Like faddish buzzwords and songs, multimedia is all around us. Sure, multimedia can mean the snazziest new games, but it also can mean simple presentations. In this chapter, let's talk about the forms that multimedia takes.

Multimedia Right Under Your Nose

Let's keep it simple, at least for the time being. If you take seriously our definition that multimedia is simply the use of two or more media, creating multimedia requires only that you place a picture, sound, video, or animation into a document (such as a word processing document). And you thought multimedia was complicated stuff.

Okay, so this wouldn't be the most sophisticated multimedia in the world and, frankly, we'll devote only a little bit of this book to that sort of thing. Yet in a very real way, this is multimedia.

Indeed, many meat-and-potato applications like word processors make it easy to add multimedia elements directly into your documents. It takes just a couple of menu selections in most applications and there you are. Many core applications like word processors even include some tools to create basic interactive multimedia.

The problem with creating multimedia in this way, of course, is that most of us distribute these documents in printed form. Unless you know some tricks I don't know, you'll lose sound and video when you print a document. Also, complex drawings and photos rarely print well. However, if you distribute your files to others with discs, this is a good way to start in the multimedia business.

Chapter 22 discusses in more detail how to make multimedia with your core applications.

Now Presenting . . .

Presentations are a very common type of multimedia. We've already mentioned the old-fashioned types of multimedia presentations that focused around a slide projector and a tape recorder.

In their day, these presentations were considered quite advanced. Now, of course, multimedia presentations are much more sophisticated. By combining the multimedia elements—text, sound, video, animation, and images—you can create presentations that are remarkably slick.

Kiosk presentation   A multimedia presentation placed in a public place, such as an office lobby. A kiosk presentation in your lobby could contain information about your organization, its products, and employees.

You can use multimedia presentations for such diverse tasks as selling products or for lobby "kiosk" presentations that provide basic information about your organization. The best part is that you don't have to be a rocket scientist or Nobel Prize winner to create these presentations. Chapter 22 describes some of the basics of creating these presentations with readily available and relatively simple software tools.

CD-ROM-a-Rama

CD-ROM is a buzzword (as if we need any more) that everybody's buzzing about. It is quickly becoming the most common method for distributing multimedia applications.

For the record, CD-ROM stands for Compact Disc Read-Only Memory. In computer parlance, the information CD-ROMs store is read-only. That means that you can use, or *read*, the information on the discs, but you can't change the information or add to it.

It is important to remember that CD-ROM is not multimedia per se. Rather, CD-ROM is a storage medium like the ever-familiar floppy disk, but with much, much, much more storage capacity.

The large capacity is one of the really amazing things about CD-ROM. Instead of taking up many board feet of shelf space, an encyclopedia can fit on a tiny little disc. A shelf full of CD-ROMs contains as much information as a decent-sized library.

Since CD-ROMs are a storage medium, it is important to remember that not all CD-ROMs are multimedia discs. There are, for example, many CD-ROMs that store huge text databases of people, places, and things.

SPEAK LIKE A GEEK

CD-ROM CD-ROMs look and, in many ways, act like audio CDs. However, CD-ROMs store computerized information. Because of their relatively large storage capacity, CD-ROMs have become the most popular medium for storing multimedia applications.

The current generation of CD-ROMs can store about 650MB of data, or as much as you can store on 500 3.5-inch floppy disks. Here's another cool statistic: A CD-ROM drive can store the equivalent of 500,000 pages of text. If you placed each page end to end, well, you'd have a heck of a long trail of paper.

Another reason that CD-ROM and multimedia are a good match is the read-only nature of the discs. After all, much like the author of a traditional paper-based best-seller, once a multimedia vendor has created the ultimate CD-ROM multimedia title, he isn't going to want anybody messing around with it. Read-only is just fine, thank you!

CD-ROM drive   The drive in which you use CD-ROMs. This is similar to using floppy drives with floppy disks. You stick the CD in the drive and it reads the information on the disc.

So what sort of multimedia can you get on CD-ROM? Several later chapters go into greater detail, so let's just say for now that the possibilities are endless. You want games, CD-ROM has them. Encyclopedias, training guides, tour guides, comedy? No sweat. Thousands of commercial titles are available and more are becoming available every day.

You need a special drive, not surprisingly called a *CD-ROM drive,* to play CD-ROMs. Oh, sure . . . just put in another drive, easy as pie. As you'll learn later, adding CD-ROM drives to your current system is not easy as pie (personally, I find pie-making to be difficult at any rate).

TECHNO NERD TEACHES...

CD-ROM technology is complicated, but here's the ten-cent tour. The CD-ROM is a polycarbonate disc coated with a film, usually composed of aluminum alloy, which, in turn, is covered by a plastic coating. Data is stored by creating an organized series of tiny (very tiny) pits in the aluminum layer of this high-tech sandwich.

Now comes the cool part—lasers. The CD-ROM drive's laser shoots a low-powered beam at the disc, which hits the aluminum film. A diffused light reflection or no light indicates the presence of a pit. A strong reflection of light means there's no pit. The drive then assembles the patterns of where there's a pit and where there isn't a pit and translates that information into data, such as text, sound, video or animation.

CD-ROMs are similar but not identical to audio CDs . Does that mean you can attach your audio CD player to your computer and play CD-ROMs, or play audio CDs in your CD-ROM drive?

Here's the definitive answer: yes and no. With special software, which is easy and inexpensive to come by, you can play audio CDs in most CD-ROM drives that are attached to computers. Typically, though, you can't attach a CD-ROM drive to your stereo unless you attach it to your computer at the same time.

As for playing multimedia discs in your audio CD player, usually, the answer is no. However, sometimes you can. Read the information accompanying the disc to find out.

Many people like to be where the action is, and in the multimedia world, that means CD-ROM. Because it is the most popular medium for multimedia, you'll be reading a lot about CD-ROM and CD-ROM drives in this book.

Electronic Books Do Everything (but Turn the Page for You)

"Electronic books" isn't an official name, but rather is an informal name for a class of applications that tend to:

- ☛ Be business-specific. That is to say, they contain information that is of interest in the workplace, but not to the population at large.

- ☛ Be distributed on floppy disks or be located on a computer network, which is a bunch of connected computers that can share resources—like printers and electronic books. However, as the price of duplicating CD-ROMs drops, more electronic books will be distributed on discs.

- ☛ Replace previously published corporate documents, like policy and procedure manuals, personnel guides or other stuff you have to read sometimes at work but don't want to.

- ☛ Use the multimedia capabilities of more mainstream products, such as word processors or programs that specialize in managing and retrieving text.

Also, some people use the term electronic books to describe traditional books that have been converted to electronic format. While interesting, these books haven't caught on yet as much as the more earthly office-related electronic books.

Electronic books   Electronic versions of books—no big mystery. Electronic books are most popular in business, where they replace formerly paperbound books and other books that gather dust in office bookshelves. A typical blockbuster: a policy and procedure manual.

Don't get me wrong—electronic books are good things. They tend to be cheaper to produce and are easier to update than the paper books they replace. That makes them more useful and economical than paper books.

Increasingly, these electronic books have multimedia embedded in them. That means if you use electronic books, you'd better hightail it to the chapters in this book about installing a sound board and about getting your computer ready to handle video and animation.

The more of these applications there are, the closer we move toward the mythical paperless office, another fantasy from the fifties. It's just that, compared to the whizzy-neat multimedia applications you can buy for entertainment and education, these applications are, well, a bit on the dreary side.

It Even Asks What You Think!

Okay, so you have this multimedia application and it has all this sound, video, animation, and even old-fashioned text and pictures. Simply putting all those things on a disc might make it a multimedia application, but it doesn't make it a *good* multimedia application.

There are several things to look for in a multimedia disc. These items are discussed in greater depth in other chapters, but let's begin the discussion here just to get you thinking.

First, a good multimedia application makes wise use of media. Video might be exciting, but it sometimes isn't the best way to get a point across. Good multimedia uses the most effective medium for each task.

Second, a good multimedia application should make it obvious how to find more information. Typically, good applications include on-screen cues, such as an arrow with text underneath it saying something like, "Click on this arrow for more information about Acme Widgets."

Third, whenever possible, it should be interactive. Interactivity can be simple, such as the arrow leading to more information about widgets.

Good multimedia also can be complex, for example, a training application that leads you through a series of questions. Each step in the experience depends on how you answer the previous question. This personalizes the multimedia experience since it lets you direct the process.

The Last Word—for Now

It's just a start, but this chapter has told you what multimedia is and scratched the surface on the basic elements (sound, video, images, and text) that go into creating good multimedia. Subsequent chapters describe each element in detail, help with chores, such as installing and tweaking multimedia hardware, and even describe some of the basics of creating your own multimedia applications.

You should know, however, that there are types of multimedia that we won't cover in this book. To paraphrase something out of one of the great discs, er, books: "the kids will lead us." Kids, with their video games, have been into multimedia longer than most of us. The games kids play today are truly sophisticated multimedia. More interestingly, the set-top game boxes from vendors (such as Nintendo, Sega, and 3DO) are a possible gateway into the information superhighway everybody's been talking about.

The information superhighway is another of those buzzwords that everybody talks about but about which nobody knows anything. It refers to some vague notion that we somehow will have incredibly large amounts of information available to us through our computers, our televisions, or both. That information may be the great works of literature and research, or some of the lesser works of film and television.

Nobody knows what the information superhighway will be like once it gets here, at least as it pertains to multimedia. Sure, talking back to the shopping channel might be interactive multimedia, but forgive me if we wait for future editions of this book before diving into that sort of thing too heavily.

Even though there's a mind-boggling future ahead for multimedia, it is quite ready for prime time now. The strong sales of multimedia hardware and software for PCs is evidence of that fact. That's why this book focuses on what is available today for mainstream users of PCs in the home and office. That's plenty of grist for the mill.

Someday, though, you'll be able to tell your grandchildren, or any other tyke that wanders onto your knee, "I was around in the early years of multimedia. Let me tell you the story of my first CD-ROM."

And just like kids have done with elders for millennia, the little booger will look you in the eyes adoringly and promptly fall asleep or divert herself with a toy while you prattle on.

The Least You Need to Know

Multimedia is in many places and forms. Specifically:

- ☞ Old-fashioned slide-and-music presentations were multimedia.

- ☞ Today, CD-ROMs are the most common carrier of multimedia applications.

- ☞ "Electronic books" are an increasingly popular type of multimedia application. These are electronic versions of the books that clog many corporate bookshelves.

- ☞ A good multimedia application is simple to navigate and should provide direct involvement for the user.

Chapter 4
The Kids Will Love You: Multimedia at Home

In This Chapter

- ☛ A multimedia maven at home
- ☛ Why the kids will love you
- ☛ The astounding range of multimedia applications

If you diligently read the first three chapters, you should have a good idea about the nature of multimedia. Now you'll learn about specific types of multimedia applications and how they are useful for the home and office. That means you'll really impress other people with scintillating lines like: "Multimedia educational applications are superior to old-fashioned paper-based tools because their interactivity enables users to proceed at their own pace. This, in turn, facilitates the learning process."

A Day in the Life of a Multimedia Maven

This is the story of a day in the life of Margaret the Multimedia Maven. Of course, Margaret isn't real. However, this "typical" day highlights many multimedia opportunities and shows how multimedia is creeping into virtually every aspect of our lives.

On this day, Margaret showered, dressed, kissed her daughter, Melanie, and her husband, Dave the Bike Racer, good-bye, and stumbled to her car. On the way to work, she stopped at the neighborhood coffee shop for a cup of high-test pick-me-up. Sleep-deprived from a late night of multimedia high-jinx, she was stuck: What type of coffee is best to start off the day?

Fortunately, the coffee shop owner had set up a "kiosk" computer with a multimedia application to help customers make such difficult decisions. Margaret felt right at home in front of the touch-screen display.

She thought: I need a high-octane blend for a quicker wake-me-up. On the touch screen, Margaret touched a square next to the words "Dark Roasts." A voice piped: "Dark roasts are hearty coffees, boasting a rich, strong flavor and aroma." Yup, that's the one.

Next, the multimedia application displayed an on-screen list of different dark-roast choices. After touching several of the choices to hear spoken descriptions, Margaret selected French roast. The application assured her French roast was "rich, unforgettable, and somewhat acidic. The perfect high-caffeine pick-me-up after a late night of multimedia." Margaret ordered a large cup to go, musing that somebody ought to invent the capability to add aromas to multimedia.

Energized (or at least awakened) by her coffee, Margaret arrived at work only to realize that she had forgotten she had an early-morning sales call with a key customer. She grabbed her notebook computer containing her multimedia sales presentation and raced to her customer's office.

After a bit of small talk in the customer's meeting room, the presentation began with an animated, spinning corporate logo and some vibrant theme music to set the mood. Next came a video of the president of the company effusively describing the new product, called the FooBitz Plus.

After that, the presentation displayed a menu with three on-screen choices. The customer had never heard of FooBitz Plus and asked her to start with the overview. There was that spinning logo again and another video of the president going into a bit more detail about the product, then, on to the five choices providing more detail about specific parts of the product.

"Any questions?" Margaret asked when the customer finished the multimedia presentation. "No," the customer replied. "That explains it all. I'll take ten FooBitz Plusses." Since multimedia had helped Margaret close a big sale before noon, she decided to take the rest of the day off.

After dinner, daughter Melanie asked for help with a term paper about classical music. First Margaret loaded a multimedia encyclopedia and got the low-down on classical music in general. She double-clicked her mouse on the word "Romantic," and the encyclopedia took her to a section about that period of classical music.

Margaret had a special interest in the sonata form and clicked on a button to get an in-depth description. That screen had a button that, when clicked, played a passage from Mozart's "Eine Kleine Nachtmusik."

Margaret helped Melanie select and copy the relevant information from the encyclopedia to a word processor. They then loaded another disc that went into greater depth about the Romantic composer Franz Schubert, his life, and specifically, a movement-by-movement analysis of one of his works, "The Trout Quintet."

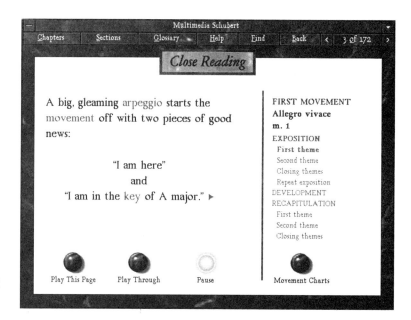

Margaret learns about Schubert.

Margaret was about to copy some information about the Trout Quintet into Melanie's paper when she heard an emphatic little voice exclaiming, "Enough, Mommy. I don't need any more help! Let *me* use the computer now!"

"Hurry up with your homework, Melanie," Dave the Bike Racer called from the living room. "I've got to use the bike repair CD-ROM to help me fix my bicycle before tomorrow's race."

Exhausted, Margaret tore herself away from the computer and went to sleep, another rewarding day of multimedia under her belt.

Okay, so Margaret is a bit obsessed with multimedia. However, the truth is that there are multimedia applications for virtually every facet of modern life. In fact, there are so many multimedia titles available, it's kind of mind boggling.

Take a look at Chapter 19 to see what goes into making a good multimedia application, then see Chapters 20 and 21 for peeks at some of my favorites. The rest of this chapter focuses on how you can use multimedia applications at home.

Impressing the Kids

It's easy to see why home use of multimedia is exploding in popularity. Multimedia is easy for kids to use and each CD packs a tremendous amount of educational information. Also, of course, multimedia is entertaining, so you and your kids will learn more—and play more interesting games.

Interestingly, the categories that classify multimedia titles for homebound users have blurred. It used to be that a title fell under either educational software or game. However, because multimedia is by nature entertaining, many educational applications are also games. And many games are also educational.

This blurring has given rise to a new category of multimedia called *edutainment.* This is an overused phrase that describes any multimedia that is both entertaining and educational.

To my mind, the term doesn't mean anything because some applications are more entertaining than educational, and vice versa. Still, it's the sort of term that marketing warriors love to repeat, whether their product warrants it or not.

The bottom line is that, no matter what type of software you get for the home, chances are your kids will love you for it. Even if they don't, you'll have fun anyway. The next two sections provide an overview of games and educational multimedia for the home.

Playing Games

Let's face it, parents. You probably want multimedia to educate your kids, but your kids want to play games. The good news is that you can have it both ways.

There is an astounding number of multimedia games available. These aren't just shoot-em-up games or games with goofy characters and even goofier background music. Many multimedia games are also educational.

Start them out young: There is a growing library of multimedia educational games for early learners. These games teach a variety of skills, including simple math concepts, memorization, and vocabulary-building.

They are fun for younger kids because the titles usually combine animation, music, and video with very little text. They're also fun because younger kids love learning—a love, lamentably, that often leaves when they start school.

A program that teaches counting.

Little tykes eventually grow out of beginning educational games. Sure, there are multimedia shoot-em-ups available by the truck load. However, you also can steer them to age-appropriate educational games. Unlike the educational games for younger kids, these games for "older" kids feature louder music, more rapidly changing scenery, and tighter deadlines to make decisions.

Some of the best of these games focus on specific subjects; for example, long-popular MathBlaster. Parents also will like the Carmen Sandiego series, which combines adventure mysteries with geography or science.

And, of course, there are the games that are pure entertainment. Some games, such as the popular Return to Zork, started as pure text games in the days before computers commonly handled graphic images, but are now full-multimedia games. These games require older kids and adults to think their way through intricate situations. Other, even more-advanced games, are like interactive movies with video clips of real actors. In these games, instead of passively watching, you help set the direction of the plot.

Flight simulators, outer space adventures, complex computerized board games—the choices are practically limitless. However, all good computer games have some things in common. First, they mix media to make them interesting.

Also, multimedia games are interactive in ways that older games can't match. For example, in a typical adventure game, you crawl down a dark hallway and meet a monster at the end. You can fight or flee. If you flee, you can go through one of three doors, each of which leads to a different situation.

This Is Too Much Fun for Education

You parents are probably thinking, "Enough games. Tell me about educational multimedia." This is one area in which multimedia really shines.

One reason multimedia is an excellent educational tool has to do with sheer storage capacity. You can put a lot of information on a CD-ROM. Also, of course, part of multimedia's effectiveness as an educational tool is due to the fact that, in many cases, watching and listening are more engaging than just reading.

An important part of educational multimedia is its interactive nature. Most of us grew up learning in a decidedly non-interactive manner: A teacher spoke and we listened. Interaction consisted primarily of answering questions, passing notes, or shooting spit balls.

With interactive multimedia, however, you tell the program what you want to learn and the order in which you'd like to learn it. With a good reference application such as a multimedia encyclopedia, you can participate in what some call "serendipitous learning."

Many multimedia applications have links that connect related topics, called *hyperlinks*. If you double-click your mouse on a hyperlink—usually displayed as different-colored type or an on-screen button—you jump to the related topic. With serendipitous learning, you can follow a path of information to find things you otherwise wouldn't find.

Hyperlinks A method of linking one bit of information to related information. When you select a hyperlink, you immediately go to the related information. Hyperlinks are useful for educational and reference works because they enable you to follow a train of thought or to explore information serendipitously.

For example, in a multimedia encyclopedia, you may start searching for "peanuts." In the article about peanuts, you may see a reference to George Washington Carver and jump to an article about him, which might include his picture. At the end of that article, there may be a hyperlink to an article about famous African-Americans that leads, in turn, to an article about Martin Luther King, Jr. That article can include a video clip showing King's famous "I Have A Dream" speech.

Now, Martin Luther King, Jr. doesn't have much to do with peanuts, but while your child was learning about peanuts, he also learned about famous black men, viewed one of the most inspirational speeches in our country's history, and had a good time while doing all this learning.

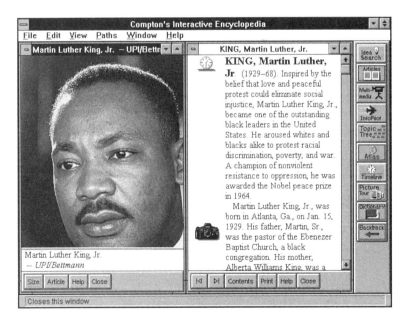

A multimedia encyclopedia.

Encyclopedias are probably the best-known multimedia educational applications, but there are many more. For example, there are multimedia dictionaries designed specifically for kids.

I saw another example recently that chronicled the formation of the earth and about 500 prehistoric species. As a paper book, this information would collect dust in your kids' school library, but as multimedia, it is fascinating. There are many exciting science discs available with subjects ranging from prehistory to space travel.

As stated in the previous section, there are many titles that mix play with education, a particularly effective method of learning for younger kids. You can also buy multimedia titles that prepare older kids to take college entrance exams or teach people of any age foreign languages. Just about anything you want to learn, you now can learn with multimedia.

There also are many lighter reference works available. I recently saw a CD-ROM chock full of thousands of movie reviews and film clips. How about multimedia applications showing exotic vacation destinations, discs of sports records, and videos of famous sports events? Still other discs focus on specific periods of history or a specific topic, such as cars or the Romantic period of classical music.

The Least You Need to Know

Multimedia is tailor-made for home uses. In this chapter you learned:

- ☞ Many educational multimedia applications are fun because they mix a variety of media and are interactive.

- ☞ This combination of fun and education blurs the lines between the two types of media.

- ☞ There are multimedia titles for kids of all ages that, by taking advantage of multimedia strengths, can be more educational and more fun than traditional books.

You say, How much more blank could a
page be? and the answer is, none.
None more blank.

Chapter 5
Your Boss Will Love You: Multimedia at Work

In This Chapter

- ☛ Multimedia at work is a hard sell
- ☛ Cost-justifying multimedia
- ☛ Multimedia in training and sales
- ☛ Multimedia in public places

Convincing people that multimedia is a good thing for the home is easy. Convincing your boss that it is a good thing for work is about as easy as convincing him that you need a bigger office. So, as a service to help you advance your career, or at least get some multimedia stuff at work, this chapter discusses multimedia applications at the office. It's a hard sell, but maybe we can make it a bit easier.

The Multimedia Hard Sell

Even in organizations that have embraced computer technology, acquiring multimedia capabilities can be a tough sell. In many cases, though, multimedia is very cost-effective.

Here's a tip to corporate high-tech warriors. In many organizations, it's easy to cost-justify CD-ROM drives. After all, the number of text-only databases available on CD-ROM is large, and increasing every day.

You can acquire databases ranging from a complete nationwide telephone book (yes, you're probably in it) to discs with scientific journal abstracts and legal precedents. These are highly useful discs, but because they use only one medium—text—they aren't multimedia and we don't cover them in this book.

Once you have the CD-ROM drive, consider it a foot in the door for multimedia. As the rest of this chapter shows, there are many cost-effective multimedia applications for business. Once the higher-ups understand the benefits of spending money for text-based CD-ROMs, the leap to getting the rest of the hardware and software necessary for multimedia isn't huge.

The next several sections discuss specific business-oriented applications to make it easier to convince people your organization needs multimedia.

Training Camp

One of the first areas in which multimedia caught on was training. Training is an ideal use of multimedia, because we learn more effectively by watching and hearing than we do by simply reading static text.

Not all types of training benefit from multimedia. For example, many people will better learn to use a complicated new software program with the traditional full-day sit-down session with a professional trainer. When you are starting from scratch learning a complicated process, using a live trainer is often more flexible and effective.

However, other types of training work well with multimedia. For example, I saw one training presentation that focused on how to handle workplace emergencies involving toxic materials. Another highly effective multimedia training application taught effective business communications skills. It featured role-playing videos in which actors used both effective and ineffective communications skills. The disc clearly explained each, and provided exercises for improving your communications skills. Multimedia training is also very effective for re-learning an old subject (such as studying French after not speaking it since college), or honing an existing skill.

Multimedia training is cost-effective because it is cheaper and easier to schedule than skilled trainers. Also, it can more effectively train because of its interactivity. The user can pace himself, learning the specific skills he needs in the order he prefers to learn them. And some training, like the communications skills disc I mentioned, can be more effective when done in private.

Interactivity is the key to good multimedia. Interacting with a well-designed training presentation can help the user focus precisely on the skills he must learn. For example, an experienced person who only needs to brush up skills need not waste time learning basic skills, as is the case with more traditional in-person group training situations.

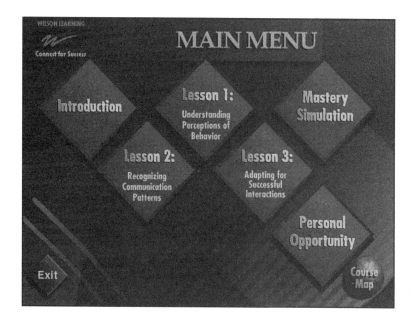

An interactive training program.

Another benefit to interactive training is that the training disc also can serve as a reference. The disc on handling toxic substances in the workplace is a good example of that. After training, the organization kept the disc for quick reference and once even used it during an emergency.

Many interactive training presentations are available, either commercially or from universities and government agencies.

Sales Presentations That Sing

Remember how in Chapter 4 Margaret the Multimedia Maven sold ten FooBitz Plusses simply by showing her customer a multimedia presentation? Easy, huh?

Most of us either have made sales presentations or sat through them. In the past, sales presenters used "audio-visual aids." In other words, the salesperson used an overhead projector, or, if she wanted to get fancy, a slide projector. The ATFY (Average Time to First Yawn) for these presentations typically is less than three minutes.

Admittedly, Margaret's success with a multimedia sales presentation was exaggerated for fun, but multimedia sales presentations can be highly effective when properly used. That, and the fact that they are relatively easy to create, explains why they are becoming common in the business world.

The next figure shows Margaret's multimedia sales presentation. You can't hear the background music or see the videos in motion, but it provides an idea of how multimedia sales presentations work.

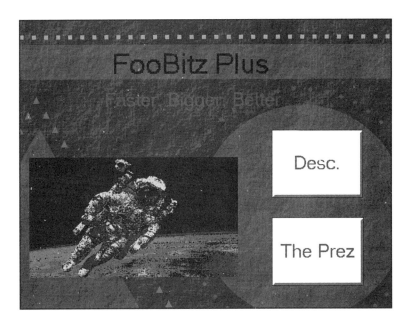

Margaret's sales presentation.

There are several keys to a good multimedia sales presentation. One key is interactivity. Sometimes, customers don't need to see a presentation from start to finish. A good multimedia presentation lets the customer jump in where he wants. A good presentation also provides as much depth as the customer wants, as shown by the section in Margaret's presentation about technical issues.

Of course, multimedia also enables you to put your product in its best light. In some cases, you can simply send the presentation to customers, letting them educate themselves about your products or services before you meet with them in person.

While you can hire professionals to create multimedia presentations, you also can create your own presentations with commercially available software. As discussed in Chapter 22, some of these tools are so simple to use that, with just a little practice, you can create surprisingly professional presentations.

Kiosk Presentations to Direct Traffic

You walk into the lobby of an office building and there's an information desk. However, the attendant is busy with a personal call and can't help you find the office you want or announce your presence to the person with whom you're meeting. What to do?

A good kiosk multimedia presentation may be the answer. It can contain information about the organization, its products, and its employees and can even help you find a specific person's extension number. Put a phone next to the kiosk, and you don't even need the person at the information desk anymore.

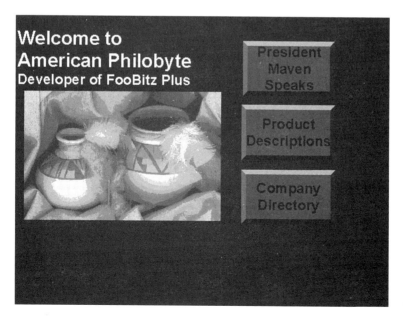

A kiosk presentation.

Here's a bit more detail about a typical lobby kiosk presentation. The opening screen might be a video of the company president welcoming you to the building and providing a brief overview of the company and its products.

Beneath the video are three buttons. Clicking on one button leads to text descriptions and images or videos of the company's products. Clicking on the second button leads to a history of the company, including videos from the corporate archives. Clicking on the third button leads to a company directory in which you can find the office number and phone extension for each employee.

Kiosk presentations also are appropriate in many other situations. In a shopping mall, a kiosk presentation can help shoppers find the stores that carry specific types of products. A kiosk presentation in an airport can help travelers find specific services and airlines. You can place a sales presentation on a public computer located in a store. You can even create a kiosk presentation that actually is a public survey, asking passersby to answer questions.

As with sales presentations, creating basic kiosk presentations can be simple, although more complex presentations may require a professional developer.

Research, Research, Research

Much research that is useful in the workplace is contained on text-based research CD-ROM. Examples include discs containing detailed information for medical researchers or filings with the Securities and Exchange Commission. Even though CD-ROMs store this information, these are not multimedia applications since they contain only text.

However, there also are many multimedia-based research discs that are useful in the workplace. Simple examples of these titles are travel related. If you've planned a business trip to the Far East, there are multimedia discs that teach local customs, list places to stay, and show points of interest.

If your organization has an in-house librarian, ask him or her to help you find multimedia applications. If there is no such person in-house, look for advertisements in trade journals.

Dust Off Your Electronic Bookshelf

As mentioned in Chapter 3, "electronic books" are an increasingly common type of multimedia application. There are some commercial electronic books available—typically electronic versions of best-sellers or classic novels. However, the most common use of electronic books is in the corporate setting, where they replace the dusty, old tomes that often clog our office bookshelves. For example, you might turn a policy and procedure manual or a training manual into an electronic book.

It is simple to add multimedia to text-based electronic books. For example, an electronic policy and procedure manual can include videos showing how to accomplish a specific procedure. Even when electronic books don't make use of multimedia, however, there are still advantages to them. They will usually contain either hyperlinks connecting related information, or text retrieval to help quickly find specific items in the book. Also, electronic books are easier and cheaper to upgrade, so they tend to be more up to date.

Converting huge documents can be extremely time consuming, though, requiring rekeying or extensive use of scanners. Also, you may run into problems if the people in your organization who use the electronic books use several different types of computers (such as mainframes, PCs, or Macintoshes). In that case, you must use special, and sometimes complex, software that enables people using different systems to read the same document.

Eloise, My E-Mail Just Talked to Me!

In the business world, the notion of adding voice annotation to documents is starting to catch on. For example, if you create a spreadsheet with a Windows spreadsheet program, you can embed within the document a voice explanation of a specific section. Then, when somebody double-clicks on a special icon representing the voice annotation, they'll hear your voice explaining why sales of FooBitz Plus exceed earlier projections. (The answer: effective use of multimedia sales presentations!)

Voice annotation A simple form of multimedia. With voice annotation, you add a spoken explanation to normal workaday documents, such as spreadsheets or word processing documents.

TECHNO NERD TEACHES...

Creating voice annotations in Windows is simple, but I can't go into detail here. Basically, you use special software and a microphone to record your voice. The computer translates the sound into a digitized format, which it can read and play back when someone clicks a button in a document. If you want to learn how to record sounds, check your Windows documentation.

Of course, you also can attach still images and video to documents. Most applications make this process as simple as making a menu choice and selecting a multimedia file.

Why bother adding multimedia to workaday documents? Adding a spoken explanation to a spreadsheet explains unexpected results quickly. Adding an image to e-mail shows rather than tells what you are talking about. True, these are relatively small multimedia applications, but they can increase your effectiveness on the job.

The Least You Need to Know

It's a hard sell, but you can, with effort, convince your colleagues and superiors to use multimedia in the workplace. In this chapter, you learned that:

- ☛ Multimedia is a cost-effective tool in the workplace.

- ☛ Training and sales presentations are more effective using multimedia.

- ☛ Kiosk presentations are often useful for providing information in public places, such as building lobbies.

- ☛ You also can add multimedia, such as sound clips, to business documents to make them more informative.

Part II
Priming the Multimedia Pump

The pump is primed, and you're probably ready to drink from the refreshing well of multimedia. It's nice to know that you can use multimedia for fun and games and learning and all kinds of neat stuff.

But let's get real—multimedia isn't magic that works just because you want it to. It requires special hardware and software. Part II walks you through the stuff you'll need to run multimedia on your PC.

Chapter 6

You Gotta Have It: Video and Sound

In This Chapter

- Looking at multimedia monitors
- Video color and speed
- Video adapters: out of the closet
- Making noise with sound cards
- The music's in the file

Mangling metaphors and analogies gives meaning to the otherwise hum-drum lives of writers. So here I go: A multimedia system is like your body, because both have parts that must work together.

Now I'll mangle another analogy by comparing multimedia to a sport like, say, bicycle racing. Each activity has specific equipment that is at its core, such as a bicycle for racing or a CD-ROM drive for multimedia. The successful racer—and multimedia maven—optimizes this core equipment.

This chapter focuses on two core pieces of your multimedia system: your video and sound system. The next chapter discusses the other hardware pieces that are part of all computers, whether or not you use multimedia. All this information will help you make more informed decisions when buying your PC or adding specific components to your computer.

The Better to See You With

You old-time science fiction fans may remember plots with advanced species from other worlds that had no need for inefficient mechanisms like eyes. They were so advanced they could see using the amazing power of their brainwaves, or some such malarky.

Well, as a species, we're not there yet. You need a video system to view text, images, video, and animation—all the elements used to create multimedia. A computer's video system has two sibling parts: a video adapter and a monitor. Of the two, the monitor is the bratty, spoiled, big brother who gets all the attention.

The next two sections tell you which capabilities and features to look for in a monitor, to maximize your appreciation of multimedia.

Your Monitor Is Refreshing

You already know that your monitor is a sibling to your video adapter, but it's also a close cousin to your television. Since I was born in the early years of the television age, I'm still a bit in awe of television technology.

Get this: monitors and televisions use "guns" in the back of the unit, which constantly shoot a stream of electrons onto the screen. The electrons trigger the display of red, green, and blue phosphors on the screen, and these phosphors comprise the image. A phosphor is, well, phosphorescent; it glows when light hits it.

The problem with electrons is that they don't stick around long. The display of electrons quickly deteriorates and must be rapidly refreshed by more electrons. Of course, the electron gun also must change the order and color of the on-screen phosphors as the application—or television program—requires.

If the monitor refreshes the display slowly, the image appears to flicker, which can cause eyestrain and give you a headache. That's why you should look for monitors with the highest possible *refresh rate*. This is true even if you don't use multimedia, but it is critically important if you do. Videos shown on a monitor with a low refresh rate appear flickery and sometimes herky-jerky.

TECHNO NERD TEACHES...

Although this section is about monitors, here's an important thing to remember: Most characteristics of your video system—like refresh rate—must be built into both the monitor and the video adapter. You'll waste your money if you buy an expensive monitor but plug it into a mediocre video adapter.

Refresh rates measure how quickly the monitor adds new vertical and horizontal lines. Of the two, the vertical refresh rate is more important. Do not buy a monitor that doesn't refresh vertical lines at least 72 times per second. This refresh rate is called 72 Hz. A vertical refresh rate of 76Hz is common and preferable.

Also, make sure to buy a multisynching monitor. This monitor can automatically change refresh rates as conditions change, such as when you go from a graphics screen to a text screen.

You Say You Want a Resolution

Those phosphors I was talking about earlier, charged by the stream of electrons, create tiny on-screen dots called *pixels*. The image you see on the monitor is actually the combination of all these pixels in a specific order. The number of pixels in a square inch of the screen is the *resolution*. The higher the resolution, the more detail appears on-screen.

SPEAK LIKE A GEEK

Refresh rate   Refers to the frequency with which a monitor replaces lines of electrons that appear on-screen. The electrons trigger red, green, and blue phosphors that make up the image. Higher refresh rates create steadier images, are easier on the eyes, and also display multimedia elements better.

Pixels   Talk about tiny … pixels are little dots created when an electron shot from the back of your monitor hits a phosphor in the front. Each pixel glows either red, green, or blue. The organized combination of pixels makes up the image. How tiny are these pixels? These days, each square inch (even in a low-end monitor) is at least 640 pixels by 480 pixels.

Virtually all monitors sold in the last few years support standard VGA resolution, which is 640 pixels per inch by 480 pixels. VGA is the bare minimum for multimedia applications. However, it is quickly becoming outdated as higher resolutions become more common.

TECHNO NERD TEACHES...

If yours is an older computer system and you want to use multimedia applications, pay special attention to your video system. Many older video systems—those more than four years old—don't support VGA resolution. Instead, those older monitors may support EGA or CGA resolution, which are out-of-date standards. Most multimedia applications won't run on EGA or CGA systems.

Also, some older systems use a monitor that displays only text and no graphics at all. You can't use this type of monitor for multimedia either.

Most monitors sold in the last couple of years support Super VGA resolution, which refers to either 640 x 480 resolution with 256 on-screen colors or 800 x 600 resolution. Many monitors, especially those sold recently, support even higher resolutions, specifically 1024 x 768 and even 1240 x 1024.

While VGA resolution is adequate for most current multimedia, Super VGA is better, particularly on 14-inch and 15-inch monitors. At this resolution, Super VGA shows all the details of an image, and they are less "grainy" than those displayed on a VGA monitor.

When buying a monitor for multimedia, don't settle for less than a resolution of 800 x 600. An added bonus is the capability to display even higher resolutions, like 1024 x 768, but you won't use these higher resolutions very often, particularly with 14-inch or 15-inch monitors.

Connect the Dot Pitch

It's hard to believe that the moving pictures we see on-screen are made up of an ever-changing series of dots. In fact, it's kind of mind boggling—and it gets even more mind boggling.

Another key element in making a sharp image is *dot pitch*. Dot pitch refers to the distance between on-screen pixels. The "tighter" the dot pitch, or the closer together the pixels, the sharper the image tends to be; the "looser" the dot pitch, the grainier the image.

Dot pitch is important for any use of your computer but is especially important for multimedia, because sharp images, text, videos, and animations are more life-like. And life-like multimedia means more fun, right?

Here's the mind boggling part: those little dots are *really* close together. In today's marketplace, there's no need to buy a monitor with a dot pitch looser than .28mm. Monitors with dot pitches as tight as .25mm are available and are not much more expensive than monitors with looser dot pitches. That's an incredibly small increment—at least *I* think so.

Remember, though, that the sharpness of the monitor's image depends on more than dot pitch. For example, the tightest dot pitch in the world won't help make a poorly focused monitor easy to view.

TECHNO NERD TEACHES...

Although your monitor and television are related, there are many differences between them. Your monitor, even running in standard VGA mode, achieves much higher resolution than does your television. Also, most modern monitors are non-interlaced, but televisions usually are interlaced. *Interlacing* is a method by which only every other line is refreshed on-screen. This enables higher refresh rates, but it contributes to a flickery image. Also, of course, your television has built in sound capabilities and a receiver to receive television signals; your monitor doesn't need these capabilities.

Your Monitor's True Colors

If there's one area in which your monitor plays a more important role than your video adapter, it's in the display of colors. Right away, you'll know if your monitor displays colors well. Reds will appear really red, for example, and the colors will seem bright and alive.

You may be wondering why color purity is particularly important for multimedia. Well, one reason is that still images displayed on a monitor with poor color lose some of their life and vitality. More noticeably, though, if your monitor doesn't display colors well, videos will be blotchy. This is particularly annoying when the video shows somebody's face.

There are no statistics or benchmarks for color quality. Rather, you must rely on your own subjective feelings. When you buy a monitor, pay special attention to the color.

There is, however, one color capability a monitor—and the video adapter—absolutely must have: The capability to display at least 256 colors on-screen at a time. Most multimedia applications make this a minimum requirement.

These days, most monitors can display at least 256 colors, but it's still best to double-check when buying. Many older monitors can't handle that many colors, so if you are using an older system, make sure the monitor has this capability. And remember, 256 colors is a minimum requirement; support for more on-screen colors is preferable.

The following table summarizes the elements that make a monitor good for multimedia applications.

Monitor Feature	Multimedia Benefit
Bright, true colors	More life-like videos, animations, and images
High refresh rate	Solid, non-flickering image
High resolution	Displays finer details of images
"Tight" dot pitch	Sharper image

Video Adapters: Out of the Closet

Out of sight, out of mind. Too often, that's how people think of the *video adapter*. It gets plugged into the inside of your system unit, so once you close the cover, you forget about the video adapter. That's a bad attitude, though, because video adapters play a significant role in how well multimedia appears on-screen.

As explained in Part III, you install expansion cards by placing them in special slots in your computer's motherboard (see the following figure). Once you install the card in the motherboard, you connect your monitor to it. Like a CD-ROM interface, the video adapter acts like a go-between, analyzing instructions from your applications and passing those instructions on to your monitor so it displays information on-screen.

Video adapters are important for multimedia because moving images—video and animation—require a lot of sophisticated video technology. If you use a mediocre video adapter, you won't like the way your animations and videos appear on-screen, no matter how much money you spend on your monitor.

When buying a video adapter, make sure it supports the monitor characteristics discussed in the last section. That is, it must support a fast refresh rate, at least 256 colors, and adequately high resolutions.

SPEAK LIKE A GEEK

Video adapter A card that you plug into your PC's motherboard. It contains all the electronic stuff needed to display images on your monitor.

Motherboard The big plastic board inside your computer. Everything connects to the motherboard. It contains the basic hardware and software needed to run your computer. For example, located on the motherboard are random-access memory (RAM) chips and your computer's central processing unit, which is the main chip that runs your computer.

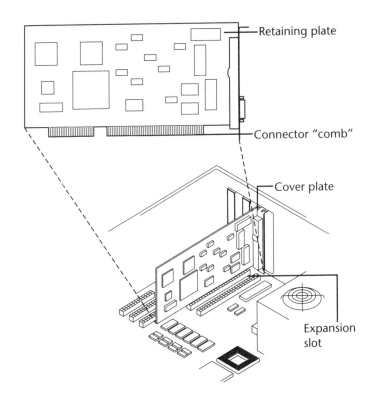

Retaining plate

Connector "comb"

Cover plate

Expansion slot

Installing an expansion card.

Faster! Faster!

I saw a bumper sticker the other day: Faster is Better. The bumper sticker didn't say faster *what*, but the sentiment seems to be universally accepted in our society. I'm not a fast freak, but I do think fast video systems are important to multimedia. In fact, besides support for your monitor, the most important thing that a video adapter provides is speed. Two sets of chips located on a video adapter directly impact the speed with which it displays information on-screen.

The first is the *graphics chip*. Just as a computer has a central processing unit that does the core computing work, video adapters have a core graphics chip that does much of the processing necessary to display nontext information like video. Like everything else, some chips are faster than others.

Speed is critically important when displaying multimedia. If your video adapter isn't fast enough, videos and animations won't play smoothly. That's because both types of media consist of a series of frames played in rapid order to give the illusion of motion.

If your video adapter is slow, it won't be able to process and display all the frames in a timely fashion. To compensate, it eliminates frames at irregular intervals. This, in turn, causes jerky motions. Also, if your video adapter isn't fast, complex still images like photographs will take a long time to display on-screen.

The second set of chips on a video board that have an impact on speed are *random-access memory (RAM) chips.* Like the RAM on your motherboard, your video adapter uses RAM to temporarily store parts of the video processing—this speeds up video display. (See Chapter 7 for more information on RAM.)

If faster is better in our society, so is *more.* And the more RAM on your video card, the faster your multimedia will display. If you will be using multimedia, don't buy a video adapter with less than one megabyte of on-board RAM. More RAM than that is preferable. Keep in mind, though, that you'll pay for speed: Faster video chips and additional RAM cost money.

Making Noise

Now on to the next of the senses—sound. Can you imagine watching a cartoon without goofy music and sound effects playing in the background? Of course not! How about watching a silent movie? Ix-nay. It wouldn't be fun (although once it was considered quite exciting).

The same holds true for multimedia. You can combine all the text, images, video, and animations you want, but without sounds, many multimedia presentations fall flat. The CD-ROM drive and CD-ROM interface (discussed in Chapters 8 and 9) are two of the major hardware pieces you need to run multimedia on your PC. To hear the sounds on a CD-ROM, you need two more pieces of hardware: a *sound card* and speakers. And, of course, you need the music itself.

Sound card   Another of those expansion cards that plugs into your computer's motherboard. A sound card analyzes the contents of sound files (such as WAV or MIDI files, which you'll learn about in the next few sections) and plays them through speakers or headphones. What does a computer sound like without a sound card? The best you'll get are the odd beeps and boops.

A sound card doesn't make sounds by itself, however. To hear sounds and music, you need special sound files. Let's talk about those files before we turn our attention back to sound cards.

Digitized and analog sounds Normally, sounds are *analog*. These are sounds you hear every day, and they consist of sound waves. The different tones are, essentially, peaks and valleys in the wave. However, computers can't understand and play sound waves. Digitized sounds, then, are audio files that computers can read and play back.

Waveform (or WAV) files Waveform files, often called WAV files, are files that store digitized sounds. They are a frequently used type of sound for multimedia and are called WAV files because they are digital versions of sound waves found in the real (a.k.a. noncomputing) world. Also, files containing these sounds often have the .WAV file extension name. WAV files can contain music, but typically they contain sound effects or recordings of sounds.

I Love That Old-Time (Digitized) Music

CD-ROM discs look like audio CDs. They feel like them. But chances are, little of the music or sounds you hear on multimedia applications come from audio CDs. And, like my father used to say, there are good reasons for that.

For one thing, most of the music on audio CDs is copyrighted, so multimedia developers are not necessarily free to use it. Other sounds and music available for multimedia often are copyrighted as well (but sometimes not). Also the sound in multimedia is often narration or sound effects—not the sort of sounds usually found on audio CDs.

As a result, multimedia usually consists of other types of sound. These sounds are *digitized*, or sounds that a computer and sound card can understand and play back. The two most common types of sounds used in multimedia are *waveform* files (sometimes called *WAV* files) and *MIDI* files.

Catching the Wave

We live in a noisy world, particularly if you are a city dweller, but noise—or more politely, sounds—are critical to multimedia. WAV files contain digitized recordings of music or sounds, such as dogs barking, cars backfiring, or birds chirping. Also, recorded voice narrations usually are WAV files.

The sounds in WAV files are recorded in much the same way you record sounds with a tape recorder. However, instead of storing the sounds on magnetic tape, you store them in digital form on a computer-based storage medium like your hard disk or a CD-ROM.

Caught in the MIDI

The other commonly used type of sound used in multimedia is *MIDI*, which stands for Musical Instrument Digital Interface. MIDI files usually have the .MID file extension name. While WAV files can include all kinds of recorded sounds, such as voice narrations and sound effects, MIDI files are synthesized music. MIDI files contain the instructions your computer needs to play back this music.

This is one place in which your sound card is important. The instructions in the MIDI file enable a synthesizer to play the music. Your sound card acts like a synthesizer and plays back the MIDI music.

Until recently, MIDI files almost always sounded like music created by synthesizer keyboards. That is, they sound like imitations of real instruments, which is what they are. However, sound card technology is changing rapidly, and new methods of reproducing sounds are yielding more realistic musical recordings.

MIDI   Stands for Musical Instrument Digital Interface. It is a type of synthesized music created with a computer that you can play through virtually all PC sound cards.

Both WAV and MIDI sounds are relatively simple to incorporate into multimedia applications. Chapter 25 tells you where to obtain both types of files should you want to create your own multimedia.

The Sound Card and the Glory

As we discussed earlier, if you use a PC and want to hear WAV or MIDI sounds, you need a sound card. Without a sound card, the most you'll get out of your PC are puny sounds like *bing* and *boop*, not the music, voice narrations, and other recorded sounds used in multimedia.

Like a video adapter, a sound card plugs into your computer's motherboard. In simple terms, when a multimedia application needs to play sound, it transmits the instructions for playing the sound through the motherboard to the sound card. The sound card then analyzes the sound file, interprets its digital contents, and plays the sound, either through speakers or headphones.

One method that a sound card uses for creating sounds (such as WAV sounds) is by playing *samples*. A sample is, as the name implies, a sample of the actual recorded sound. The more samples in a sound file, the more realistic the sound. The rate at which the sound card plays samples of the sound is the *sampling rate.*

Another method of recreating sounds is *FM synthesis.* FM stands for frequency modulation. It requires a special chip on the sound card but, these days, virtually all sound cards have this chip. In FM synthesis, the sound card pieces together a series of sounds so they resemble other sounds, such as musical notes. The results of these tones are usually stored in MIDI files.

A new technology, sometimes called *wavetable synthesis*, is increasingly being found on newer sound cards. This technology stores actual recorded samples of instruments and sounds in a special chip on the sound board or, sometimes, on your hard disk.

Sound cards with this technology replace synthesized tones with the recordings of the actual instruments. The result is music that sounds more realistic than synthesized music because it is based on samples of real instruments.

TECHNO NERD TEACHES...

You can use sound cards for more than just playing sounds and music as part of multimedia. For example, you can use sound cards to record both MIDI and waveform sounds. In fact, many sound cards include a MIDI port that enables you to plug a synthesizer into your sound card. That way, you can play a keyboard and record the music on your computer as MIDI files. Sophisticated music software exists for editing this music and even printing sheet music.

Another interesting use of sound cards is voice recognition. This is the sort of stuff you see in the Star Trek series, when somebody interacts with a computer by speaking to it. Today's voice recognition isn't nearly as sophisticated as that on the Starship Enterprise, but it is becoming more sophisticated quickly. Some voice recognition programs come with their own, more specialized expansion cards. However, many voice recognition programs use standard PC sound cards.

Hearing Noises

Many CD-ROM drives have jacks into which you plug headphones. Sound cards have a jack into which you plug headphones or speakers.

The headphones are particularly familiar: they're the same headphones you use with your walk-around stereo. The speakers also are familiar, although usually less elaborate and expensive than you use for your regular stereo system.

Because sound cards usually have only a minimal capability to amplify sound, the speakers you use for multimedia should be self-powered. This means you can plug them into an electrical outlet to provide additional amplification.

Also, speakers used with computers usually have special shielding for the magnets they contain, because magnetism can damage the data on your hard and floppy disks and can distort the image on your monitor.

You can buy speakers for your PC for as low as $20, but if you spend a little more for better speakers they'll really make your multimedia applications come to life. Take the time to try out several different speakers. Choosing the right sound is a very subjective thing, and you'll notice quite a difference within a small price range.

The Least You Need to Know

Even if you don't use multimedia, you'll need a monitor and video adapter. This chapter told you about those pieces and what is important when running multimedia. Specifically:

☞ One of the most important capabilities your monitor can provide for multimedia is crisp, pure colors. The lack of crisp, pure colors will detract from the quality of multimedia.

☞ Your monitor also must have a refresh rate fast enough to avoid a flickering image—at least 72Hz and preferably higher. If your monitor flickers, you'll suffer from headaches and eyestrain.

☞ You also should look for a "tight" dot pitch when buying a monitor. Dot pitch refers to the distance between the on-screen dots, called *pixels*, that comprise the image.

☞ Your video adapter, while hidden in your computer, is an extremely important factor in providing high-quality video. It must support your monitor's capabilities. It also must provide fast video, or visual multimedia elements like images and video will suffer.

☞ The sounds and music you hear in multimedia usually are stored in two computerized formats: MIDI and waveform files (also called WAV files).

☞ To play multimedia music, you need a sound card and either speakers or headphones.

Chapter 7
Hardware Is Easy

In This Chapter

- How multimedia often requires a hard disk
- The role of random-access memory
- Of mice and other pointing devices

If a computer's video system is its eyes, the stuff we talk about in this chapter is the guts of your computer. Like your own guts, these things aren't very fun or interesting. However, it's important to know about them, even if you don't see these parts every day.

Hard Drives Are Easy

We elders in the world of PCs remember that way back in the Stone Age of computerdom, say ten or twelve years ago, few computers came with hard drives as standard equipment. A big hard drive was 20MB, which is barely enough for storing a single program these days.

Now, of course, hard drives are virtually always part of new computers, with standard storage capacities of 10 or 20 times the size of those formally "huge" hard drives.

Newcomers to multimedia often are surprised to learn that even CD-ROM multimedia applications often require a hard drive. There are two simple reasons for this: hard drives are faster than CD-ROM drives, and you can't add data to CD-ROM drives as you can to a hard drive.

Because of their slow speed, it can be tortuous to load the basic files needed for a multimedia application from a CD-ROM drive. That's why many multimedia applications copy the files needed for starting up, and other frequently used files, to your hard drive.

Another reason that hard disks are important for multimedia is that some multimedia applications need to create or alter information. A simple example is a multimedia game that keeps track of your progress and score. It can't store that information on a CD-ROM because you can't add information to the disc. Rather, the game requires a medium on which it can change data, like your hard disk.

That's why, when buying a new PC or adding a hard drive, you should keep your multimedia needs in mind. If you plan to use a lot of multimedia and you are buying a new PC or adding a hard drive to an existing PC, think large.

Each multimedia application can add as much as ten megabytes of files—sometimes more—to your hard disk. That means you should get as much hard disk storage space as you can afford. I have about 600 MB, and with my CD-ROMs using more than 100 MB of that, I'm already wishing I had more.

To repeat the lesson of this section: If you are going to use multimedia, think BIG when selecting a hard disk capacity. While the specific amount of disk space you need varies from person to person, here's a rule of thumb: Get more than you think you'll need. The inviolable rule about hard disk space is that, however much capacity you have, you'll fill it up.

RAM Tough

You perhaps know that one of the things stored on your computer's motherboard is random access memory (RAM). RAM is like, you know, like... wow!—like a strange concept, dude.

In one way, RAM is like a hard drive or a CD-ROM drive because your applications store information there. However, RAM is conceptually more difficult to understand than a disk drive. You can hold a CD-ROM or a hard drive in your hand. Drives read information that is stored on specific parts of a disk. That's why they sometimes are called *physical drives*.

While you can hold RAM chips in your hand, the information stored in RAM isn't in a clearly definable place, like a specific location on your hard drive. The information is in memory. It's kind of like trying to figure out where a thought is located. It's truly a strange concept.

Random-access memory (RAM) Where your applications store much of the information needed to run on a moment-to-moment basis. RAM is composed of a series of chips. The more RAM you have, the more quickly and efficiently your multimedia applications operate.

Because physical drives store information in a specific location, the information remains on the drive even if you turn off your computer. The information in RAM disappears when you turn off your computer.

RAM operates more quickly than physical drives but is not nearly as plentiful as physical storage. As a result, the information stored in RAM tends to be transient information your programs or applications need to operate efficiently. Often, this isn't the information you access, but it's the core code needed to run the program—stuff only your computer and programmers know or care about.

Reading that information from RAM makes your applications operate faster than reading it from a hard disk, kind of like how thinking a thought is faster than reading it from a page.

Because CD-ROM drives are slow and because multimedia elements are also slow to operate, the more RAM your computer has, the more efficiently your multimedia applications will work. Make sure your PC has a minimum of 4MB of RAM. More, of course, is better—much better. My PC has 8MB of RAM and I wish I had more.

TECHNO NERD TEACHES...

While more RAM is better, faster RAM is often beside the point. True, some RAM chips operate more quickly than others, but the differences tend to be slight. If you're buying a new computer, be more concerned with quantity than speed, because PC vendors tend to equip their computers with the fastest RAM chips they can handle. If you are adding RAM, be wary of mixing RAM chips of different speeds; check with your PC's owner's manual before buying.

Doing the Processor Thing

Let's get to the heart of the matter: your computer's central processing unit (CPU). This is the chip that sits on your motherboard and is more responsible than anything else for determining how efficiently and quickly your computer operates.

Every computer has a CPU and the CPU has a hand in most computer operations. It's the chip that processes the hidden code that runs your programs. It also is involved in processes, such as displaying information on-screen, even if other chips, such as the graphics chip on your video adapter, also play a role.

SPEAK LIKE A GEEK

Central processing unit (CPU)   The main computing chip in your computer. It is involved in virtually every computing operation from calculating numbers to displaying information on-screen.

Over time, the power of the CPUs in PCs has increased dramatically. The first PCs, released in the early 1980s, had 8088 (pronounced *"eighty eighty-eight"*) CPUs. While quite snazzy at the time, these chips were laughably underpowered by today's standards. In fact, those early PC processors didn't even have enough power to run the current version of Windows.

After the 8088 chip, the next chip was the 80286 (pronounced *"two eighty-six"*) chip, which once seemed incredibly powerful but is laughably incompetent today. Then came the 80386 (*"three eighty-six"*) chip. There are still a fair number of PCs with this chip in operation, although very few PC vendors still sell 386 computers. At this writing, the most commonly used chip is the 80486 chip, although it is rapidly being supplanted in popularity by the newest (and not so laughable) generation chip, called the Pentium chip.

TECHNO NERD TEACHES...

Note that these CPU names were coined by Intel Corporation, the huge company that has long had a stranglehold on the chip market. Now, there are other companies making competing chips that work virtually identically to Intel's chips, which is good news for price-conscious consumers. In the past, a chip was always referred to by the numbers in its name, regardless of which company manufactured it. Recently, however, Intel got smart and chose a real name for their latest chip: the Pentium. Since Pentium is a registered trade name, other vendors use different names for their versions of this chip.

Besides added capabilities to each new wave of chips, each generation of chip operates more efficiently than the previous one, which increases speed dramatically. Somewhat different from the efficiency at which the chip operates is the intrinsic speed of the chip, which also has increased dramatically over time.

The early, highly inefficient 8088 chips operated at a speed of 4.77 megahertz (abbreviated as MHz). Because today's Pentium chips are much more efficient, even if they operated at 4.77MHz, they would be many times faster than the 8088 chips. Besides this increased efficiency, today's chips also have faster intrinsic speeds. One version of the Pentium chip, for example, operates at 100MHz.

SPEAK LIKE A GEEK

Megahertz (MHz) Measures how frequently something happens. This isn't like once a week, or annually. Rather, megahertz refers to how many millions of times per second something happens. With computers, it refers to how many millions of instructions, or tidbits of your computer program, the system can process per second.

The connection between CPUs and multimedia is straightforward: Buy the most powerful CPU that you can afford. Multimedia taxes almost every part of your PC, but the more powerful the CPU, the faster multimedia applications run and the more satisfying your multimedia experience.

Shopping Is *Not* Fun

Buying a computer is enough to break the spirit of anybody whose idea of a good time is shopping. Major new models of CPUs are introduced every couple of years. In the meantime, the price of existing CPUs is always decreasing, providing ever more bang for your buck.

The relentless march toward more powerful technology combined with decreasing prices causes many people to delay purchasing on the assumption that, if they wait, they'll get more for less. That's true, of course. But it will always be true, no matter how long you wait.

TECHNO NERD TEACHES...

If the future operates like the past, here are some buying guidelines. When computers with a new CPU first appear, a typical unit costs about $4,000.

If you're shopping for value, wait until the price is roughly half the original price, about a year to a year and a half after initial introduction. Prices will decrease after that point, but they will decrease relatively slowly.

If you're a shopping fanatic, you may not want to wait. You can have your new computer now and upgrade it later. Make sure you clarify with your vendor whether it is upgradable. If it is, you simply add the new chip to your computer and off you go. Easy, yes. Cheap, no. You impatient people should know that upgrading is an expensive process; it will cost you hundreds of dollars—how many hundreds depends on which chip you are upgrading to.

Eeek! A Mouse

In the last (but not least) category is an important message: You need a mouse, or something like a mouse, for multimedia.

To review a computer basic, a *mouse* is a pointing device you move around with your hand. Moving the mouse on your desk moves an on-screen pointer. Most multimedia programs let you make choices, such as deciding the next screen to view, by positioning the pointer with the mouse, then clicking.

It's this simplicity when making choices that has led most multimedia developers to require them. This is particularly true of interactive presentations in which you determine the direction you want the application to take. These days, most PCs come with mice. If you don't have one and you want to use multimedia, you'll need to buy one.

Besides the standard type of mouse, you also can buy other types of pointing devices. For example, a trackball is like a mouse turned upside down. Instead of moving the mouse, you roll a ball that's located within the device with your fingers, kind of like rubbing the mouse's belly. When you move the ball, the on-screen pointer moves. Some people prefer trackballs—it's strictly a matter of personal preference.

If you're of the game-playing persuasion, another pointing device you may want is a joystick. A joystick resembles the stick you often see on shoot-em-up arcade games. It requires a special port on your computer, often referred to as a game port. Most computers and some CD-ROM interfaces and sound cards come with game ports.

Fortunately, if you don't have a mouse or other pointing device, they're relatively inexpensive. Top-end mice run about $100, but you can find good mice for half that amount, or less. A good joystick tends to be about as expensive as a high-end mouse.

The Least You Need to Know

In this chapter, you learned about the parts of every computer that are important when using multimedia. Specifically:

☞ Multimedia applications—even those that come on CD-ROM disks—require hard disk storage space. When selecting a computer, make sure you have a lot of disk storage.

☞ The more random-access memory (RAM) you have, the faster multimedia will operate.

☞ The faster your computer's CPU, the faster multimedia operates. And the faster multimedia operates, the more you'll enjoy it.

☞ A mouse is virtually mandatory for most multimedia applications.

Chapter 8

The Scoop on CD-ROM Drives

In This Chapter

- How CD-ROM drives work
- CD-ROM drives interacting with your computer
- Standards and nonstandards

A word of caution before we begin: The stuff you'll learn in this chapter is important to know as you get started with multimedia, but keep it under your lid. It's not top secret, but it doesn't exactly make for the most scintillating conversation. You'll get a reputation as a techno-nerd if you start spouting off this information around the office water cooler.

The last two chapters told you about computers in general and how they relate to multimedia. In this chapter, you'll learn about one of the pieces you need to run multimedia on your PC—the CD-ROM drive.

You need to learn all you can about hardware because multimedia technology is changing at an incredibly rapid rate, and uninformed buyers can easily make purchases they soon regret. Believe me—I know. Also, some of you brave souls will install the multimedia hardware yourselves. In either case, you need the background this chapter provides to understand more about the pieces and how they work.

While you won't want to talk about this stuff, the knowledge will help your self-esteem. You can be smug because you'll know more than some yo-yo who is blathering on and on about what he thinks multimedia is.

Spinning Discs: About CD-ROM Drives

The most visible part of a multimedia system is a CD-ROM drive. Ironically, it is not a mandatory part of multimedia. That's because a CD-ROM drive is merely a way of storing and playing data, like your hard drive.

However, because multimedia items, such as videos and sound, require a lot of storage space and because CD-ROMs have an abundance of storage space, they have become, hands down, the most popular method of storing multimedia. CD-ROMs are such a popular method of storing multimedia that many people incorrectly believe that CD-ROMs *are* multimedia.

It might surprise you to find out, however, that many CD-ROMs aren't multimedia discs at all. Many of the CD-ROM titles that are of interest to business are large text databases, not multimedia.

At any rate, since most commercially available multimedia is available on CD-ROM, CD-ROM drives are a good place to begin discussing the hardware and software you need for multimedia. That's what the next several sections do.

A Certain Magnetism

Even if you're a raw recruit to the world of computing, you're probably familiar with floppy disks and floppy drives. The basic drill for using CD-ROM drives and floppy drives is about the same: To access data on the disk, you insert the disc into the drive. Also, like hard drives and floppy drives, you can get a CD-ROM drive that fits inside your system unit (called an *internal* drive), or you can get one that sits to the side of your computer (called an *external* drive). Turn to Chapter 10 for more information about the differences between internal and external drives.

Of course, CD-ROM drives work differently from floppy drives. The industry also calls floppy drives and hard drives *magnetic media* because a magnetic substance, such as iron oxide, coats the disks. That's why (like the well-known magnetic medium of cassette tapes) data on a disk can be distorted or eliminated if placed next to a magnetic object. The disks store the data (or music on a tape) in a very specific order, and magnets can damage or delete the data.

It's the Pits

If you want magnetism, you won't find it on CD-ROMs. CD-ROMs store data on polycarbonate discs coated with a film, usually composed of aluminum alloy. Data is stored by creating an organized series of very tiny pits in the aluminum layer of this high-tech sandwich.

As I told you in Chapter 3, the CD-ROM drive shoots a laser beam at the disk. The drive analyzes the reflection of the laser beam to discern whether a pit exists at any given point in the disk. The drive reads the pattern created by the pits and translates that pattern into data.

You would think that because they use something as cool as a laser, CD-ROM drives would be superior to magnetic drives in every way. They're not, although their relatively large storage capacity makes them extremely convenient for multimedia. With today's most commonly used CD-ROM technology, you can't add or delete information on CD-ROMs as you can with magnetic drives. Another disadvantage of CD-ROM drives is that they display information more slowly than traditional hard drives.

One of the key measurements of the speed of any drive—whether it is a floppy drive, hard drive, or CD-ROM drive—is its *access time*, usually measured in *milliseconds (or ms)*.

Currently, the average access time of most hard drives is between 10–20 milliseconds. By contrast, at this writing, even a fast CD-ROM drive has an average disk access speed of about 200 milliseconds, or about 10 times slower than most hard drives. As always, of course, technology is marching forward and CD-ROM drives are getting faster.

Access time   Refers to the average amount of time a drive takes to find the data and start reading data from a disc. The lower the disc access time, the faster the disc responds to your requests for data.

Millisecond (ms)   The measure most often used to count the length of time a drive takes to start reading data from a storage medium, such as a floppy disk or CD-ROM. One millisecond is a thousandth of a second. Obviously, a millisecond is a very brief interval—in my experience, this is about the length of time it takes to think a nasty thought and then regret it.

Like a Greek Chorus on Speed

If this book had a Greek chorus, it might say something like: A millisecond is a teeny, tiny measure of time, so even the difference between 20 milliseconds and 250 milliseconds is hardly noticeable. So what's the big deal?

As has long been the tradition, Greek choruses ask good questions. If you're a particularly laid-back person, the difference in speed between a hard drive and a CD-ROM drive may not be a big deal. It will be noticeable, however, and it can be annoying. That's because reading the data on the disk is just one step of the process. The drive—whether it is a hard drive, floppy drive, or CD-ROM drive—must translate that data into something your computer understands and present that data to you, typically either on-screen or as sound. These processes involve other parts of your computer, such as your computer's main processing chip, central processing unit (CPU), video adapter, and monitor, to name just a few. These items also require time to operate.

The nature of multimedia can exaggerate the problem of slow speed. Video, animation, and sound require ongoing processing to play the entire clip.

In other words, it takes more than a single action by the CD-ROM drive to display a two-minute video. It requires an ongoing interaction between the drive and the other parts of your computer. A slow CD-ROM drive produces a ripple effect that causes delays as you wait for multimedia items to start playing. It can also cause a herky-jerky playback.

A CD-ROM Drive's Spin Cycle

Maybe by now, you're getting the idea that all these milliseconds add up. What's a multimedia maven to do?

Well, there are ways to speed up the CD-ROM process. The most notable method—or at least the method that gets the most attention—is to increase the speed at which the CD-ROM drive's motor spins.

A couple of years ago, CD-ROM vendors released the first so-called *double speed* drives, which doubled the speed at which the CD-ROM spins in the drive. This, in turn, dramatically increased disk access time.

Remember, however, that because there are other processes involved in reading information from CD-ROM drives, doubling the spin rate doesn't necessarily double the access time.

At this writing, vendors are still selling single-spin drives, but double speed drives have become the norm. As always seems to be the case in the high-tech world, double speed drives are coming down in price rapidly while faster technology is becoming available. Triple speed and quadruple speed drives already are on the market, and as sure as the sun rises in the morning, they eventually will replace double speed drives.

Gimme Some Cache

If you don't want to twiddle your thumbs waiting for the next big jump in CD-ROM drive technology, go ahead and buy a double speed (or greater) CD-ROM drive. Besides that solution, though, there are two other ways to speed up CD-ROM drives.

The first is to use a faster CD-ROM interface. We'll discuss CD-ROM interfaces in Chapter 9, but the short story is that they are expansion cards that connect your CD-ROM drive to the rest of your computer. Suffice it to say, some CD-ROM interfaces are faster than others.

Another way to speed up your CD-ROM drive is to use a *disk cache*. Disk caches are little programs that have long been popular for use with hard drives. They work by storing recently used data in a special place in RAM. The theory is that applications tend to keep re-using the same information. So instead of repeatedly reading information from a disc, the computer stores it in that special place in RAM. This speeds things up because RAM is much faster than even a relatively fast hard drive.

SPEAK LIKE A GEEK

Disk cache A utility program that stores recently used information in your computer's RAM. This speeds up the access time because accessing data from RAM is faster than accessing it from a mechanical device, such as a CD-ROM drive. Not all disk cache utilities work with CD-ROM drives, but those that do also will speed up your hard drive.

When applied to a CD-ROM drive, a disk cache dramatically increases performance. How much, you ask? I tested several disk caches on my double speed CD-ROM drive and used a special benchmark program to measure the results.

Without a disk cache, the average access time on my drive is about 300 milliseconds. With a disk cache, the average access time is 60 milliseconds. In other words, the difference is quite noticeable. Your results may vary, but no matter how fast your CD-ROM drive, it's worthwhile to use a disk cache.

TECHNO NERD TEACHES...

Even a disk cache can't turn a sow's ear into a silk purse. A disk cache significantly increases the performance of a single–speed drive, but it still won't make it as fast as a double–, triple–, or quadruple–speed drive. There are several reasons for this. First and foremost, disk caches don't cache all the information on a disk—only the most recently used information. The cache speeds up access to that information, but it doesn't make the drive spin faster, so the drive still accesses a lot of other information relatively slowly.

If you don't know your version of DOS, or even whether you have a copy of SMARTDrive, at the DOS prompt, type **VER** to see the DOS version number. To see if your SMARTDrive version can handle CD-ROM, type **DIR SMARTDRV.EXE** at the DOS prompt and press **Enter**. If you have SMARTDrive, a file displays. If it shows the date November 1, 1993 or later, it is capable of caching a CD-ROM drive.

Where Do I Get the Cache?

Where do you get one of these magical disk cache utilities? Well, there are many vendors who would be ever so happy to sell one to you, but chances are you already have one. That's because a competent disk cache utility, called SMARTDrive, comes with all versions of MS-DOS and Windows sold in the past year or so.

For some of you, though, there is a gotcha with SMARTDrive. While SMARTDrive has long been a part of DOS, only very recent versions of DOS—starting with MS-DOS 6.2—include a version of SMARTDrive that works with CD-ROM drives.

If your version of SMARTDrive caches CD-ROM drives, you must load it like you load any program. It then works when you use all your other programs. The easiest way to load a disk cache is to place the commands for loading it in your AUTOEXEC.BAT file. This file contains commands that execute automatically when you start your computer (AUTOmatically EXECute—get it?). Read your DOS user's manual for more details. If you don't have a version of SMARTDrive that caches CD-ROM drives, either upgrade to the most recent version of DOS or buy a cache utility from another vendor.

Which Cache Is the Best?

If you're a curious consumer, or a closet power-user, you might ask which is the best disk cache. Funny you should ask: Of the four or five disk cache programs I've tested that work with CD-ROM drives, I've found they all provide about the same performance improvements, give or take about ten percent.

The utilities did vary, however, in other areas. Some provide more capabilities for tweaking how the cache works. This sort of tweakability is of greatest interest to technically savvy people (a.k.a. techno nerds) The tweaking results in relatively small improvements in performance. Still, these small improvements are what techies love to talk about, so they do have some value.

Another consideration is that some caches require less of your computer's memory than others. If you are perpetually short on RAM, this may be an important consideration when selecting a disk cache.

Data Transfer Rates Exposed!

This section needs a hot heading because, let's face it, *data transfer rates* aren't the most scintillating topic. But they are important. As the name implies, the data transfer rate measures how much information (or data) a CD-ROM drive can transfer from the drive to your PC in one second. Some consider it a better measurement of a CD-ROM drive's capabilities than disk access speeds because it more accurately reflects how efficient your drive is. That's because access time measures only a drive's response time to a request for information. The drive's data transfer rate, on the other hand, tells you how much information the drive can process per second.

Data transfer rate   The amount of information that a CD-ROM drive can read and send on to the computer for processing in a second. Your computer measures the data transfer rate in kilobytes per second.

A high data transfer rate is important if you access large files. In the multimedia world, videos, animations, and many sound files are large files indeed. As a result, give greater credence to the data transfer rate than to access time when choosing a drive that you'll use primarily for multimedia.

While lower access time numbers are better, higher numbers are more valuable with data transfer rates. You measure the data transfer rate in kilobytes of information per second.

A double speed drive should provide a data transfer rate of at least 300 kilobytes per second. Triple speed drives have a data transfer rate of at least 450 kilobytes per second, and quadruple speed drives have a data transfer rate of 600 kilobytes per second.

In the Buffer

Another part of the CD-ROM drive you need to be familiar with is the *data buffer*. Buffers aren't terribly exciting, but you should know about these little guys because they have a direct impact on your CD-ROM drive's performance.

Data buffer   A section of memory that temporarily stores information until your PC can process it. Many different types of applications use buffers, but for our purposes, we're talking about buffers built into CD-ROM drives. An adequate buffer is important to keep information flowing consistently from the drive to the computer.

Say you listen to my advice (as well you should!) and buy a CD-ROM drive with a high data transfer rate. At times, that CD-ROM drive will pump out information as fast as all get out.

That, of course is great. However, it can also cause a problem if it pumps information faster than your PC can handle it. If that's the case, the information needs a place to wait until the PC can deal with it or the whole multimedia shebang slows down. That place is a *buffer*. A buffer is a bit of memory dedicated to the task of storing data until your computer can display it.

In truth, buffers aren't the exclusive domain of CD-ROM drives. Your keyboard, for example, has a buffer with which you may be familiar. Say you save a large file and start typing before your hard drive finishes saving. At first, nothing appears on-screen, but when the hard drive finishes, the stuff you typed appears. You're smart, so take a guess as to where that information you typed was hiding while the hard disk thrashed away? You got it: in your keyboard's buffer.

CD-ROM buffers work pretty much the same way, and have the same benefit. They help make sure that the data moves from the CD-ROM drive to your PC's other resources in an even flow. This prevents data loss and slow-downs as your PC struggles to keep up.

Don't buy a CD-ROM drive without a data buffer, even if the drive has a fast access time or high data transfer rate. The minimum acceptable buffer size is 64 kilobytes, but buffer sizes can be as large as 256 kilobytes or more. The bigger the buffer, the faster and more consistently your drive operates.

Standards Issues

Say that one day a bolt falls off your child's backyard swing set. You find the bolt on the ground, but not the nut that tightens the bolt. You have two choices: You can ignore the problem and hope your child isn't hurt too badly when the swing set falls apart, or, being a good parent, you can put the bolt in your pocket, go to a hardware store and get a new nut. Since you love your child, you choose the latter.

At the hardware store, you go to the nut section, where it takes about one minute to find the specific nut you need for your bolt. Just to be sure, you try turning the nut on the bolt and, sure enough, it works perfectly. You return home and, zip-zap, your child's swing set is safe again.

You're probably thinking: Excuse me, but what has this to do with multimedia? Well, nothing directly. However, there is an important connection indirectly. The reason you had so little trouble finding the correct nut was that nuts, bolts, screws, and the like have standardized threads.

Standards We all have standards. Standards are generally agreed-upon ways of doing things. Standards exist for items ranging from nuts and bolts to virtually all sorts of computer equipment. There are several international organizations that focus on creating and imposing standards.

That means that a bolt created by one manufacturer works with a nut created by another. That's what a *standard* is. If there were no standards, you would probably spend a day or a week looking for the right twenty-five cent nut to work with your child's swing set. If you couldn't find such a nut, you'd have to throw away the swing set and buy another.

Okay—enough about swing sets. Let's talk about standards as they pertain to multimedia. If there were no standards, you might buy a CD-ROM, plop it in your CD-ROM drive and find that it doesn't work. Fortunately, however, there are several standards that apply to CD-ROM drives and discs. If the CD-ROM drive you purchase adheres to these standards, you should have no trouble using virtually all CD-ROMs currently available.

Read Chapter 10, which discusses the features to look for in a CD-ROM drive, to learn more about these standards. My purpose here is simply to alert you to the fact that standards do exist. Most CD-ROM drives available today adhere to these standards, but it still is possible to find drives that don't.

The Least You Need to Know

In this chapter, you learned:

☛ CD-ROM drives use a laser beam to read a pattern of pits on a disc and translate that pattern into data.

☛ One measure of a CD-ROM drive's speed is its access time. The access time is how long it takes from the time you ask for information until the drive starts providing it. The lower the access time, the better.

☛ That CD-ROM drives don't operate as quickly as hard drives, but there are ways to speed them up, such as by using a disk cache utility.

☛ Standards exist for how CD-ROMs are formatted. You should make sure that your CD-ROM drive adheres to all these standards.

(zen text)

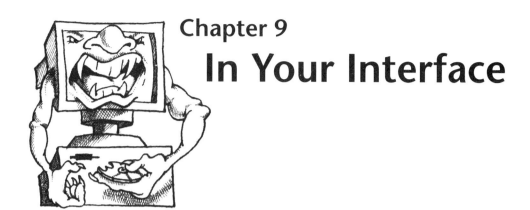

Chapter 9
In Your Interface

In This Chapter

- ☞ Interfacing with CD-ROM drive
- ☞ SCSI isn't scuzzy
- ☞ More discussion about drivers

The human body is a series of interconnected and interdependent parts. If one part breaks down, the rest of your body doesn't work very well. Also, all the pieces have to be *properly connected*. If you have a nose on the side of your head instead of the front of your face, you have a serious problem.

Same goes for a CD-ROM drive. You must properly connect everything before you can expect the thing to work. You must have a monitor and video adapter to show information on-screen, a sound card and speakers so you can play and hear sound, a big hard drive, and lots of RAM. You have to hook up all that stuff correctly or the multimedia experience is a no go. (Installation instructions are in Part III of this book.)

Not only do you need to hook it up the right way, but your CD-ROM drive also must know how to communicate with all this other expensive equipment. The thing that helps your CD-ROM drive interact with the rest of your computer is a *CD-ROM interface*.

Let's Interface, Baby!

Often, the term interface refers to how you communicate with software programs. When used in this way, for example, the system of menus and commands for your word processor comprise that program's interface.

CD-ROM interface An expansion card that plugs into your computer's motherboard. You connect your CD-ROM drive to the interface, and the interface, in turn, enables the drive to access the resources, such as video and sound, in the rest of your computer. Like other items you plug into your computer's motherboard, CD-ROM interfaces also are sometimes referred to as adapters or cards.

In the context of CD-ROM drives, an *interface* is the piece of hardware that enables the drive to communicate with the rest of the parts of your computer. It's an expansion card that you plug into a free expansion slot in your computer's motherboard.

After you insert the CD-ROM interface into a slot in your computer, you connect the CD-ROM drive to the interface with a cable. Some CD-ROM drives are placed directly inside your computer and others sit outside of your computer. Both types must be connected by cable to the CD-ROM interface (although as you'll learn in Part III, some of the specifics of the connection are slightly different).

After you hook up all this stuff, your CD-ROM drive becomes an integral part of your computer, and you can access the information contained on CD-ROM discs.

Beginning SCSI-ness

Acronyms can be fun, particularly when the name of the organization is stretched to make an interesting acronym. One of my favorites, for example, is the club for tandem bicyclists in Wisconsin called Couples on Wheels (COWs).

Multimedia also has a clever acronym. By far the most commonly used type of CD-ROM interface is a SCSI adapter (pronounced *"SCUZ-zy"*). SCSI stands for Small Computer System Interface, and it is an industry standard.

A standardized SCSI adapter actually can support other types of devices besides CD-ROM drives, such as hard drives and tape backup units. As will be discussed in Chapter 13, you can connect multiple devices—as many as seven—to a single SCSI interface. This process is called *daisychaining*.

Some CD-ROM drive vendors provide a version of the SCSI adapter designed to work only with that specific drive. There are advantages and disadvantages to these proprietary interfaces.

You'll learn more about SCSI adapters later in this book. The purpose here is more simple: to introduce you to this bit of computer lingo.

Wrapping Up Interfaces

Let's say you want to view a piece of multimedia that shows a still image and plays a narration at the same time. Here, in rough terms, is how it works.

1. The CD-ROM drive uses a laser to read the pattern of pits on the disk. The drive has a microprocessor that decodes this pattern of pits and turns it into data.

2. The drive then sends the data representing the image and sound to the CD-ROM interface, which connects to your computer's motherboard.

3. The CD-ROM interface sends the information to the motherboard. Built-in software which determines the interactions between the parts of your computer routes information appropriately.

4. The image information goes to your video adapter. The sound information goes to your sound card.

5. Those cards perform the processing tasks necessary to handle the image and sound. Then, like magic, the image appears on your monitor and you hear the narration through your speakers.

This, of course, is a simplified explanation. Getting all these parts to work harmoniously is difficult at times. That is why (as you'll learn in Part III) you may find it difficult to install the pieces that make multimedia work.

Software Stirs the Drink

By now, you've probably memorized the basic ingredients for a multimedia PC: a CD-ROM drive, a CD-ROM drive interface, a sound card, and speakers or a headphone. You probably think that you plug all these pieces in and you're done, right? Well, not exactly.

Believe me, you are a long way from done. First, you must make sure that the other parts of your computer, such as your monitor and hard drive, are up to the task of multimedia. Chapters 6 and 7 discuss those hardware and software issues. Also, I'd be remiss in my duties if I didn't mention the software you need to make all this multimedia stuff work. No, I'm not talking about the CD-ROMs or other actual multimedia applications. I'm talking about something far less interesting but equally essential.

Most of the hardware discussed in this chapter requires at least one bit of software to make it work. As you recall, this program is called a driver. It is a small computer file that you must load before using hardware. It allows the hardware to interact with the other parts of your computer.

Specifically, you usually need drivers for your CD-ROM drive, CD-ROM interface, and your sound card. Without the drivers, your computer won't even know that these bits of hardware exist or what to do with the information they are processing.

Think of a software driver as, well, a car driver. Without a driver, a car is just a hunk of metal and plastic. Without software drivers, your multimedia hardware is just a bunch of metal that doesn't do anything or go anywhere. These drivers come with the hardware; you don't have to buy them separately. Besides these drivers, you also must use a special software program for your CD-ROM drive that comes with recent versions of DOS. This program is MSCDEX, which stands for Microsoft CD Extensions, and it comes with all versions of DOS sold in the last couple of years.

You also need a number of drivers to play sounds, videos, and animations in Windows. Some of these drivers come with Windows, some come with your hardware, and some come with your multimedia applications. Again, you shouldn't have to buy these drivers separately.

Usually, you can set your computer to load these drivers automatically whenever you start your computer. You do this by placing the command that loads the driver in your AUTOEXEC.BAT or CONFIG.SYS files, which are listings of commands that your computer automatically executes when it starts. (For information on editing your AUTOEXEC.BAT or CONFIG.SYS files, check your DOS documentation.)

For playing multimedia in Windows, you place commands in special setup files to run these drivers. Two of the most prominent files in which you place these commands are SYSTEM.INI and WIN.INI. (For more information on SYSTEM.INI and WIN.INI, see your Windows documentation.)

If this sounds threatening, it needn't be. Usually, your hardware and applications come with special installation programs which, among other things, modify your AUTOEXEC.BAT, CONFIG.SYS, SYSTEM.INI and WIN.INI files to automatically load these files. Read Chapter 16 for more details about installation programs.

Still, you should know about these drivers, even if you buy a multimedia-ready PC. That's because new capabilities you add to your PC may conflict with existing multimedia drivers, and, chances are, you'll need to know what to do to make them work together.

Oops—we're getting a bit ahead of ourselves. The purpose here is simply to describe the pieces you need for multimedia and provide a basic explanation about how those pieces work. Part III describes the installation process for this combination of multimedia hardware and software. It's a process that isn't always pleasant but becomes simpler if you understand the role of each piece of the puzzle.

The Least You Need to Know

Were you paying attention to this chapter? If you were, you'd now know:

- ☞ The CD-ROM interface is the expansion card to which you attach your CD-ROM drive. It acts like a go-between, passing information back and forth between the drive and the rest of your computer.

- ☞ The most common type of CD-ROM interface is a SCSI interface.

- ☞ You need special programs called *drivers* (usually included with the multimedia hardware) to make the hardware work with other elements of your PC.

Hey, now's a good time to take a break. Relax. Close your eyes. Roll your head around. Your neck is a well-cooked piece of asparagus.

Chapter 10
Shopping, Anyone?

In This Chapter

- The MPC standards
- What you need in a CD-ROM drive
- Data buffers—wow!

Some people just love to shop. To me, shopping for computer equipment is a real hassle. So many choices, so much money... and the technology is changing so rapidly. Who can keep up with it all?

That's why previous chapters told you about the capabilities to look for in a computer that you'll use for multimedia and described the multimedia-specific hardware and software you'll need. This chapter is a natural follower because it tells you what to look for when selecting multimedia-specific components.

Let's face it—shopping for computers and computer components will never be fun. However, maybe, just maybe, we can take some of the fear and loathing out of it.

I Want My MPC

In much the same way that a group of Main Street merchants gets together to promote downtown shopping, a group of self-interested hardware and software vendors got together a few years ago. The problem they were trying to solve was the same one that this chapter addresses: People become easily confused about the hardware and software they need to run multimedia applications.

The result of this get-together was the first MPC (Multimedia Personal Computer) standard. The idea was that if your PC meets the MPC standard, it will run multimedia applications efficiently. The group, called the Multimedia Marketing Council, even came up with a logo for computers that comply with the standard and software that run on those computers.

What a relief, huh? Actually, it turned into a not-so-funny joke. At the heart of the first MPC standard were the following components:

- ☞ CD-ROM drive with a minimum of 500 millisecond access time and a 150 kilobyte per second data transfer rate. This refers to a single speed CD-ROM drive.

- ☞ Computer based on a 80386 or greater central processing unit

- ☞ 2MB of RAM

- ☞ 30MB or greater hard drive

- ☞ 8-bit sound card

The Multimedia Marketing Council was well-intentioned, perhaps, but unfortunately there was a problem. Systems that just barely met this standard ran multimedia about as quickly as molasses in January. Based on this standard, many people bought PCs that were woefully underpowered and almost immediately out of date. Sure, multimedia worked on these computers, but it didn't work well.

Because the original MPC standard was old before its time, the Multimedia Marketing Council came up with a newer standard called, quite imaginatively, MPC Level 2. This standard is a bit more realistic, although a skeptic might claim that it still leads people to buy underpowered computers. The updated MPC standard calls for:

- ☞ PC based on the 80486 or greater CPU

- ☞ 4MB of RAM

- ☞ 160MB hard drive

- ☞ 16-bit sound card

- ☞ CD-ROM drive with a 400 millisecond average access time and data throughput of 300 kilobytes per second. This refers to a double speed CD-ROM drive.

- ☞ VGA monitor

Isn't it nice that these concerned vendors took the trouble to help us out? Here's my suggestion: Don't rely on the MPC standards. There's no magic about them; they're just a series of loose guidelines developed by self-interested vendors.

If you are considering buying a computer and multimedia hardware, consider MPC Level 2 a minimal starting point. It's adequate for many of today's multimedia applications, although far from optimal. As technology and multimedia complexity increases, MPC Level 2 equipment will become very underpowered.

Instead of rushing out and buying the first computer you see that has the MPC logo slapped on it, glean all the knowledge you can from the previous chapters, which discuss the parts of all computers required for multimedia and the multimedia-specific components. Also read the rest of this chapter thoroughly; it makes recommendations about multimedia-specific hardware and software.

Keep in mind that the MPC Level 2 standard is a minimal standard for today and will be out of date before long. If you can afford it, spend more to get greater capabilities.

When you finish the rest of this chapter, you should have a pretty good idea about the equipment you need, and the benefits and drawbacks of the various options.

Taking a CD-ROM Drive for a Spin

Of the major multimedia hardware you need, the CD-ROM drive is the most visible. To review two of the important points (from Chapter 8):

- ☞ **The speed of the drive.** Single speed drives are rapidly becoming out of date. Double-speed drives are the minimum speed you should buy. Triple and quadruple speed drives are available and prices for those drives undoubtedly will come down over time.

- ☞ **Access time.** This number measures the difference between the time when the computer asks for information and when the drive actually finds it. Access time is an important measure of a CD-ROM drive's performance.

- ☞ **Data transfer rate.** This number is particularly important for multimedia fanatics. It measures the amount of data that the CD-ROM drive can transfer at a time. Because multimedia files (such as video files) usually are large, the higher the transfer rate, the faster multimedia will operate.

While the motor speed, access time, and data transfer rate of the drive are important when choosing the drive you want, there are also other factors. Specifically, you should keep in mind:

- ☞ The size of data buffers.

- ☞ Whether the drive adheres to certain standards that enable it to read most CD-ROM discs.

- ☞ Whether you want the drive installed inside your PC like a floppy or hard disk drive, or whether you want an external unit.

The following sections discuss the last two issues in greater detail. Don't be afraid: I'll keep it simple. These topics are important because they will make you a better consumer.

So You Have Standards

We all have standards to which we adhere (or try to). Your CD-ROM drive has standards, too. If you buy a drive that doesn't meet some basic standards, you could be an unhappy camper.

Why standards? Well, as explained in Chapter 8, without standards, pieces developed by different manufacturers don't work together. That holds true whether the items are nuts and bolts or whether they are CD-ROM drives and discs.

One area in which standards have evolved is the physical formatting of CD-ROMs. Formatting in this case refers to organizing the information on a disc in a consistent and predictable manner so that the CD-ROM drive can read it.

The idea behind these standards is similar to the idea behind formatting hard and floppy drives. The drive has to know where to look for information or it will, at best, be inefficient. Standards provide a structure for the placement of information on a disk, and also provide the drive with help finding specific information.

One of the earliest standards—and still the basic standard—for CD-ROM discs is the *ISO 9660 standard*. ISO stands for—are you ready for this?—the International Standards Organization. This is a group that develops standards for a variety of different product types.

If your CD-ROM drive doesn't support the ISO 9660 standard, you're in a world of hurt. That's because the vast majority of CD-ROMs adhere to this standard. These days, you'd have to work pretty hard to find a drive that doesn't support ISO 9660, but it is possible.

You might use these standards to test pesky know-it-all salespeople. If they've never heard of the standard, they're unlikely to be the most knowledgeable source of information. If you're going to drop a wad of money, you certainly deserve to work with people who have the knowledge to help you.

ISO 9660 The basic standard for the format of CD-ROMs that helps determine the way your computer places information on a disc. It provides standardized tools that enable the CD-ROM drive to find that information. Since virtually all CD-ROMs support this standard, it is essential that your CD-ROM drive support it also.

A twist on these standards is the capability for a CD-ROM drive to play audio CDs as well as CD-ROMs. This capability is CD-DA (for digital audio). Again, virtually all CD-ROM drives have this capability, although you need a sound card connected to your CD-ROM drive to make it work.

Assuming you have a sound card, you can play the sound through your speakers. Otherwise, most CD-ROM drives have a jack into which you can plug headphones. If you really want to get ambitious, depending on your sound card, you can even attach your drive to an amplifier and play sounds through a "normal" stereo system.

To play audio CDs, you need a special program. Usually, this program comes with your CD-ROM drive or your sound card. You merely load the utility and the audio CD, and then listen away.

The CD-ROM Drive As Photo Album

Just as we use our multi-thousand dollar PCs to play goofy little games, we also can use them as substitute photo albums. A recent development has been the slow, but growing, acceptance of Kodak's Photo CD format. With this format, you take photos as you normally would, but you tell your photo finisher to publish the photos in digital form on a special CD-ROM.

Not all photo developers can develop film in the Photo CD format. I hate free plugs, but here's a useful one: To find out the location of nearby photo finishers who handle Photo CD format, call 1-800-235-6325. This is a special line sponsored by Kodak.

You can buy a special Photo CD player that connects to your television for viewing your photo CDs. However, most CD-ROM drives also can access and display photos stored in this format.

While most recent CD-ROM drives support this format, it's still worth double-checking before you buy. This format is growing in popularity, particularly among those who create multimedia presentations and those who create documents with desktop publishing programs. Photo CD enables you to incorporate photos into these applications without first scanning them or going through complex printing processes.

You also should make sure that your CD-ROM drive supports *multisession* Photo CD capabilities. Typically, you add information to a CD-ROM once and only once. Multisession support refers to the capability for the CD-ROM drive to read information that you place on the disk in more than one session. How economically and environmentally correct!

This is a common need with Photo CDs because often the contents of more than one roll of film can fit on a single CD. Multisession support enables a photographer to add photos to a disc over a period of time, which is more cost effective than creating a new disc each time. Increasingly, CD-ROM drives have multisession Photo CD capabilities, but, at this writing, some still do not.

SPEAK LIKE A GEEK

Photo CD format
Developed by Kodak, a means of placing photographs on a CD-ROM. It is steadily gaining in popularity as a computerized format for photos used in multimedia presentations and by desktop publishers. Before you buy a CD-ROM drive, make sure that it supports the Photo CD format and also multiple Photo CD sessions.

CD-ROM XA and Away

An on-again-off-again CD-ROM standard is CD-ROM XA, which stands for CD-ROM Extended Architecture. This standard isn't widely accepted, and it's hard to know whether it ever will be. However, you should know about it because some parts of the standard are relevant today. CD-ROM XA enables multimedia developers to precisely combine more than one medium, such as a graphic image and sound. It also is necessary for viewing Photo CDs. This standard doesn't replace the older ISO 9660 and HSF standards, it works in conjunction with them.

SPEAK LIKE A GEEK

CD-ROM XA CD-ROM Extended Architecture, a format that makes it easy for multimedia developers to combine more than one medium, such as still images and sound, relatively seamlessly.

At this writing, few CD-ROM drives on the market are fully CD-ROM XA compliant, but most drives are at least partially compliant—compliant enough for Photo CD. A part of the MPC Level 2 standard requires

CD-ROM drives to be able to play files that mix media using the CD-ROM XA standard. However, the MPC Level 2 standard does not require full compliance with the standard.

It isn't certain whether this situation will change over time. Relatively few multimedia titles (and drives) provide full support for the CD-ROM XA standard although many titles include portions of mixed multimedia. In the future, you may only need to make sure that a CD-ROM drive you buy can play XA files, something that most drives on the market can do.

SPEAK LIKE A GEEK

Internal and external drives An *internal* CD-ROM drive fits inside a computer's drive bay the same as a floppy drive. An *external* drive is a self-contained unit that remains outside your PC when connected to your computer's CD-ROM interface.

Is Yours an Innie or an Outie?

It's happening already! Increasingly, PCs are coming with CD-ROM drives as standard equipment. These standard-issue CD-ROM drives are *internal drives* built into the PC, just like floppy and hard drives.

If you add multimedia capabilities to an existing PC, you have a choice. Most CD-ROM vendors offer the same drive in an internal version and an external version that you can place on top of your computer or on your desk (see the following figure). Here are some of the pros and cons of internal and external CD-ROM units.

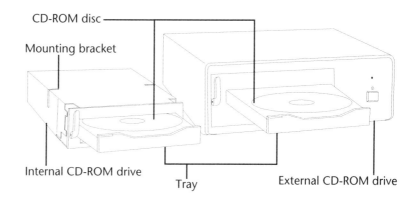

CD-ROM disc

Mounting bracket

An internal and external CD-ROM drive.

Internal CD-ROM drive

Tray

External CD-ROM drive

Ease of Installation

Hands down, external units are easier to install. That's because you don't have to worry about putting them into a drive bay. A *drive bay* is a part of your PC that holds drives.

If you ask your PC vendor, he'll undoubtedly tell you that it's trivially simple to slide a new drive into a drive bay. Well, somewhere in this universe that may be true. In my world, before you slide a new drive into a drive bay, you often must build a frame around the drive and add rails so it slides in easily.

Sometimes this is simple, sometimes not. Sometimes the drive comes with the frame and rails, sometimes not. Even if the drive does come with the frame and rails, sometimes they're the right size, sometimes not.

On the other hand, you just plop an external drive on top of your PC, connect it to your CD-ROM drive interface, plug in the power cord, and off you go.

Your PC's Internal Capacity

Even if you have the right frame and rails, there may not be a place inside your PC for the CD-ROM drive. That's because some PCs come with empty drive bays in case you want to add new drives, and some don't.

Before you buy an internal unit, make sure you have an available drive bay. To do this, either ask the person from whom you bought your PC or take the lid off your PC and look. Look either above, below, or to the side of your current hard and floppy drives. If there's a drive-sized gap, that probably means you have a free drive bay.

Also, think about your future expansion plans. If there's only one free drive bay and you think you may want to add an additional hard drive, maybe you should get an external CD-ROM drive. You can buy external hard drives, but they're harder to find than external CD-ROM drives, and they're expensive.

Portability

Getting an internal drive installed is difficult enough. What if you buy a new computer and want to switch the drive to that computer? Again, external drives are the hands-down winner. Simply unplug the drive from the CD-ROM interface, carry it to the new computer, and plug the drive into that computer's CD-ROM interface. What could be simpler?

External drives, of course, are easier to move around. Remember, though, that they do take up space that internal drives don't require.

Cost

You're probably saying, "Bottom line me, baby!" If you are, please knock it off and talk normally. If cost interests you and you can ask without using that obnoxious phrase, here's the deal. You'll spend at least $50 more and as much as $150 more for an external drive than you will for an internal drive.

Sure, there are different expenses for external drives, such as an external case. However, I'm not sure why these different parts would add up to such a large premium for the external drive. At any rate, be prepared to pay a premium for the external drive.

Capabilities

There should be no difference in the performance between an internal drive and an external drive. Most vendors offer the exact same drive for external or internal usage. The only difference is the location and, in the case of the external drive, the case around it.

Driving a Caddy

This last section about CD-ROM drives discusses a few less important points: Disk caddies, double doors, and self-cleaning lenses. Why bother discussing them if they're trivial? The answer is simple: salespeople.

We all buy stuff that we're not completely familiar with, whether its cars, CD-ROM drives or new ultra mega-foobitzes. Some of us, lamentably, depend too much on salespeople to guide us as we buy.

Sales is a tough job, and there are many dedicated sales professionals who know the products they are selling inside and out. However, there are also salespeople who would rather talk about easier stuff. These guys love talking about whether a CD-ROM has double-doors, a self-cleaning lens, and whether you must put the disc in a caddy before you insert it into the drive. For normal uses, these things are about as important as chewing over the different types of floor mats you can select with a new car.

Of these features, the most important is a self-cleaning lens. This refers to a drive's capability to keep the lens clean so that it can properly focus the laser beam on a specific part of the disc.

Admittedly, not all CD-ROM drives come with a self-cleaning lens, but most do. If you have a choice, get the drive with the self-cleaning lens. If your CD-ROM drive doesn't have a self-cleaning lens, don't despair. You can buy inexpensive kits to clean the lens.

The other two items—double doors and disk caddies—aren't as important. A double door is precisely what it sounds like—it's a complex door covering the slot into which you place the CD-ROM. A disk caddy is a separate container for the disc. You put the disc into the caddy, then slide the caddy into the drive.

Double-doors keep dust out of your drive, which is a good thing. They're of greatest use in particularly dusty environments. Where I live, we're not the greatest house cleaners, but as dusty as it is, I don't feel compelled to have double doors on my CD-ROM drive.

SPEAK LIKE A GEEK

Self-cleaning lens   The capability of a CD-ROM drive to automatically clean the lens that focuses the laser beam on the CD-ROM. This ensures that the drive accurately finds data. While a good feature, you can always buy an inexpensive add-in kit to clean your drive's lens if the drive doesn't come with this capability.

Disk caddies protect the disk from scratches and other damage. This is a benefit in rougher environments, like shop floors or high-volume usage situations, such as libraries.

If yours is a "normal" environment where you plop a disk into the drive a few times a day, double doors and disk caddies are fine. No problemo. If your drive doesn't have these features, fine. No problemo. A single door will adequately keep the dust out.

For normal home and office uses, don't listen too seriously to a salesperson who insists that these are must-have features. Similarly, if the drive the salesperson is trying to sell *doesn't* have these features, he or she may minimize them.

At any rate, you're better off spending your time asking the salesperson about the drive's data transfer rate, average access time, or the standards to which the drive adheres. If his or her jaw doesn't break when it hits the ground, you may actually get some useful information.

The Least You Need to Know

This chapter told you about multimedia standards and what to look for in a CD-ROM drive. You learned:

- ☞ The MPC standards (particularly MPC Level 2) aren't particularly useful but do serve as a starting point for making buying decisions.

- ☞ Don't buy a single speed CD-ROM drive. Double speed drives, however, are relatively inexpensive and triple and quadruple speed drives are gaining in popularity.

- ☞ Make sure your CD-ROM drive adheres to commonly accepted standards.

- ☞ External CD-ROM drives are easier to install.

Chapter 11
Multimedia Bits and Pieces

In This Chapter

- ☛ Getting scuzzy
- ☛ The sound and the fury

You're unlikely to have much fun with multimedia if you don't have a CD-ROM drive. That's why the preceding chapter taught you the important features to look for when buying one of those little guys. Don't put your wallet away, though. Now that you have your CD-ROM drive, there are still two absolutely essential pieces of multimedia hardware you need: a CD-ROM interface and a sound board. This chapter gives you the low-down on these two pieces of hardware.

When you finish this chapter, you'll have enough information to start the fun stuff—shopping. We'll talk about shopping in Chapter 12.

SCSI—Just Like It Sounds

A CD-ROM interface is the card you put in your system unit that enables your computer to work with your CD-ROM drive and enables your CD-ROM drive to work with everything that's hooked up to your computer. Historically, the most common type of CD-ROM interface has been a SCSI (pronounced "SCUZ-zy") interface.

SCSI   Stands for Small Computer System Interface, a common type of CD-ROM interface. It has the advantage of being usable by many other types of devices besides CD-ROM drives. With a SCSI interface, you can daisychain multiple devices to a single card. However, you may find SCSI interfaces complex to install.

While some CD-ROM drive vendors automatically include an interface with their drives, typically a SCSI interface, many vendors do not. When buying your drive, find out whether the vendor includes an interface with the drive. Some vendors that don't automatically include an interface will still sell you the SCSI adapter, and this adapter usually is well-tuned to work with that specific drive.

SCSI interfaces have several advantages:

☞ Once you plug a SCSI adapter into your PC, you can use it for other devices besides CD-ROM drives. There are, for example, hard drives and tape backup units that work with SCSI adapters.

☞ You can *daisychain* multiple SCSI devices, one to another. This means that you can use many different peripheral devices but only one adapter card.

☞ SCSI adapters tend to process information faster than other types of adapters you can use with CD-ROM drives.

There are disadvantages to SCSI adapters. Most notably, they can be difficult to install.

At this writing many, but not all, CD-ROM drives use a standardized SCSI interface. This interface adds $100 to $200 to the cost of the drive, which is a bit more expensive than other types of CD-ROM interfaces. (I use the qualifying phrase "at this writing" quite a lot in this book. That's because in the multimedia world, things are changing rapidly and what is a common practice one day is out of date the next.)

Here's another downside to SCSI adapters: while SCSI is a standard, there still are differences in the *capabilities* of SCSI drives.

The SCSI-2 standard is an enhanced and updated version of the original SCSI standard. There are also some SCSI drives that are still available that adhere to the original SCSI standard. Drives attached to the older-style SCSI interfaces will be slower than those attached to SCSI-2 interfaces.

How much faster is SCSI and SCSI-2 than other interfaces? Many users will find that the difference isn't enough to worry about. Still, in the multimedia world, speed is important because of the size and complexity of multimedia files. That's why demanding users demand standardized SCSI interfaces.

If you choose a SCSI interface, make sure it is SCSI-2. A SCSI-2 adapter is only marginally more expensive than an old-fashioned SCSI interface and is more up to date.

Proprietary Information

Hey, I like a good SCSI interface as much as the next guy, but that isn't the only way to connect your CD-ROM drive to your system. Two other types of CD-ROM interfaces are proprietary interfaces and an old stand-by, your parallel port.

A *proprietary interface* is one that comes with the CD-ROM drive and works only with that drive. Proprietary interfaces are usually variations of SCSI. They can be both good news and bad news, depending on how you use your computer.

Proprietary interface   A proprietary interface is one that works only with a specific CD-ROM drive. Often a variation of the SCSI standard, these interfaces simplify installation but make your system slightly slower. Also, you can't daisychain devices, one to the other.

The best news is that proprietary interfaces usually are easier to install than standardized SCSI interfaces. That's because generic, standardized adapters, such as a SCSI adapter, must work with a variety of different devices, not just CD-ROM drives.

Since proprietary adapters need only work with one specific device—your CD-ROM drive—the vendor can do a lot to simplify the connection. Besides making proprietary interfaces easier to install, this also tends to make them less expensive than standard SCSI adapters.

Some sound cards come with SCSI adapters built in. Sometimes these are standard SCSI adapters, and sometimes they are proprietary adapters. Often, this occurs in a bundle, in which you buy the sound card and the CD-ROM drive together from a single source.

Bundle Multiple items that you can buy at the same time. In a multimedia upgrade bundle, for example, you'll get at least a CD-ROM drive and a sound card. You also might get a CD-ROM interface, discs, and all sorts of other goodies.

Some CD-ROM drives work only with proprietary adapters. This is okay if you don't plan to use other SCSI devices. However, CD-ROM drive vendors who sell drives that work only with proprietary interfaces won't always inform you of that fact. As a result, you could later buy another SCSI device, daisychain it to your CD-ROM drive, and find that it doesn't work. Make sure that, when you buy your CD-ROM drive, you know what kind of interface you are getting.

There are some downsides to proprietary adapters. For one thing, unlike generic, standardized SCSI adapters, you can't use a proprietary adapter to daisychain several devices together, such as your CD-ROM drive and a tape backup device. Also, proprietary interfaces tend to be slower, although the difference is not too significant.

Which is best: a proprietary adapter or a generic SCSI adapter? The answer depends on how you use your computer and multimedia. If performance is of paramount concern, stay away from proprietary adapters. The performance differences vary from interface to interface, but proprietary adapters can be as much as 20% slower than generic SCSI interfaces.

Also, if you plan to use other SCSI devices, such as a tape backup device or a SCSI hard drive (or a second CD-ROM drive), don't use a proprietary adapter. You'll need a standard SCSI adapter for those other devices, so you might as well get one from the get-go when you buy your CD-ROM drive.

If you want to avoid installation headaches, if you aren't fanatical about performance, and/or if money is an issue, proprietary interfaces could be the way to go. I've used both, and I've settled on the slow but easy proprietary interface that came with my sound card. I don't get to participate in "mine is faster than yours" discussions with my techno-dweeb friends, but then my system is almost hassle-free.

Parallel Universes

There is one other type of adapter you can use for CD-ROM drives: your *parallel port*. This is the same port you use for your printer and the like.

Talk about simple: You plug the thing in, and you're just about ready. Why don't all CD-ROM drives use parallel ports? Actually, there are several reasons.

First, parallel ports are in short supply. Chances are, your printer already has a claim on yours. Second, this type of connection tends to be sl-o-o-o-w. Third, CD-ROM drives that work with a parallel port are usually expensive.

As a result, parallel port connections tend to be for specific uses, such as for portable CD-ROM drives. This means you can take your CD-ROM drive with you as you travel.

I Have an IDE

An IDE controller is the adapter used in most newer PCs to control hard and floppy drives. Typically, IDE controllers are speedy. More importantly, though, they are easy to use. Most people don't know this, but adding a new hard drive to a computer that uses an IDE controller is simple. All you do is connect the hard drive to the IDE controller with a cable. The hard part is fitting the new hard drive into the PC.

Currently, few CD-ROM drives work with IDE controllers. However, there are signs that this is changing. Stay tuned. This could be an interesting development.

A Sound Investment

You already know that, besides a CD-ROM drive and a CD-ROM interface, the other bit of multimedia hardware you'll need is a sound board. You don't want just any sound board—you want bright, trilling highs, deep, booming lows, sound that will make you say, "Wow!"

Fair enough, but first let's do a quick review. As you learned in Chapter 6:

☛ WAV files contain recorded music and sounds that are in digital format, which your computer can play. The sound card plays the sound by playing a rapid sequence of sound samples.

☞ MIDI files are data files that contain information on instruments and notes. Synthesizers use this information to recreate music.

☞ A new type of sound is emerging called wavetable synthesis. This is for music and involves storing samples of musical instruments either on the sound card or on your disc. The sound card uses the samples to play back music, making the music sound more realistic. By the way, this is only for MIDI files.

☞ Last but not least, you need a sound card and speakers (or at least a headphone) to play sound and music.

☞ Don't be cheap when buying speakers. Multimedia sounds much better through good speakers.

So far, so good. Now what should you look for in a sound card? Read on.

A Bit of Music—Eight and Sixteen Bits to Be Exact

Remember the old ditty, "Shave and a haircut, six bits?" Try going to your favorite hair stylist and offering six bits for a shampoo and a simple styling job. Hah! Even my father, who is, uh, somewhat depleted in the hair department, pays many times that much for a cut—five bucks.

Samples   Just like it sounds, a sample is a snippet of a sound played back by your sound card. The more samples your sound card can play back, the better the sound quality.

With sound cards, you'll probably deal with units that are either 8-bits or 16-bits. And "bits" doesn't refer to money, but to quality. A 16-bit card gives you higher-quality sound than an 8-bit card.

Specifically, this bit business refers to the number of sound *samples* that the sound card can record and play back. The more samples, the better the sound quality. The sampling rate is measured in kilohertz, which is the number of samples per second, in thousands. An 8-bit card has a limit of 22 kilohertz (or KHz for short), which means that it is providing 22,000 samples per second. That sounds like a lot, but it still produces muddy sound with a severely limited dynamic range.

By contrast, 16-bit cards have a limit of about 44KHz, or double that of 8-bit cards. This theoretically provides audio-CD quality, but that's a bit of a stretch. The sound quality simply isn't as good.

These days, fewer and fewer 8-bit cards are available; you can get a decent 16-bit card for under a hundred bucks. As a result, don't bother with an 8-bit card unless money is really tight.

Not surprisingly, you can pay more for sound cards if certain features are important to you. 16-bit sound cards that support wavetable synthesis are becoming more popular, so, while they are somewhat more expensive than standard 16-bit cards, prices are dropping. The results are pleasing.

Kilohertz (KHz) The number of actions per second a device takes, measured in thousands. In this case, it refers to the number of sound samples a sound card uses per second. The more sound samples used, the more realistic the sound quality.

More Sound Decisions

By now, you can tell that I think that buying an 8-bit card is penny-wise and pound foolish, as multimedia grandmothers like to say. What else should you look for in a sound card?

First, make sure it is SoundBlaster compatible. The SoundBlaster was one of the first widely sold sound cards for PCs. As a result, it has developed into a kind of unofficial standard. Many people write applications with sound that requires SoundBlaster compatibility. Most cards these days are SoundBlaster compatible, but it's best to make sure.

SoundBlaster compatible This refers to the capability of any sound card to act like a SoundBlaster sound card. The SoundBlaster was one of the first best-selling cards; many multimedia applications require that your sound card act like a SoundBlaster card.

Some sound cards use digital signal processors (DSPs), which offload from your computer's central processing unit some of the work needed to play complex sounds. These cards are good because you can play ever more complex sounds without bogging down your system. If your applications will be sound-intensive, make sure that your sound card uses a DSP.

The rule of thumb for buying sound cards is simple: buy as much quality as you can afford given your projected use. Yes, you can get a good 16-bit sound card for under $100 that is more than adequate for most of today's CD-ROM discs. If you spend several times that amount, multimedia sound will really knock your socks off—and you'll be prepared for the future.

Here's one final buying tip for sound cards. If at all possible, listen before you buy. The differences in sound quality between even similar sound cards is surprising.

The Least You Need to Know

In this chapter and in previous chapters, you learned about all the pieces you need to play multimedia and you received some guidance about which features are best for you. Specifically, you learned:

- ☛ Standardized SCSI and SCSI-2 CD-ROM interfaces provide the fastest performance and the most flexibility, but they can be a hassle to install.

- ☛ Proprietary SCSI interfaces are simpler to install and are less expensive, but they usually perform slower and are less flexible.

- ☛ Don't buy an 8-bit sound card. 16-bit sound cards are inexpensive and more than adequate for most of today's multimedia applications.

Chapter 12
Shopping Tips for Nerd Wannabes

In This Chapter

- ☞ Buying multimedia PCs from mail order
- ☞ Buying multimedia PCs locally
- ☞ Adding multimedia to existing PCs

Well, you've made it through multimedia boot camp. It was tough, but you hung in there, and now you can protect your country from infidels who don't understand multimedia.

With tough boot camp behind you, and for some, dangerous installation action ahead, there's only one thing to do—go shopping. If you know what you're buying and buy wisely, you should survive. This chapter will help you decide what to buy and where to buy it.

Good luck, multimedia soldiers.

Buying Ready-Mades

The phrase "I can't get my head around it" is apt when talking about buying a multimedia computer. The choices are mind boggling, and because these things aren't cheap, the risks are high.

So let's simplify. When buying a multimedia system, you can:

☞ Buy a new computer that is multimedia-ready. Such computers have all the multimedia components you need already installed and ready to go. That's the subject of this section.

☞ Add multimedia hardware and software to an existing PC. That's what the next section is about.

Why buy a ready-made multimedia PC? Glad you asked—if you didn't, I wouldn't have a chance to pontificate.

The answer is obvious: Buying a multimedia-ready PC is easier. Hands down. You ask the salesperson for the PC, and hand over your plastic or write the check. Later, you open the box, pull the PC out, and plug it in. No problemo, right?

Well, yes and no. There still are a few matters to consider.

Do I or Don't I?

Question One: Should you buy a new computer at all, or should you upgrade your present system? It's a no-brainer if you don't currently have a computer, or if your computer is inadequate to handle multimedia. If you want multimedia, you have to buy the goods.

What if you have a computer but think that it either will soon be out of date or is on the borderline in its capabilities to handle multimedia?

A good starting point is the MPC Level 2 standard discussed in Chapter 10. This standard describes a computer that is powerful enough to handle most—but not all—current multimedia applications. It won't necessarily handle all titles quickly, and it will be out of date in the foreseeable future, but it will handle most multimedia needs in the short term.

To review, the key PC parts of the MPC Level 2 standard are:

☞ PC based on the 80486 or greater CPU

☞ 4MB of RAM

☞   160MB hard drive

☞   VGA monitor

If your basic computer meets these minimal standards, if you want to add multimedia, and if money is an issue, go to the section of this chapter that describes multimedia upgrade kits. Kits provide the pieces you need to convert an existing PC to a multimedia PC.

If you are going to buy a multimedia computer, you have two options: You can buy a multimedia-ready PC, or you can buy a more generic computer, and then buy and install the parts yourself.

If you buy a new ready-made multimedia computer, you will save yourself the headache of installing the multimedia elements yourself. Depending on where you buy it, it won't necessarily cost you more money, and may even cost you less than buying the PC and then buying the individual parts and installing them yourself.

For some, though, there is a downside to these ready-made multimedia PCs. The downside is that you can't always get precisely the pieces you want.

Vendor A may sell the CD-ROM drive you want but not the sound card you covet. Vendor B may sell both the CD-ROM drive and the sound card you want, but not the hard drive or video system you want. Because of this, our first multimedia buyers rule of thumb is to be flexible about the precise components in a ready-made system.

Two Thumb Rules

One important rule of thumb is to beware of sellers who offer generic equipment. It is tempting to buy this generic equipment because it is less expensive than brand-name equipment. Some generic equipment is perfectly fine—but some is not.

So the second rule of thumb is that you have the right to know the brand of each component in your multimedia PC and also the performance specifications. Despite the inevitable assurances from your salesperson, all hardware is not equal. Do not assume that a generic double speed CD-ROM drive from a vendor you never heard of is equal to a double speed drive from a better-known vendor.

If you want to find reputable vendors, pick up one of the computer magazines at your local bookstore. They often rate vendors and manufacturers: the good ones and the bad ones. You should also ask friends and co-workers about their experiences.

Mail-order vendor Buying "mail order" usually means purchasing an item over the phone and having it delivered to your home or business.

And the Lucky Seller Is . . .

Once you've decided to buy a ready-made multimedia PC, your next choice is where you buy it. Broadly speaking, you have two options: You can buy it locally from a store or you can buy it through mail order.

Mail-order vendors for all kinds of things ranging from clothes to computers became the rage in the '80s. There are many reputable mail-order resellers who sell quality computer equipment and who back up their systems. Even so, there are pros and cons to buying through mail order.

Cost. In general, when comparing computers of similar quality, mail-order systems are less expensive than those you buy in a store, even if you take shipping costs into account. That is changing in some locations, however, as computer "superstores" open in more cities. Mail-order firms run some of these superstores.

Quality and reliability. You can buy high-quality systems via mail order and low-quality systems in a local establishment. Or vice versa. Some of the top-tier mail-order firms offer a lot of quality and charge a relatively small premium for it.

Once again, the rule of thumb about quality is that it pays to know the brand and performance specifications for each important part of your computer. Computers are commodity items composed of commodity parts. A reliable vendor won't be afraid to give you this information. A vendor who refuses to provide this information may be hiding something.

Service and support. If there's one thing that scares many people about buying via mail order, it's service and support. The common notion is that you're more likely to get good service and support locally than from a distant vendor.

That assumption, of course, depends on the mail-order vendor and on the local store. I've had truly wretched service locally and truly stellar service through mail order. And vice versa.

One inevitable problem with mail-order vendors, though, is that when something breaks, you must box it up and send it back. Sometimes, you send it to the vendor who sold it to you, and sometimes, you must send it to the original manufacturer of the equipment. Last year, for example, my mail-order monitor took a four-week vacation while the manufacturer (supposedly) fixed it. Luckily, I had a spare—most people aren't as fortunate.

In theory, at least, if you buy locally, you can get your equipment in and out of the shop faster. In theory, you'll avoid shipping delays and costs (most mail-order vendors make you pay one-way shipping costs). Also, with a local vendor, maybe, just maybe, you can get a loaner or even a house call.

The rule of thumb on service is that, whether you buy mail order or from a local store, make sure you know in advance what you can expect for service. Ask how long service will take and what service will cost after the warranty runs out.

Mail-Order Vendor, Where Are You?

Where do you find a mail-order vendor? That's the easy part—they're coming out of the woodwork. The easiest way to find these vendors is to buy a computer magazine. There will be dozens of ads for these vendors.

With so many mail-order vendors from which to choose, here's another one of those thumb rules: Don't buy from strangers. Whether you buy from a mail-order firm or locally, talk to people who have dealt with the seller before. Also, ask tough questions. If a salesperson doesn't give you precisely the information you want, don't buy from that person.

It's a tough world when it comes to buying PCs. They cost a bundle, and you can feel like a complete idiot when they break and you can't get them fixed. Believe me, I know. So be careful.

Upgrade Kits—Rolling Your Own

It's scary to buy a new computer. So you think you'll take the easy way out and upgrade your current computer to handle multimedia. Quick, easy, and cheap, right?

Well, maybe. Quick? Upgrading your computer is sometimes quicker than buying a new one, sometimes not. Easy? It depends on if you install the multimedia components yourself, which can be a painful process, or hire somebody else to do it. Cheap? Well, upgrading is cheaper than buying a new computer.

Before you even consider upgrading your computer, take a good look at it. It may not even meet the minimum standards for a multimedia PC. If you have an old 386 and an EGA monitor, you better buy a new computer. Sell your 386 to some high school or college kid.

If you upgrade, you'll probably wind up buying a *multimedia upgrade kit*. This is a collection of the multimedia-specific pieces you need for your computer. Upgrade kits almost always include a CD-ROM drive and a sound board. They also typically include a CD-ROM interface and speakers.

You can buy all the pieces that come in an upgrade kit one at a time. If you have both the time and a clear idea of precisely the components you want, that isn't a bad idea. It might be slightly more expensive, but you'll get exactly what you want.

Upgrade kits, also sometimes called *bundles* because they bundle together many different pieces, are the easiest and often least expensive way to go. That's because, obviously, all the pieces are in one place.

Caveat Emptor, Baby

As with so much else in this world, buyer beware. If you buy an upgrade kit, make sure:

- ☛ You know precisely which pieces are in the kit. For example, an upgrade kit may includes a CD-ROM drive, but not a CD-ROM interface.

- ☛ You buy name brand pieces. I'm hardly a name-brand fanatic, but in this case, it pays to buy name brands, at least for the critical components, such as CD-ROM drives and sound boards. There are many, to put it politely, off brands out there. Some work well, some don't.

- ☛ You have somebody to call for help if you install the pieces yourself. I'm not talking about a friend with a shoulder to cry on, although you may want one of those, too. I'm talking about a company with on-going technical support. (The next section of this book discusses installation issues.)

- ☛ A warranty on each piece in the bundle.

This list leads to a final rule of thumb about upgrading to multimedia: Don't be afraid to ask questions. Sometimes, we feel like idiots for asking what we fear are simple or basic questions. Just as often, somebody like a salesperson or a support technician helps make us feel like idiots.

It's your money. Ask as many questions as you need to feel comfortable before you buy.

Where, Oh Where, Should I Shop?

As with buying PCs, you can order your multimedia upgrade via a mail-order establishment or buy it locally. In some cases, if you buy locally the store will install your multimedia for you at a nominal charge. If that is a possibility, think seriously of taking advantage of it.

A final and important note about bundles is in order. So far, I've only talked about the hardware pieces you need for a multimedia PC. Almost always, the software drivers you need to make those pieces work come with the upgrade kit. Make sure before you buy.

If you find talk about hardware and software and how to buy it to be tiresome, take heart, because we're almost done. All that's left is the fun part. The fun part, of course, is multimedia titles.

Often, as part of the multimedia bundle, you'll get multimedia CD-ROMs. CD-ROMs also often come with multimedia-ready PCs. Besides getting you started in the world of multimedia, these bundled discs also serve to remind us about why we're going to all the trouble of buying hardware and installing it.

You deserve to be discriminating about the discs that come with your multimedia bundle. If you're choosing between two similar multimedia upgrade bundles, the quality of the included multimedia titles should be the tie-breaker.

The Least You Need to Know

Congratulations! You now know what to look for when buying a PC on which you will run multimedia applications. You also know what's important (and what's not) in the specific components, such as sound boards and CD-ROM drives, that actually play the multimedia.

In this chapter you learned how to buy this hardware and software, and from whom. You know that:

- ☞ You should seriously consider buying a new PC if you want multimedia but your current PC doesn't meet the minimal MPC Level 2 specifications.

- ☞ You can buy a "ready-made" multimedia PC and save the trouble of installing the multimedia components yourself.

- ☞ You can buy an upgrade kit containing the components you need to upgrade an existing PC to a multimedia PC.

- ☞ You can buy both multimedia PCs and upgrade kits from a local dealer or via mail-order firms. There are advantages and disadvantages to each. You should first talk with others who have dealt with that vendor in the past to make sure they're reputable.

Part III
The Pain: Installing Multimedia

Uncle Louie—now there was a guy who understood the concept of pain and gain. He was perfectly happy to put himself through untold pain fixing or installing something himself. Sometimes it was to save money, other times it was for the satisfaction of saying he did it himself.

This part of the book is for all you Uncle Louies. If you have a PC and want to add multimedia, you've got to read this section. Part II told you about the hardware and software you have to install. Part III teaches you how to actually install it. Too bad Uncle Louie didn't have a book like this.

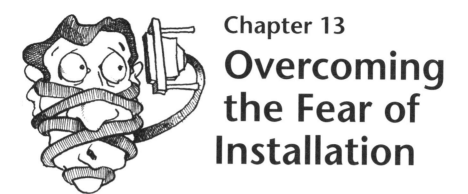

Chapter 13
Overcoming the Fear of Installation

In This Chapter

- The ideal multimedia installation
- Installation in the real world
- Potential installation problem areas
- Installation aids

If you're reading this chapter you're either:

a) Insatiably curious (and perhaps a bit strange) or,

b) Installing your own multimedia components.

This is the first chapter in the section for those who are rolling their own multimedia PCs. This chapter provides important background about the sorts of problems you may encounter when installing multimedia components.

That's what this section *is*. What it *isn't* is a manual for installing your specific hardware and software. That's because the installation process is different for each adapter and drive.

However, use this section along with the documentation that came with your multimedia components. The combination should give you enough knowledge and confidence to help you successfully accomplish your multimedia installation without feeling like an idiot.

If you can get through installing the multimedia components into a PC without feeling like an idiot, you'll be much further ahead than I was at this stage of the game.

The Installation Dream

Let's dream for a minute. Let's dream that installing multimedia components is fast and trouble free. In this dream, installing a CD-ROM interface and a sound card is easy, and goes something like this:

1. Insert the CD-ROM interface in a free slot in your computer.

2. Connect your CD-ROM drive to the CD-ROM interface. You do this with a cable that should come with the drive.

3. Most CD-ROM interfaces come with an installation program. Place the floppy disk containing the installation program in a disk drive and run it.

4. Insert your sound card into another free slot in your computer.

5. Run the installation program that comes with your sound card.

6. Connect your sound card and your CD-ROM drive. A cable for this should come with the drive.

7. Insert a disc in your CD-ROM drive. Enjoy.

The Installation Reality

What a wonderful dream! Unfortunately, though, it's time to wake up, because installing multimedia hardware and software often isn't quite that simple. However, installation needn't be difficult if you understand how everything works.

Some of you will recognize this scenario. Creepy crawly things in the night petrify a child. So the parent comes in and tries to reason with the kid. That fails, so the kid sleeps with the light on.

If you've experienced this as a child, a parent, or both, the next few sections will feel familiar. That's because they shine the light on the things in your computer that go bump in the night.

Specifically, there are three basic computer functions that are the most frequent sources of problems when you install new devices, such as sound cards and CD-ROM interfaces. These are "invisible" functions because you don't see them on-screen (other than your screen going blank when they cause your system to crash).

This chapter isn't going to turn you into a techno-dweeb. It's not even important that you fully understand these technical issues. Rather, the idea is to help you understand that these issues *exist*. This will help for two reasons.

First, the installation process practically demands that you have some understanding of these issues. Second, having a basic understanding of these issues will help you solve problems should they go bump in the night after installation.

High (and Low) IRQs

No person is an island, and neither are computer components. When you install any new device (such as a CD-ROM interface or sound card) in your PC, that device must communicate with other parts of the computer. It's kind of like how your heart and lungs work together to bring in new oxygen to replace the old.

The inside of your computer is a busy place. Many components must use the computer's resources, such as its memory and the capabilities of the central processing unit (CPU), at the same time.

If every component had to wait its turn, the inside of your computer would resemble a Monday morning traffic jam. Fortunately, though, your computer has some mechanisms that keep the traffic moving right along.

The first mechanism helps components, such as your CD-ROM interface and sound card, communicate with your computer's central processing unit (CPU). Sometimes there are problems because, unlike polite people who wait their turn, computer components get to *interrupt*.

SPEAK LIKE A GEEK

IRQ Stands for *interrupt request*, a method of briefly interrupting other computer processes so that information can flow from your CD-ROM interface, sound card, or from any other adapter to other parts of your computer system. If two devices have the same IRQ address, certain parts of your system may stop working or your system may crash.

These "interrupts" tell the CPU that the software, in this case, a CD-ROM, needs the services of another part of the computer and that the CD-ROM interface is waiting for this attention. This interruption expedites the processing of information on the CD-ROM.

Each device has its own special interrupt number, called an IRQ number, so the CPU knows who's interrupting. It's like a family with a lot of kids, each with his own sound effect. Susie rings a bell to tell her parents she needs their attention and Bobby blows a horn. In a family, this would be irritating, but in a computer, it helps create order.

It is important to know three things about IRQs:

☞ Sharing IRQ numbers is tricky. In fact, only one device can use an IRQ at a time.

☞ There are a limited number of IRQs available.

☞ When an IRQ conflict occurs, your system can crash.

The result is that when you install your CD-ROM interface or sound card, you must give it an IRQ number that no other device uses. Usually, the expansion card comes preconfigured with an uncommon IRQ. Also, the installation programs for both adapters may help you figure out which IRQ to use.

Most PCs have 16 IRQ addresses. Some, however, are reserved for basic computer functions. For example, your keyboard uses IRQ 0, your communications ports use IRQ 3 and IRQ 4, and your parallel port uses IRQ 7. Typically, IRQs 10, 11, 12, and 15 are free for use by other devices, like your CD-ROM interface or sound card.

The trick, obviously, is to select an IRQ that another item is not using. We'll talk later about some of the general ways to avoid IRQ conflicts before they happen and how to fix them when they do.

I Don't Give a DMA

Another way that your computer sorts out the data traffic that runs from one component to another is to use *DMA* channels. DMA stands for direct memory address and it is the pathway, or channel, that data takes from the device, like a SCSI adapter, to your system's random-access memory (RAM).

Typically, PCs have eight DMA channels. As with IRQs, don't assign more than one item to a single DMA channel. Also like IRQs, some basic computing functions use certain DMA channels, but most are free. Typically, for example, DMA channels 1, 3, 5, 6, and 7 are free.

While IRQ conflicts can often cause system crashes, DMA conflicts more typically result only in a device not working. For example, if your CD-ROM interface uses the same DMA channel as another device, the CD-ROM drive may not work.

What's Your (Base) Address?

If you are trying to find somebody's house, what do you do? You find the address, right? In some ways, computers work the same way.

Devices, such as sound cards, require memory. As a result, these devices need specific chunks of memory. These memory segments have addresses, called the device's *I/O port address*. In computerese, I/O refers to input/output, or the flow of information in and out of the computer.

As with IRQ addresses and DMA channels, you don't want to assign the same I/O port address to more than one device. Typically, this isn't as much of a problem as finding an unused IRQ, but it is a problem that definitely crops up from time to time.

As with DMA conflicts, if you have an I/O port address conflict, at least one of the devices involved in the conflict probably won't work.

It's Darkest Before the Dawn

Don't worry about all that technical mumbo-jumbo—you won't be tested. This is complex stuff and we're only skimming the surface, technically speaking. The purpose is to tell you just enough so you'll have some idea about what problems can occur.

Not to panic you or anything, but the problem of finding the right IRQ, DMA channel, and I/O port address can get worse over time. That's because virtually every device you add requires these items. For example, in my installation nightmare of a system, I have:

☞ A sound card

☞ A proprietary SCSI adapter

☞ A network adapter

☞ A tape backup device

The tape backup device was the last thing I added and it took me an afternoon and an evening to get it to work. And I don't even have an internal modem, which would require its own IRQ, DMA channel, and base address. Or a video capture card or . . .

Whew! Enough with things that go bump in the night. Now, at last, it's time to turn to the good news. Despite those creepy, crawly IRQs, DMAs, and I/O port addresses, you can successfully install your multimedia components without a lot of grief. It happens all the time.

The next two sections describe some preliminary methods for solving conflicts before they occur.

Some Light on the Horizon

When a child scared of the dark turns on the light in his room, he is gaining knowledge—in this case, the knowledge that horrible creatures aren't lurking. Knowledge is power.

Fine, you're probably saying, I now know some of the problems that can occur when I install stuff (such as my sound card and CD-ROM interface). So what do I do about these problems?

Fortunately, help is available to you. The next two sections describe, in general terms, two things that can help simplify the installation process. We'll discuss actually using those items in the next chapter.

Doing the Installation Thing

The first bulwark against installation headaches is the installation programs you use for your CD-ROM interface and sound card. If you're lucky, these programs will help you sort out DMA, IRQ, and base address problems.

Specifically, a good installation program will first detect which IRQs, DMAs, and addresses already are in use, and will suggest using those that aren't in use. Then, a good installation program will place the correct drivers in your DOS and Windows startup files so that it runs automatically.

TECHNO NERD TEACHES...

A startup file is a file that contains commands and that runs automatically. The DOS startup files are AUTOEXEC.BAT and CONFIG.SYS, and your computer executes commands in those files when you first start it.

The key Windows startup files are WIN.INI and SYSTEM. INI. Windows uses the information in those files when you first type **WIN** at the command prompt.

Besides testing for IRQ, DMA, and I/O port address conflicts and modifying your startup files, a good installation program will have diagnostic capabilities. These capabilities can test for problems after installation to make sure that everything is working right. This is useful, for example, if you install a sound card, and then install another device that, without your knowledge, uses the same IRQ.

The next figure shows a screen for an installation program, in this case, the program that installs a sound card.

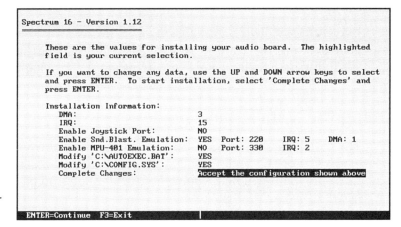

```
Spectrum 16 - Version 1.12

    These are the values for installing your audio board.  The highlighted
    field is your current selection.

    If you want to change any data, use the UP and DOWN arrow keys to select
    and press ENTER.  To start installation, select 'Complete Changes' and
    press ENTER.

    Installation Information:
        DMA:                          3
        IRQ:                          15
        Enable Joystick Port:         NO
        Enable Snd.Blast. Emulation:  YES  Port: 220    IRQ: 5    DMA: 1
        Enable MPU-401 Emulation:     NO   Port: 330    IRQ: 2
        Modify 'C:\AUTOEXEC.BAT':     YES
        Modify 'C:\CONFIG.SYS':       YES
        Complete Changes:             Accept the configuration shown above

 ENTER=Continue   F3=Exit              |
```

A sound card installation program.

Finding Your Address

There are programs available that can determine which IRQs, and I/O port addresses are in use and the specific device that is using them. You can avoid conflicts if you use these programs before installing new components in your PC.

"WOW!" you're probably saying. "Such a program could save me a lot of trouble. Where do I get one?"

Well, happy times, campers. You probably already have one. Included with recent versions of MS-DOS is a diagnostic program called Microsoft Diagnostics, or MSD for short. It's not a very imaginative name, but it is a very useful program.

MSD has several diagnostic capabilities. For our purposes, the most useful of those capabilities determine which IRQs and I/O port addresses are in use.

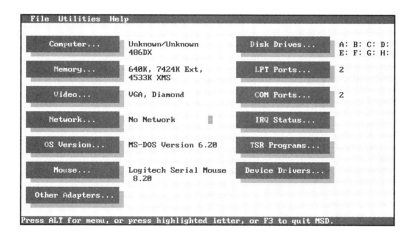

Microsoft Diagnostics.

After beating my head against the wall with several installations, I'm now in the habit of running MSD before I begin. That way, I have a running shot at preventing a conflict that could bring down the whole shebang. I mark down the used IRQs and make sure that the new device doesn't use them.

You run MSD from the command prompt. Switch to your C:\DOS directory, which is the default name for the directory in which you keep your DOS files. If you're a nonconformist and use a different drive and directory for your DOS files, go to that directory. Then, at the command prompt, type **MSD** and press the **Enter** key.

In the opening screen, click on the button that says **IRQ status**, or simply press **Q**. MSD shows the following screen.

```
 File  Utilities  Help
                            IRQ Status
  IRQ  Address    Description      Detected              Handled By

   0   07EE:04B7  Timer Click      Yes                   SNAP.EXE
   1   D84D:1923  Keyboard         Yes                   Block Device
   2   052E:0057  Second 8259A     Yes                   Default Handlers
   3   052E:006F  COM2: COM4:      COM2:                 Default Handlers
   4   052E:0087  COM1: COM3:      COM1: Logitech Seria  Default Handlers
   5   052E:009F  LPT2:            Yes                   Default Handlers
   6   052E:00B7  Floppy Disk      Yes                   Default Handlers
   7   0070:06F4  LPT1:            Yes                   System Area
   8   052E:0052  Real-Time Clock  Yes                   Default Handlers
   9   F000:F1A0  Redirected IRQ2  Yes                   BIOS
  10   052E:00CF  (Reserved)                             Default Handlers
  11   052E:00E7  (Reserved)                             Default Handlers
  12   052E:00FF  (Reserved)                             Default Handlers
  13   F000:F2E8  Math Coprocessor Yes                   BIOS
  14   052E:0117  Fixed Disk       Yes                   Default Handlers
  15   052E:012F  (Reserved)                             Default Handlers

                             OK

 IRQ Status: Displays current usage of hardware interrupts.
```

A listing of IRQs.

Notice that the crowded screen includes:

☞ IRQ number

☞ I/O port address of the device using that IRQ

☞ Device using that particular IRQ

Make a note of the information you find with MSD before you start installing. For obvious reasons, it's good information to have.

Jump in and Take a DIP

We've covered a lot of ground here, so maybe it's a good time to review. You learned about three technical issues—IRQs, DMA channels, and I/O port addresses—that can cause problems when you install your multimedia equipment.

You've learned that some installation programs will help determine whether problems exist and, in some cases, help you solve them. You've also learned that there are diagnostic programs, such as the MSD program that comes with DOS, that can detect IRQ, DMA, and I/O port address conflicts.

Now, let's talk in general terms about what you do with these problems once you encounter them. The answer: jumpers and DIPs.

Huh? If you thought a jumper was somebody who took a dive off a bridge and a DIP was somebody who already knows about all this computer stuff, you have another think coming.

Jumpers and DIPs are the things on the expansion cards, in this case, either your CD-ROM interface or your sound card, that you use to set IRQs, DMAs, and I/O port addresses.

The idea is to try to avoid problems by running diagnostics and the installation program *before* you insert the cards in the computer. If the diagnostic test or installation program determines that there's a conflict, you change the settings with a jumper or a DIP.

If you haven't heard of these before, they might sound funny. However, they're relatively straightforward affairs. In fact, in our high-tech world, they're kind of old-fashioned.

A jumper has a row of pins (see the following figure). Usually, the row is two pins wide. By covering or uncovering pairs of pins in a specific order with little plastic coverings, you change the settings.

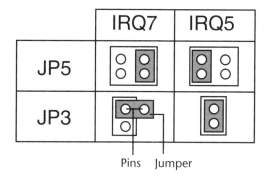

Pins   Jumper

Jumpers connect pins in various layouts.

You pull coverings on and off with another old-fashioned device, such as tweezers. You can determine what a setting is by eyeballing the jumpers and comparing it to a chart that should be in the documentation for the device you are installing.

There are really only two small difficulties with using jumpers. First, the little plastic doodads that cover the pins are pretty small. You'll be tempted to use your fingers to pull them off or put them on.

If you're ham-handed like certain writers we could mention, resist this temptation. That's because they employ a secret, sadistic design so that when you use your fingers, the plastic covers not only fall, but they fall in the darkest, most inconvenient place available.

The second problem is that there may be multiple banks of jumpers, each of which determines the setting for a different item. If that's the case, you must, of course, be careful to use the correct bank. You'll need to get that information from the manual for your device.

TECHNO NERD TEACHES...

I know, I know, this talk of jumpers is very technical, and you're probably getting frustrated. If you need help, check with the manual or call your local computer geek.

DIP switches   A series of on-off switches you use to change settings for things, such as IRQs and DMAs. You can use a small pointing device (like a pen) to move the switches.

DIP switches are a bit easier to deal with. DIP switches (DIP stands for Dual Inline Package) consist of a bank of switches located on the expansion card. Each switch can be in one of two positions. Some DIPs refer to the positions as on and off, others as 0 or 1.

Actually, you'll run into DIP switches from time to time in areas other than computers. For example, my automatic garage door opener uses DIP switches for changing the security code. These really are handy little devices.

At any rate, the manual for your device should tell you which bank of DIP switches to use for switching each function and how to set each switch in the bank. Like jumpers, DIPs are tiny little critters, so you need to find something small and pointed, but not too sharp, to push the switches up or down. I use a tiny Philips screw driver.

Just like any oldie but goodie, DIPs and jumpers are on the way out. You can change the IRQs and DMA channels on some SCSI adapters with software. If that's the case with your device, you simply follow on-screen directions.

We're also starting to see a new standard, called Plug and Play, in which you simply place cards into empty slots and they configure themselves, just like magic. As Plug and Play becomes widely accepted, the installation dream described earlier in this chapter gets ever-closer to reality. For now, though, the majority of devices still use jumps and DIPs.

The Least You Need to Know

This chapter described some basic multimedia installation information and procedures. You learned that:

☞ IRQs briefly interrupt your computer's CPU and request that it pay attention to a specific function, such as your CD-ROM drive. PCs typically have 16 specific IRQs, and if two devices use the same one, your system can crash.

☞ DMA channels route information from a device, such as a CD-ROM interface, directly to your computer's memory. Again, there should be only one device per channel.

☞ I/O port addresses refer to the specific chunk of memory that a device uses. As with IRQs and DMAs, two devices using the same address can cause a device not to work.

☞ A good installation program will help walk you through the process of selecting unused IRQs, DMA channels, and I/O port addresses. It will also help properly install the software needed to run your device.

☞ There are utility programs, including one that comes with DOS, that help you determine which base addresses and IRQs are in use. These are useful for installing devices without hassle.

☞ On many expansion cards, you change IRQs and DMAs with either jumpers or DIP switches.

☞ If all this techno-babble is confusing, read the manual for the trouble-making device, call the manufacturer's technical support number, or call a computer expert.

This is a virtual text page. There's virtually no text on it.

Chapter 14
Poking Around Inside Your System Unit

In This Chapter

- ☛ Getting ready to install multimedia
- ☛ Checking for problems

Now, let's get ready to install the multimedia hardware. Don't panic; we're not going to actually install anything until the next chapter. We're just going to prepare.

To start: take a slow, deep breath, and then let it out. Breathe in again, then let it out. Keep this up until you stop shaking. If you prefer, use the relaxation technique of your choice.

Remember this, though: This book can only provide generalizations about installation because you install every device differently. If you use it in conjunction with the user manuals that come with your hardware, you will maximize your chances of success.

Here's another thing to remember. This chapter talks about installing a sound card, a CD-ROM interface, and CD-ROM drive. You can use the principles described in this chapter, though, to install any combination of those items or any other device into your computer.

So don't be nervous—breathe in and breathe out a bit more—then let's dive right in.

Are You Ready?

The Boy Scouts have it right: Be Prepared. Upgrading a PC to handle multimedia can feel like a daunting task, but it needn't be if you have knowledge and preparation.

The last chapter provided the knowledge about the technical elements that can create problems when you're installing multimedia components. The next couple of sections will help you prepare for the task so that it goes smoothly.

The Preflight Checklist

Just like taking off in a jet, there are certain things you need to do before you take off with a multimedia installation.

First, lay out all the pieces in front of you to make sure they're all there. Lay them out on a flat surface near your computer. For a full-boat multimedia upgrade, the pieces may include:

- ☞ CD-ROM interface

- ☞ CD-ROM drive

- ☞ Sound card

- ☞ Floppy disks containing the installation programs and drivers for the drive, interface, and sound card.

- ☞ Instruction manuals

- ☞ This book

- ☞ If it's an internal CD-ROM drive, there may be some additional hardware for fitting the drive in the drive bay securely.

- ☞ Miscellaneous cables and dealy-bobs that I'll explain in this chapter.

☛ Depending on your upgrade bundle, there may be things, such as speakers, headphones, CD-ROMs, a disc caddy, an in-flight magazine, a bag of nuts, or whatever. For the time being, however, you won't need these things.

You won't need much in the way of tools to install multimedia hardware. About all you'll need for sure are both regular and Phillips screwdrivers and a tweezers. Needle-nose pliers may be useful in some circumstances and maybe a sharp knife for opening the boxes containing the equipment. A tip: Don't keep a hammer near by. It could cause some real damage if things get frustrating.

True confession: I'm not the most organized person in the world. However, it pays to keep yourself very organized while installing hardware and software. That's why you should lay everything out in front of you. Also, don't start until after you've read this chapter and the manuals that came with your hardware and software. That will give you a good idea of the steps you need to go through for a successful installation.

Next, make sure you have an emergency disk. An emergency disk is, at the very least, a bootable floppy disk containing the basics you need to start your computer and run it. The simplest way to create a bootable floppy disk is to format a disk in your A: drive with the **FORMAT /S** command. (See your DOS documentation for details.)

Better still, if you have a utility program, such as The Norton Utilities or PC Tools, use them to create an emergency disk. When you create an emergency disk with utilities like those, you not only can boot start your computer, but you also can restore your computer's most rudimentary settings should a system crash alter them.

Also, emergency disks created with these programs make it easier to restart your computer if you use a disk compression utility, such as DOS DoubleSpace or DriveSpace, or Stac Electronic's Stacker.

You may be thinking, "If there's a good chance that we'll install multimedia without problems, why do we need these safeguards?" Well, you need these safeguards for the same reason that airline seats float and your steering wheel inflates on impact. Just in case. Don't worry.

I've never needed the airbag in my car, but I have needed an emergency disk—several times. Believe me, at some point, whether it is while you are installing multimedia or some other time, you'll be glad you have an emergency disk. I was.

Popping the Top

Next, turn off your computer and take the cover off, in that order. You may need to consult with the documentation that came with your PC to learn how to take the top off your computer.

If you've never seen the inside of a computer before, you may be baffled. There's a lot of stuff in there. Don't worry; you don't have to know what most of the stuff in there does. Just remember a few common-sense rules, like keep small kids and animals away while the cover is off.

Important! Before you touch any computer components, ground yourself. No, I'm not talking about the breathe-in, breathe-out stuff, although that's a good idea, too. I'm talking about touching something metal just before touching anything in your computer. Static electricity can do plenty of damage, a truism brought home the hard way on a dry winter day recently. That was one of the times I needed my emergency disk.

Starting to Roll

You've laid out your equipment and tools. Check. The CD-ROM drive, CD-ROM interface, and sound card manuals are open and nearby. Check. So is this book. Check. You have an emergency disk. Check. You've turned off your PC and taken off the top. Check, check.

Now, let's gather some information. First, let's see how many open *slots* you have for adapters and what type of slots they are. A slot (sometimes called an *expansion slot*) is where you plug in expansion cards, such as your sound card or CD-ROM interface.

TECHNO NERD TEACHES...

There may be some confusion because of the names used to describe things (such as CD-ROM interfaces and sound cards). Yes, they are interfaces and cards, but sometimes, you'll hear them referred to as adapters. Basically, it's all the same thing. Whether it's an interface, card, or adapter, it's a thing you plug into an expansion slot in your computer.

Look in your system unit for other expansion cards that look, more or less, like your sound card or CD-ROM interface. These cards will be plugged into the expansion slots. Even if you haven't added any expansion cards yourself, there are likely to be one or two cards that came with your computer.

For example, your video card should be in one slot. You also might have a controller card for your hard and floppy drives in another slot.

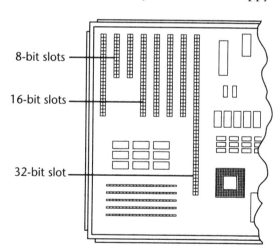

8-bit slots

16-bit slots

32-bit slot

Expansion slots range from an 8-bit size to a 32-bit size.

You'll probably notice as you look at your motherboard (and at the preceding figure) that expansion slots come in several sizes. Specifically, they are 8-bit slots, 16-bit slots, and 32-bit slots. (Remember that the bit business refers to the amount of data that the adapter can exchange with the motherboard.)

Look at the adapters you are going to add to your system and examine the length of the gold-plated connector. The two most common types of cards are 8-bit cards, which have the shortest connectors, and 16-bit cards that are longer. Make sure there are free slots of the appropriate type for your cards.

If there aren't free slots, you have a few options. You can move around the cards already in your computer to free up a slot. For example, you might have an existing 8-bit card in a 16-bit slot—that sort of thing works just fine. You might need to pull out the 8-bit card and put it in an 8-bit slot to free up a 16-bit slot.

TECHNO NERD TEACHES...

If you need to take out a card, do it very carefully. With both hands, get a good grip on the card, but try not to touch anything except the green plastic. Using firm but controlled strength, pull the card straight up out of its slot. Resist the urge to pull the card back and forth and wrench it out of the slot. Remember—you're dealing with a fairly delicate piece of electronic equipment. Keep it in a safe place until you learn how to install an expansion card in the next chapter.

If you want to install a SCSI interface and a sound card but there is only one free slot, you may need to buy a sound card with a built-in SCSI adapter. It will be a hassle—you'll have to return the stuff you've already bought and get new stuff. But that's a better solution than returning everything, closing up the computer, and forgetting about multimedia. You don't want to do that, do you?

Dock of the Bay

Next, check for a free *drive bay* (the area in your PC where you insert a drive) if you are inserting an internal CD-ROM drive. If you don't know where to look for a drive bay, first locate your floppy drives. If there's a free drive bay, it's likely to be above, below, or next to the floppy drives. It will be an empty gap about the size, say, of a floppy or CD-ROM drive.

Finding the drive bay may be difficult. If you haven't done so already, and if your computer case allows it, you may have to remove the front panel of your computer to see if there's a free drive bay. If there's not a free drive bay, you'll need to use an external drive. If you already bought an internal drive, you'll have to trade it in.

Once you've found it, don't actually do anything with the drive bay yet. I'm giving you information about it prior to the actual installation of the drive so you can make sure you bought the right kind of drive. It would be a let-down if you got all the way to the next chapter and realized that you need an external drive instead of the internal one that you've already taken out of the box.

Waiting to Interrupt

Sorry to interrupt you, but it's time to do a bit more research. Specifically, you must find out what *interrupts*, or IRQs, are available.

Run MSD or a program like it (see the previous chapter for information on MSD). Print the list of available IRQs or write it down. You'll need this information a little later.

Next, read the manuals for all the adapters you are installing to get a general idea about the lay of the land. Where are the jumpers or DIP switches you may need to use? What are the default IRQ or DMA channel settings?

If this part of the process finds a conflict, don't change the jumpers or DIPs yet. Just note that the tests showed a problem.

Not everybody agrees, but I suggest installing the cards without changing jumpers or DIPs, even if your diagnostic utility indicates a potential conflict.

That's because more than one device can use an IRQ; they just can't use the IRQ at the same time. If the overlap is with a rarely used device or a device you are unlikely to use at the same time as your CD-ROM adapter or sound card, you might, just might, be okay. It's pretty risky, and you should probably only do it as a last resort.

For example, if you have a tape backup device, you're unlikely to use it while you're enjoying multimedia. You may have to switch the device off if you can (which is easy with external units), but it is possible that it and your CD-ROM interface card can co-exist. Or maybe not. There's only one way to find out.

The Least You Need to Know

Phew! That wasn't so bad, was it? In this chapter, you learned:

- ☞ You should take some time to prepare for an installation by laying out all the pieces and skimming the manuals for the CD-ROM interface, drive, and sound board.

- ☞ Have an emergency disk ready, in case of emergencies.

- ☞ You can prepare for problems by checking the IRQs used by your system before you actually start installing the hardware.

- ☞ You install your sound card and CD-ROM interface into empty expansion slots in your computer.

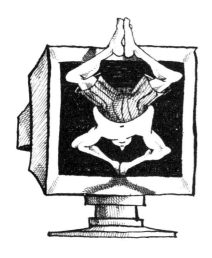

Chapter 15

Diving In: Installing the Hardware

In This Chapter

☛ Preparation basics

☛ Open it up

☛ Plug it in

We're at that point—at last, we get our hands dirty, figuratively speaking. We have all the pieces ready to go, we've selected free slots, and we've tested for potential IRQ conflicts. We've examined the hardware and glanced through the manuals. Nothing left to do but to do it.

Surgical Basics

If you were a surgeon, here's where things would stand. The patient (computer) is open and you have to put your hands in. If you haven't done this before, this is definitely one of those breathe-in, breathe-out times.

It can be daunting, but there's really nothing to worry about. That is, there's nothing to worry about if you follow a few simple rules.

☛ Never, ever, ever work inside your computer while it is turned on. That's one way to cook yourself, and your computer, in a hurry.

☛ Never force anything. Don't screw things in tighter than necessary or force things, such as your CD-ROM interface, to fit. If you have to use too much muscle, chances are you'll break something. However, firm pressure is necessary at times. Beware: There's a fine line between firm pressure and forcing.

☛ Keep all liquids, such as your high-caffeine sodas, coffee, or whatever, away from the opened computer (or a closed computer, for that matter).

☛ Also keep all small animals and children away.

☛ Stay calm. The breathe-in, breathe-out stuff isn't just a joke. If you become frustrated and confused, you can make a hasty mistake you'll be sorry about later. Take time, when necessary, to calm yourself.

☛ Always ground yourself electrically before you touch anything inside your computer. One way to ground yourself is by touching something metal that's also grounded (like power supply casing). I've mentioned this tip before; it is worth repeating.

Backplane The flat panel of an expansion card that usually has ports so you can plug cables into the card. A backplane plate is the metal plate that covers up the hole in your computer that would otherwise be covered up by an expansion card's backplane.

Home, Home on the Backplane

OK, are you ready?

First, a bit of mechanical work. After you select the slots you want to use, you must take off the backplane plate for each slot. A *backplane plate* is a little piece of metal that covers the hole in the back of the computer that's next to an empty slot.

See, when you put an expansion card in the slot, part of it has to be accessible through the back of your computer so you can plug cables into it. (For example, you plug speakers into the backplane of your sound card, and you attach your monitor to the backplane of your video adapter.) However, when you don't have an expansion card in a slot, you need something to cover the hole so dust and gook doesn't get in your system unit. That's what the backplane plate is for. If you look at the back of your system unit, you're bound to see several.

Don't use a screwdriver that's magnetized. This type of screwdriver is great in other circumstances for holding on to screws. Remember, though, that magnetic devices can damage your computer's data.

Use a small screwdriver to remove the screw holding the backplane plate into the chassis. Do this for each backplane plate you want to remove.

Caution Number One: Don't let any little screws fall into your computer. They're a pain to get out and they can wreak havoc (causing short circuits), if you leave them in. If a screw does fall in, do whatever it takes to remove it, including unplugging everything and turning the computer upside down. Your best bet, though, is to try to grab the screw with tweezers.

After you remove the backplane plate, save it and the screw in a safe place. If you ever remove the card, you'll want to put the backplane plate back.

Playing the Slots

With the backplane plates removed, insert the cards you are installing. It's most efficient to match the size of the connector at the bottom of the card to the size of the slot. You can, however, fit a smaller connector, like an 8-bit card, into a larger slot, such as a 16-bit slot.

Place the card so that its gold-plated connectors ride loosely on top of the slot. Then, with the card perpendicular to the motherboard, push down with both hands.

Don't do a Godzilla routine on it, but you needn't press too gingerly, either. This is one of those times when firm pressure works. These cards are pretty sturdy; use a reasonable amount of pressure. At any rate, you soon should feel the card snap into place.

Often, things stick out a bit from the backplane of the expansion card. For example, the SCSI connector can stick out a quarter or half an inch. These things can catch on other parts of your computer and prevent you from inserting the card, no matter how much pressure you put on it. If the card simply won't plug in, this might be the problem.

If your computer doesn't start after inserting expansion cards, the problem is likely to be an IRQ conflict. Less likely, but also possible, is an I/O address conflict. The problem is unlikely to be a DMA channel conflict. Those conflicts merely prevent a device from working; they usually don't prevent a system from starting.

Now, take a breath in and let the breath out. Do it again. Do it several times. When you're calm, move your screwdrivers and electronic parts away from the computer. Then, leaving the cover of the computer off, turn on your computer. This is an experiment that probably will have one of two outcomes: Either your computer will start successfully, or it won't.

If it starts successfully, you may see some additional information flash by on your screen. That's because some expansion cards, particularly SCSI adapters, will tell you if the computer, upon starting up, "sees" the card.

If your computer starts, but you see a message saying, essentially, that the computer doesn't recognize the CD-ROM interface, don't worry. It likely means that you haven't yet installed the drivers to make the CD-ROM interface work. Or it could mean that the card isn't in the slot correctly. Turn the computer off, then check to see if you have firmly seated the CD-ROM adapter in the slots.

If your computer doesn't boot successfully, take the new cards out one at a time. In other words, if you inserted a sound card and a SCSI adapter, take the SCSI adapter out first and reboot.

If your system starts up, the conflict is with your SCSI adapter. If it doesn't start up, turn off the computer and remove the sound card. If your computer starts up, the problem is with the sound card. Don't, however, forget when you test it this way, that you could have conflicts with both cards.

If your computer doesn't start with both cards removed, it's time to trot out the emergency disk.

Using the DIP switches or jumpers on your CD-ROM interface or sound card, change the IRQ to one that is free. (Remember . . . you checked for available IRQs with the Microsoft Diagnostics program.) After you change the IRQ, replace the card and try starting your computer again.

Here comes news that's hard to break to you. Just because your system started doesn't mean that you have no IRQ, DMA channel, or base I/O address conflicts. Sorry, a booting computer only means that you don't have any conflicts that prevent the computer from starting. Once you actually start using stuff, conflicts can become apparent.

Here's another thing you may not like to hear: Sometimes one conflict masks another. Don't assume that if you resolve one conflict, you've resolved them all.

Driving It Home—Externally

Next, make sure the power is off, then install and connect the drive. Let's talk about external drives first because they are simpler. Take the SCSI cable (which should have come with the drive), and attach it to the connector in the back of the drive and the connector in the backplane of the CD-ROM interface.

The SCSI cable will be a short, thick cable. The hard part is that, because SCSI cables are usually pretty short, you will probably have to keep the drive near your PC, which can be a bit clumsy during installation.

TECHNO NERD TEACHES...

The back of your external CD-ROM drive probably has two connectors, although some drives that work only with proprietary SCSI adapters have only one. The second connector is for daisychaining together more than one device. For now, let's assume that you aren't daisychaining devices—we'll talk about daisychaining in a later section.

Many SCSI cables and connectors have hooks to lock down the connection. These hooks typically look like eye hooks made out of thin metal. These hooks, located on each side of the plug end, clip into the edges of the connectors to ensure a firm connection.

Sometimes, though, the plugs and connectors use little screws to tighten down the connection. Whatever the method, make sure you do this. If you don't, it can come loose and your drive won't work.

Somebody I know (I won't mention names) once spent the better part of a day tracking down why the CD-ROM drive didn't work. He was certain the problem was an IRQ, DMA channel, or base I/O address conflict. Boy was I—er, *he* embarrassed to find that he didn't firmly connect the %&*@ cable to the CD-ROM interface.

Don't worry about which end of the cable you should attach to the card or drive. If it plugs in, you've made the right connection.

Remember you'll have to plug an external drive into an electrical socket. The manufacturer also should include the power cord for that.

Also remember that you must connect your CD-ROM drive or CD-ROM interface to your sound card. Most drives and adapters handle this differently, so consult the documentation that came with the equipment.

Driving It Home—Internally

Installing an internal drive is similar to installing an external drive—up to a point. Two major things are different: you must actually install the drive into the drive bay, and the connections between the drive and the CD-ROM interface are different and somewhat more complex.

First, you must install the CD-ROM drive. Start by removing the face plate in front of the drive bay if you haven't done so already. The face plate covers up empty drive bays.

Next, try inserting the drive into the bay. It may slide in tightly and securely by itself, but there's a fair chance you'll need to construct a system of rails to make it fit into the drive tightly.

Be careful when you buy drives; some of them come without rails. That's because drive bays aren't standardized and some vendors just don't want to include rails for all common sizes of drive bays. If that's the case, you can buy rails in an electronics store.

You'll need to rely on your CD-ROM drive's documentation for installing the rails. Whether or not you use rails, though, when you finish attaching them to the drive, you should be able to slide the drive securely into the drive bay.

The drive should fit so the front of the drive is flush with the front of the computer. Depending on the construction of your PC, you'll likely need to screw the drive to the drive bay with some included screws.

Next is a part that is usually easy. You must connect the drive to the adapter with ribbon cable that should come with the drive. Both sides of the cable are identical, so you needn't worry about which side you attach to which piece.

You do need to worry, however, about making sure the cable faces in the right direction. This isn't difficult. There should be either a red stripe or, in some cases, a dotted line along one edge of the ribbon cable.

The pins in the connectors are numbered and the red stripe corresponds to the first pin in the connector. Some connectors work in such a way that you can only plug the ribbon cable in correctly so that the red or dotted part of the ribbon cable automatically connects to pin 1.

> **SPEAK LIKE A GEEK**
>
> **Ribbon cable**   A flat, plastic cable that connects an internal CD-ROM drive to the CD-ROM interface. You must make sure that the edge of the cable that is red (or possibly has a dotted line) connects to pin 1 of the connector located on the interface card.

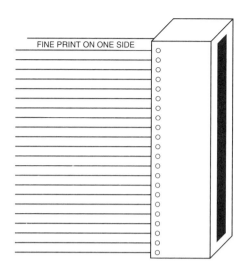

FINE PRINT ON ONE SIDE

Attaching ribbon cable.

However, often you'll have to figure out the location of pin 1 yourself. Look carefully at the card and the drive. With luck, the vendor included the number 1 where the first pin is. Also, the vendor likely describes the location of pin 1 in the documentation.

If you are sure that you don't have an IRQ, DMA channel, or base I/O address conflict, and your CD-ROM drive still doesn't work, a leading suspect is that the ribbon cable is backwards. Typically, you'll want the red stripe to be facing up at both ends of the connection, but double check the documentation, and closely examine the connectors to make sure.

A possible hassle here is that you may have to take the CD-ROM interface out of the PC to connect the cable to it. In fact, if the cable is long enough, you should connect it to the drive before you insert it in the bay.

If the cable is short, however, it helps to be double-jointed as you reach your hand into the guts of your computer to plug the end of the cable into the installed drive. Or you can borrow somebody with small hands.

Next, connect the drive to your computer's power supply. The CD-ROM drive should come with a power connector that fits into a socket in the back of the unit.

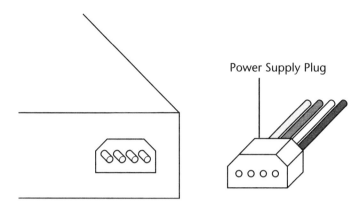

Power Supply Plug

Connecting the power.

Next, look for a spaghetti-like tangle of power cords behind the drive bays. The cords will be easy to find—they'll be black, yellow, and red. These are the power cords that connect your floppy and hard drives to your computer's power supply.

If there's an open power socket amongst all these cords, you're in luck. Just plug the other end of your CD-ROM drive's power cord into it.

If a socket isn't available, you'd better hope that the CD-ROM vendor included a *cord splitter*. This is a cord with a single connector at one end and two connectors at the other. If the vendor didn't include a cord splitter, they're usually available from electronics stores.

Be aware that a splitter may overload your power supply. It's a good idea to split off a floppy drive, as described below, because overloading won't be likely that way.

Once you have the splitter and you've plugged one end into the back of your CD-ROM drive, do this:

1. Disconnect the power cord from the back of one of your drives, preferably a floppy drive.

2. Plug one of the ends of the cord splitter to the back of the floppy drive.

3. Disconnect the other end of the floppy drive's power connection. Take the cord out of the computer.

4. Plug the other end of the power splitter into that connection.

As with the external drive, remember that you must connect the internal CD-ROM drive or CD-ROM interface to your sound card. Again, since most drives and adapters handle this differently, read the documentation that came with the equipment.

It's about this time that I usually feel like dropping a Molotov cocktail into my computer. But resist the urge. You're done with the physical labor—maybe. If you're lucky.

Pretty Daisies and Daisychains

Unlike pretty daisies, you're not likely to look at a SCSI adapter and fall in love or start pondering the meaning of life.

Still, it is kind of neat that you can daisychain together many SCSI devices to a single SCSI adapter. In simple terms, you connect the first device to the SCSI adapter, then connect the second device to the first, and so on to a maximum of seven SCSI devices. This chain of connected devices is a *daisychain*.

That's why there are usually two connectors on CD-ROM drives. One is for the cable connecting the drive to the CD-ROM adapter if the drive is the first in the chain or to the previously attached device if it isn't. The other connector is for connecting the drive to the next SCSI device in the chain.

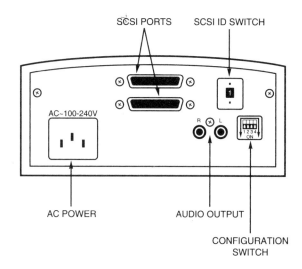

The back of an external drive with two SCSI ports.

SCSI PORTS   SCSI ID SWITCH

AC~100-240V

R   L

AC POWER   AUDIO OUTPUT

CONFIGURATION SWITCH

Usually, you can use either connector for either purpose. If the CD-ROM drive is the first item in the daisychain, connect one end of the cable to the drive and the other to the adapter. If it's not the first in the chain, attach one end of the cable to the SCSI device before it.

Terminator　A plug that you attach to the last device in a chain of SCSI devices. This plug closes the loop; without it, your SCSI devices may not work.

In either case, if the drive is the last device in the chain, you need to terminate the end connector using a *terminator*, or by flipping a terminator switch. A terminator closes the connection on the last device in the chain. Some devices use plugs, some use switches. Make sure that you only terminate the last connector in the last device of the daisychain, because the electronic signal that flows through daisychained devices stops when it gets to a terminator.

Some external drives come with a terminator, which is simply a dead-end plug that you place on the end connector. Internal drives usually have plugs called *resistors* located on circuit boards attached to the drive. If the drive isn't the last in the daisychain, you must pull the resistor out of the circuit board.

On newer devices, however, there is a terminator switch on the circuit board that you just flip. You don't need to mess with plugs or resistors.

Next, you may have to set the SCSI ID. This isn't a falsified document that gets underage people into bars. It's more like a serial number you give to each SCSI device in a daisychain. When you daisychain multiple devices, each device must have a unique SCSI ID number. If this is your only SCSI device, the default SCSI ID number is undoubtedly fine, as long as the ID is not 0.

Typically, you select this ID number with a switch, located on the back of the external unit or on the circuit board of an internal unit. You can use any available SCSI ID number, as long as it isn't being used by another device. If you need help selecting an ID number, refer to the manual that came with the drive.

Installation Is a Turn On

You've added in your expansion cards and straightened out any IRQ conflicts. The drive is in place. You've connected the drive to the adapter, the adapter to the sound card, and plugged the drive into your computer's power supply or into an electrical outlet.

Believe it or not, after you've done this a few times, we're talking ten or fifteen minutes to do all this. Really.

At long last, you can turn your machine on. No, you're not finished. Still, if everything went well, your computer should start up just fine, thank you.

The next step is running the installation programs for the CD-ROM interface and the sound card. To briefly review, they may (or may not):

☞ Check for IRQ, DMA channel, or base I/O address conflicts.

☞ Suggest using specific IRQs, DMA channels, or base I/O addresses.

☞ Alter your startup files to automatically load the relevant drivers and other software.

☞ Check to see that everything is working.

You'll have to read your manuals about the installation programs because they're all different.

There's only one last bit of business before you finish the heavy lifting of installation. Connect the speakers to the sound card. Usually, you do this by connecting the speakers together, then connecting one of the speakers to a jack in the backplane of the sound card.

Are We There Yet?

When you're on your way to Grandma's and the kids in the back seat get restive and whine, "Are we there yet?", answering with a "maybe" won't work. But it will have to suffice here.

That's because now you must reboot your computer and see if everything works. If everything works, you're there. If something doesn't work, you must enter troubleshooting mode, switching around IRQs, DMA addresses, and the like.

Here's a quick way to see if your CD-ROM drive is working.

1. Put a disc in the CD-ROM drive.

2. At the command prompt, type the drive letter of the CD-ROM drive. For example, type **E:** and press **Enter**.

   Your installation program should either ask you for the drive letter you want for the drive or automatically assign it to the next letter after your last current drive letter.

3. If the prompt for that drive displays on-screen, type **DIR**. If you get a list of files on that drive, *congratulations!* Your CD-ROM drive is working.

Chances are your sound card came with some little programs that can play WAV and MIDI files. If it did, load those programs and try playing a sound. If the sound plays, *congratulations!* Your sound card is working.

If something isn't working correctly, here's the list of leading suspects:

☞ IRQ conflict

☞ DMA channel conflict

☞ Base I/O address conflict

☞ You did not seat one or both of the expansion cards firmly in the slot.

☞ You did not correctly connect the ribbon cable between the CD-ROM drive and the CD-ROM interface.

☞ The cable connecting the drive to the sound card isn't connected correctly.

☞ You've inserted the disc in the CD-ROM drive upside down.

☞ You have bad karma.

☞ Something's broken.

Here's an important tip:
After everything is working,
fill in and mail all the
registration cards for all the
hardware you're installing.
This is useful for several
reasons, not the least of
which is that the vendor
often requires this in order
for you to get support.

If you have any of these problems, re-read the previous chapters in this book, or consult with someone who knows a thing or two about installing hardware. If all else fails, read the manual or call the CD-ROM drive manufacturer's technical support number.

After you get everything working correctly—and you will, never fear—all that's left is the cleanup work. Specifically:

☞ Turn off the computer and find the small screws that held down the backplane panel for the empty slot. Use them to firmly attach the new expansion cards to the frame of your computer.

☞ Put the top back on your computer, and any other panels you took off for the installation process. Be careful! You don't want to chew up any cables when you put the cover on your system unit.

☞ Clean up the mess of empty plastic bags, loose paper, and other garbage left behind in the installation process.

☞ Strut around feeling (quite justifiably) like you've done something great.

☞ Turn the computer back on and start enjoying multimedia!

The Least You Need to Know

This chapter really got you deep into the installation process. You learned:

☞ The first steps are opening the back of the computer, getting the lay of the land, and removing the backplane plates that cover the slots you need.

☞ Installing an external hard drive is much simpler than installing an internal hard drive.

☞ You may well have to do some troubleshooting to eliminate IRQ or DMA conflicts.

Chapter 16

Software Can Be Hard, Too

In This Chapter

- ☞ Mandatory software
- ☞ More software troubleshooting

The previous chapter described installing multimedia hardware. It also told you a little about running the installation programs that install the software that enables the hardware to work. With luck, everything should work fine after running the installation programs. However, the word *should* refers to a probable and predictable state, and we all know by now that multimedia often isn't predictable.

If you read the previous chapters and your multimedia system still doesn't work, you probably need to read this chapter. It goes into more depth about the software you need to run multimedia.

You Gotta Have It

I was an angelic sort of kid, (or so my parents believed), but I always admired the kids who liked to bedevil substitute teachers. They were so cool, in a hoodish sort of way.

Now, however, I feel like a substitute teacher. That's because I can tell you're getting a bit impatient and unruly. We finished the hard part and looming is the endless summer vacation of actually *using* multimedia, which starts with the next chapter.

However, there's still some work to do, SO SIT UP STRAIGHT AND PAY ATTENTION! The next several sections describe the software that works behind the scenes to make multimedia possible and what can go wrong with it. If you don't learn this, you'll have to go to summer school.

Let's Review

Class, let's review the four bits of software that you must load before you can use multimedia. They consist of a program and three drivers.

Who remembers what a driver is? You . . . the little geek in the corner with the pocket protector, do you know? Correct! A *driver* is a little program that tells your computer how to interact with a peripheral.

Now I'll write the names of the four essential pieces of software on the chalkboard:

- ☛ **MSCDEX.** A program you must load in order for your CD-ROM drive to work. MSCDEX stands for Microsoft CD Extensions, and in simple terms, it enables DOS to work with your CD-ROM drive the same as it works with other drives.

- ☛ **A CD-ROM interface driver.** A software driver that the vendor included with the CD-ROM interface. It helps DOS and the other parts of your computer interact with the CD-ROM interface card.

- ☛ **A CD-ROM-specific driver.** A software driver that enables your specific CD-ROM drive to work with your specific CD-ROM interface. Your CD-ROM drive vendor should have included it.

☛ **A sound card driver**. Enables your sound card to work with DOS and the other parts of your PC. Your sound card vendor should have included it with the sound card.

The name of the Microsoft CD Extensions file is always MSCDEX.EXE; however, the names of the other drivers will vary, depending on the vendor.

As discussed in Chapter 9, most installation programs automatically install these programs and drivers. The installation program should:

☛ Examine your system for the appropriate IRQs and DMA channels used by the hardware.

☛ Alter your startup files, specifically your CONFIG.SYS and AUTOXEC.BAT files, to load the files automatically when you start your computer.

☛ Modify the commands placed in your CONFIG.SYS and AUTOEXEC.BAT to reflect your system. For example, some drivers require that you name the proper DMA channel or IRQ in the command that loads them.

To run the installation program, follow the instructions in the device's manual. I would give you directions, but the instructions are different for everything. You'll probably be prompted to answer a few questions, but the installation program should do everything for you.

If you haven't been through this sort of thing before, this process might sound easy. But those of you who have been around computers for a while will instinctively feel that tightening of the stomach muscles that tells you, "It ain't always that easy."

The next few sections list some potential problems with the software. They serve as a trouble-shooting guide if you've already done the trouble-shooting on the hardware and the stupid system still doesn't work.

This discussion about loading order supposes that you're using a standard SCSI adapter as your CD-ROM interface. If you use a proprietary SCSI adapter, you may not need to worry about loading order. That's because, sometimes, proprietary interfaces don't require a CD-ROM interface driver. Proprietary adapters typically are slower and less flexible, but this is one way that they can make life a bit easier.

Lock and Load—In That Order

When you dress, you must put your clothes on in the right order. Otherwise, your underwear might be on top of your pants, or your socks would be on top of your shoes. To some extent, the same is true of the four essential software items: You must load some of them in the correct order.

Incredibly, sometimes installation programs botch this seemingly simple task. Or sometimes, you or a supposedly techno-wizard friend will muck around in your AUTOEXEC.BAT or CONFIG.SYS files and inadvertently change the order.

Of the two startup files, your CONFIG.SYS file executes first. Within that file, the proper loading order is:

1. The CD-ROM interface driver.

2. The driver for your specific CD-ROM drive.

If these drivers load in the opposite order, your CD-ROM drive won't work.

MSCDEX loads in your AUTOEXEC.BAT file. Depending on your sound card, the sound driver may load in either the CONFIG.SYS or the AUTOEXEC.BAT file. The order in which these two remaining files load usually doesn't matter.

Everything's Up to Date (NOT!)

Here's my opinion: Computing life would be a lot simpler if software like DOS and the MSCDEX program came with expiration dates like you get on a gallon of milk. This stuff changes from time to time and sometimes older versions don't work with newer technology.

DOS didn't always come with MSCDEX. If you use an older version of DOS, you may not have a copy of MSCDEX and, as a result, your CD-ROM drive won't work.

Many installation programs come with a version of MSCDEX, but some don't, expecting the program to be in your DOS directory. Often, the installation program loads the copy of MSCDEX in a newly created directory.

All this can lead to one of two problems, either of which will prevent your CD-ROM drive from working:

☞ If you have a pre-MSCDEX version of DOS and your installation disk doesn't include a version of MSCDEX, you won't have this program and your CD-ROM drive won't work.

☞ You can have two copies of MSCDEX on your hard disk and the installation program may set your AUTOEXEC.BAT file to load the older copy.

Here's how to unravel this mess. First, look for the MSCDEX.EXE file in your DOS directory (or whatever you named the directory in which you store your DOS files). Switch to your DOS directory and type **DIR MSCDEX.EXE**. If this command unearths a copy of MSCDEX.EXE, make a note of the file creation date as listed by the DIR command.

Next, check your CD-ROM drive's documentation to see if the installation program created a new directory. If it did, switch to it and type **DIR MSCDEX.EXE** again. If you find a copy in this directory, make a note of its file creation date as listed by the DIR command.

If you don't have the file in either directory, get a copy by contacting either Microsoft or your CD-ROM drive vendor. Either should send you a copy for a nominal fee, although this failing should be at least a misdemeanor for CD-ROM drive vendors. After you receive the program, put it in the directory where the AUTOEXEC.BAT file expects it to be.

If you have two copies of MSCDEX, check the command in your AUTOEXEC.BAT file to see which one is loading. If the older version is loading, change the command so that the newer version loads instead.

Do this by loading the AUTOEXEC.BAT file in a text editor (dig out your DOS documentation for specifics), such as the EDIT program that comes with DOS. Once you are viewing the AUTOEXEC.BAT file in the text editor, find the line in the file that loads MSCDEX, then type the drive and path of the copy of MSCDEX.EXE you want to load. (Make sure you save your AUTOEXEC.BAT and CONFIG.SYS files after you edit them.)

For example, if the version in your DOS directory is newer, the command in your AUTOEXEC.BAT file should look like this:

C:\DOS\MSCDEX.EXE /D: MVCD001

If you store DOS on a different drive or directory, of course, that path should be part of the command. Also, there may be some stuff (like the /D) after the command. This "stuff" modifies the command. Don't change any of that information—at least, not yet. Note, though, that what's on your system may be different from my example. We'll talk about this situation in the next chapter.

Here's a variation of the out-of-date MSCDEX problem. Sometimes, your CD-ROM will work with an older version of MSCDEX, but some specific functions won't work. For example, Photo CD doesn't work with older versions of MSCDEX.EXE.

Again, if you suspect your version of MSCDEX is outdated, contact your CD-ROM drive vendor or Microsoft for an update.

Switches and parameters
You use switches and parameters to modify a command so that it executes in a certain way.

Tote That Bale, Switch That Parameter

Now things get a bit dicey. Often, you must modify commands in your CONFIG.SYS or AUTOEXEC.BAT files with things called *switches* and *parameters*. Switches and parameters come after the command.

Just as an example, I'll show you a common command and switch that isn't related to multimedia:

DIR /W

The DIR command tells DOS to list all the files in a directory. If there are a lot of files, the files at the beginning of the list will scroll off the screen so you can't see them any more. The /W switch tells DOS to list the files in a *wide* format so that you can see more of them on-screen.

That's a simple switch. MSCDEX.EXE has several switches that determine more complex items, and so do the drivers for your CD-ROM interface and drive.

Now here's the tricky part. The installation programs should automatically modify the commands they place in your CONFIG.SYS and AUTOEXEC.BAT files with the proper switches and parameters. But SURPRISE! Sometimes, it doesn't work that way. The result is that there might be a subtle problem with a switch in your command that escapes your notice, even if you've done all the other hardware and software troubleshooting.

I can only help you a little bit here since each vendor uses different commands, switches, and parameters for their software. As a result, you must closely read the documentation that came with your hardware to learn more about these switches. If the problems still don't become clear, call the vendor's technical support number and ask for help. Unfortunately, the vendor got you into this jam, and there's not much I can do to get you out.

Here's one quick thing to check for if your CD-ROM drive or sound card doesn't work. In most cases, there must be a switch that identifies the CD-ROM device. This switch must be, at the very least, in the commands in your CONFIG.SYS file that load the CD-ROM driver and MSCDEX. Depending on your CD-ROM interface, it may need to be in the command in your AUTOEXEC.BAT file for that driver, too.

The switch typically begins with /D. Mine is

(COMMAND) /D: MVCD001.

Yours is likely to be different. Make sure that:

☛ This switch is present in both command lines.

☛ The switch is the same in both command lines. If, for example, it is MVCD001 in one command line and MVCD002 in another, your CD-ROM drive won't work.

The Least You Need to Know

The hard part is done—installing the hardware. You've also installed the software you need for running multimedia. This chapter explained more about that software. You learned:

☛ There are four essential pieces of software you need to run multimedia.

☛ You can have difficult-to-trace problems if the drivers for your multimedia hardware use the wrong switches and parameters.

☛ Your CD-ROM drive may not work if you load the drivers in the wrong order.

Part IV
The Gain: Using Multimedia

The thing about Uncle Louie was that, after the pain of installing or fixing something himself, he never tired of telling you about the gain. "I saved three dollars doing it myself!" he would crow proudly. Or, "You should see the new appliance I installed. What a wonder!"

In Part III, we went through the pain of installing the hardware and software needed to run multimedia. Part IV is the gain: We'll talk about using multimedia applications. You'll learn what makes a good multimedia application. And, like Uncle Louie, I'll brag about my Top 10 List of multimedia programs.

Chapter 17
Multimedia Does Windows

In This Chapter

- Windows' multimedia extensions
- Drivers galore
- Playing media

Geez—you're getting restless out there. I know you're sick and tired of all the technical talk and all the setting up. You want to get the show on the road. I can here you whining, *"Are we there yet?"*

Well, we're not quite there yet, but we're in the home stretch. Before we finish this section and move on to more entertaining topics, let's do Windows. This chapter provides a brief overview of how multimedia and Windows work together.

Where the Action Is

We all want to be where the action is. If you have a PC, most of the multimedia action is in Windows. The Windows *graphical user interface* (sometimes called a GUI and pronounced "GOO-ey") is an excellent match for multimedia applications. That's because Windows tends to be more intuitive than the old DOS interface: You select options by pointing and clicking with a mouse instead of issuing arcane commands as required at the DOS prompt.

Graphical User Interface (GUI) A graphical user interface (pronounced "gooey") uses things like icons and dialog boxes for navigation. This is easier than issuing text-based commands, as many DOS programs require.

In the Beginning . . .

Back in the old days when I first started using Windows, it wasn't designed for multimedia. No siree. In fact, it wasn't until version 3.1 that Windows became a good platform for multimedia. It was in this version that Microsoft added what's known in the jargon world as *multimedia extensions*.

These extensions enable Windows to play multimedia files, such as music files. They also enable Windows to interact with multimedia hardware.

There are several elements to the Windows multimedia extensions. Among these elements are:

MCI. No, this isn't a long distance telephone company. It stands for Media Control Interface, and it's Windows' way of working with multimedia hardware. Among the things with which MCI works are audio CDs, laser disk players, video cassette recorders, and software that plays .WAV and .MID files. Windows comes with a variety of MCI-related drivers for various types of hardware.

Audio support enables Windows to handle music, such as audio CDs and MIDI files.

MIDI patching lets you play MIDI files no matter which MIDI device created the file.

An expanded control panel is part of the Windows Control Panel added to Windows 3.1 that enables you to control multimedia in Windows. We'll discuss some of these later.

Happily, for the most part, you don't need to worry about these extensions if you have Windows 3.1 or better. When you install Windows, the multimedia capabilities are automatically installed, too.

Besides placing the proper software, such as various multimedia drivers, on your computer's hard drive, the Windows installation program also makes basic changes to the two key Windows startup files, WIN.INI and SYSTEM.INI.

While Windows installation takes care of the basics, there will be times when you need to add, delete, or tweak the drivers that run multimedia. The next section tells you about the tools Windows provides to do this.

Be a Control (Panel) Freak

The Windows *Control Panel* is where you go to adjust a variety of matters relating to Windows. By default, the icon (small picture) for opening the Control Panel is in the Main program group in the Windows Program Manager.

When you double-click on the icons in the Control Panel, Windows displays dialog boxes for fine-tuning virtually all aspects of Windows. For example, by default, the Windows Control Panel includes dialog boxes for changing the colors of your Windows environment, how your mouse operates, and how your printer is set up.

Windows Control Panel   The Windows Control Panel is a collection of features you use to control Windows' settings. For example, from the Control Panel you can access the Drivers dialog box, in which you can add, delete, and fine-tune various multimedia software drivers.

In versions of Windows since Windows 3.1, the Control Panel also provides some control over drivers needed to run multimedia in Windows. The Drivers icon in the Control Panel is of particular interest here. Double-clicking on this icon leads to the Drivers dialog box, which enables you to fine-tune the basic Windows multimedia drivers or add new drivers, as some products require. For example, some multimedia applications require that you have specific types of video drivers.

To add a driver, highlight it, and click the **Add** button. (You need to have the driver available on disk in order to add it.) To delete a driver, highlight it, and click the **Remove** button. If you want to change the way a driver works, highlight it, and click the **Setup** button (more on that in a little bit).

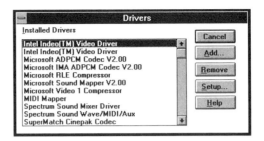

The Drivers dialog box.

Besides the basic Windows multimedia drivers, you will probably have some extra drivers in the Drivers dialog box that were put there by installation programs. Windows usually requires that any new drivers you install can be controlled through the Drivers dialog box. (In this case, the term "installation program" doesn't refer to an installation program you run when installing multimedia *hardware*, but rather the installation programs for multimedia *software*, such as those that come on CD-ROM.)

For example, many multimedia applications require a specific type of driver for the video or sound portions of multimedia applications. Usually, it's a Windows-wide driver that can be accessed by many programs. If you don't have the driver the multimedia application needs, its installation program installs that driver and gives you access to it from the Drivers dialog box.

The Drivers dialog box lists the loaded Windows multimedia drivers. It also has buttons for adding new drivers, deleting existing drivers, and a Setup button for modifying installed drivers. For many drivers, when you click on the Setup button, Windows displays a dialog box with parameters specific to that driver. Here's another area where things can get a bit dicey.

In some cases, such as with drivers installed by your sound board's installation program, you will have documentation that describes the Setup dialog box. In other cases, such as drivers installed by multimedia applications, you probably won't have any documentation for the Setup dialog box. Some drivers don't even have a Setup dialog box. When you highlight those drivers in the Drivers dialog box, the Setup button isn't available.

If your multimedia hardware—specifically your CD-ROM drive and sound card—works with some applications but not with others, there's a fair chance there's a problem with one of your drivers.

The tricky part is this: Don't mess with the Setup dialog boxes you access from the Drivers dialog box unless you know what you're doing. Read the documentation that comes with Windows or the multimedia application. If that doesn't provide the information you need, call the technical support number that the application vendor (hopefully) provided. A technical support specialist can help you troubleshoot and walk you through any changes necessary to the Windows multimedia drivers.

Now Playing . . .

YES! We're done talking about installation and drivers and all that stuff. But as long as we're talking about Windows, it's a good time to discuss two little multimedia programs that come with Windows.

These little programs, Media Player and Sound Recorder, enable you to start experimenting with the building blocks of multimedia: sound, video, and animation files. By default, you access both programs by clicking on their icons in the Accessories program group in Windows program manager.

The Accessories group.

To get you started with multimedia, let's take a brief walk through these two little programs.

Playing Media with Media Player

Talk about a self-explanatory name; Media Player plays (multi)media. You can buy players with more tools and greater flexibility, but Media Player isn't bad for a freebie. My Media Player is shown in the next figure—yours may look a little different.

Windows Media Player.

As discussed in other chapters, multimedia information is contained in files. Those files typically have specific file name extensions. The following table summarizes some of the more common multimedia files (and their file extensions) that Media Player can play.

File name extension	Multimedia type
AVI	Videos
FLC	Animation
FLI	Animation
MID	MIDI sound files
WAV	Waveform sound files

Media Player plays these types of files and also multimedia objects from any other MCI-compliant hardware, such as audio CDs. It doesn't, however, view image files. To view images, you must use a program, such as Windows Paintbrush, which also comes free with Windows.

Relatively few multimedia applications use Media Player; most have their own media players built in. But even if your multimedia application does use Media Player, you don't have to load Media Player before you start the application. The application takes care of that for you.

As you can tell in the previous screen shot, Media Player has a simple interface. It contains a slider bar that marks the progress of the media item as it plays. Beneath the slider bar is a scale for measuring the length of the media clip. Typically, the scale is in seconds, although, depending on the type of media you are playing, you can access other options in the Scale menu. Media Player has buttons similar to those found on a VCR or audio cassette player for playing the media.

If you're just starting out and are not sure which directory has sound files to play, check in the Windows directory. The .WAV files aren't very interesting, but they certainly will give you a feel for how Media Player works.

To load a multimedia clip:

1. Select **File**, then **Open**. Media Player displays the Open dialog box.

2. In the Open dialog box, select the drive and directory containing the multimedia file you want to play. Then select the specific multimedia file, and click on **OK** to return to Media Player.

3. Click on the **Play** button, which is the left-most button on Media Player. If you selected a sound, Media Player plays it. If you selected an animation or a movie, Media Player opens a little window in which the item plays.

There are several other interesting options in Media Player. You can use the **Edit Copy** command to copy media clips to the Windows Clipboard. Then, you can use the **Edit Paste** command to copy the clip into another application, such as a word processing document.

When you paste a clip into a document, Windows places an icon in the document. When you double-click on the icon, Media Player loads and plays the multimedia item. Do this right now, and you can say you've created your first multimedia application. *Congratulations!*

Also on the Edit menu are the Options and Selections commands. These commands change, depending on the type of media clip you play. They enable you to fine tune how the clip plays.

For more information about Media Player, check with your Windows on-line help.

The Recording Sound and Fury

I've always thought it was ironic that we spend thousands of dollars on computers, and then we do simple things with them, such as play games. Here's another opportunity to underutilize your computer: The Sound Recorder utility makes your expensive computer work like a simple tape recorder.

Sound Recorder enables you to record sounds as .WAV files, play them back, and like Media Player, insert them into your other applications.

The Sound Recorder Utility.

Like Media Player, Sound Recorder plays .WAV files. However, it's most useful for recording the files and performing some minor sound editing functions.

You load Sound Recorder by double-clicking on its icon in the Accessories group in Windows' Program Manager. To open a sound file, first select **File Open**. In the Open dialog box, click on the sound file you want, and then click **OK**. Play the file by clicking on Sound Recorder's **Play** button.

Sound Recorder is also useful for recording .WAV files that you place in other files; for example, you can record an explanation for a certain calculation and insert the explanation in a spreadsheet. To do this, you must have a microphone connected to the back of your sound card. Click on the **Record** button in the Sound Recorder to start recording.

Read Chapter 25 for more information about using Sound Recorder to record sounds and embed them in your other applications.

The Least You Need to Know

In this chapter, you learned:

- ☞ Windows' multimedia extensions help make Windows an excellent platform for multimedia applications.

- ☞ Many software applications require and install special drivers to properly play multimedia in Windows.

- ☞ You can add, delete, and modify these drivers from the Windows Control Panel.

- ☞ Windows comes with two utilities, Media Player and Sound Recorder, for playing multimedia and recording .WAV sound files.

Yeah, this page is blank, but don't worry—you were only charged for the pages with stuff on them.

Chapter 18
Getting Around in Multimedia

In This Chapter

- ☛ Application installation basics
- ☛ Navigating multimedia applications
- ☛ Searching for information
- ☛ Getting help

Just the Basics, Ma'am

By now, you've installed your CD-ROM drive and CD-ROM interface. You have safely tucked your sound card inside your PC. You've connected the speakers to the sound card, and the software is installed. You're ready to go. Now it's time to focus on some of the other stuff that came with either your ready-built multimedia PC or your multimedia upgrade kit.

Playing with a Caddy

If your CD-ROM drive requires a *disc caddy*, the vendor undoubtedly included one with the drive. Disc caddies protect your disc and the drive from dust and other perils like spilled coffee and stray hairs.

A disc caddy is a plastic housing into which you place the CD-ROM. You then place the caddy, with the disc inside, into the CD-ROM drive. (Quiet out there. No sniggering!)

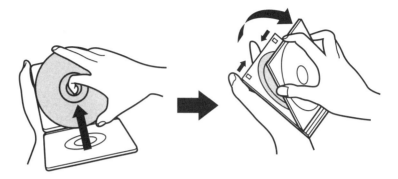

Using a disc caddy.

Some CD-ROM drives don't require disc caddies. With those drives, you open the drive door (usually by pressing the Load/Eject button) and place the disc directly into the drive. Actually, those CD-ROM drives are pretty safe, especially if they come with double doors, which is another type of "barrier device" that keeps out dust.

If your CD-ROM drive came with only one disc caddy, run out to an electronics store and buy some more. That way, you can keep your most commonly used discs in their own caddies at all times. You'll spend about ten bucks per caddy, but the expense is worth it. It's a pain to keep swapping discs in and out of a single caddy.

Using a disc caddy is simple. Usually at the back edge of the caddy are perforated buttons to push in, one on each side. As you push the buttons in with your thumb and forefinger, lift the plastic cover, then insert the disc, making sure that the printing on the disc faces up. Close the caddy and pop it in the drive.

Usually, there is an arrow at the front of the caddy indicating that you should put that end in first. But the arrow really isn't important because most drives only let you put the disc caddy in the right way.

If the caddy doesn't go into the drive, there can be two possible solutions: You're trying to put the caddy in the wrong way or there's another caddy already in the drive. In either case, it doesn't take a rocket scientist to fix the problem.

Other Tchotchkes

Growing up, my house was full of *tchotchkes* (pronounced "choch-kahs"). I'm still not sure of the official translation of this Yiddish word, but my own personal translation is "junk."

Well, most multimedia bundles come with their share of tchotchkes, although in this case, they sometimes are pretty useful.

Here's a brief, nonexhaustive list of the knickknacks and doodads that may accompany your multimedia PC or multimedia upgrade kit. Different kits are just that— different, so you may have all or none of these, or you may even have some tchotchkes I didn't think of. You can also buy them separately.

Tchotchke A gimcrack or doodad. For some, a tchotchke is the ashtray you bought at a roadside rest stop commemorating a state or tourist trap. In my house, a tchotchke was a pitcher shaped like a parrot. In the multimedia world, tchotchkes can include CD-ROM driver cleaners and headphones.

Unlike the cutesy, little figurines Mom collects, you won't want to put these in a hutch in the dining room. Rather, you should keep them near your multimedia system—you may actually need them.

CD-ROM drive cleaner. A CD-ROM drive cleaner, as the name implies, cleans your CD-ROM drive. Why not just take the darned thing outside and hose it down? If you need an answer to that question, you're probably not quite ready for multimedia.

At any rate, a CD-ROM drive cleaner cleans the innards of your CD-ROM drive, particularly the lens. The lens focuses the laser beam that reads the data on the drive. If the lens gets dusty or smudged, the drive won't read the data correctly.

In most cases, the CD-ROM drive cleaner is like a caddy and/or disc. You put the thing in the drive and let it clean away. If your system doesn't use a caddy and it doesn't have double doors to protect it from dust, I suggest using the CD-ROM drive cleaner frequently. Some people think you should only clean the lens when you have trouble with your CD-ROM drive. If you aren't sure what to do, call your CD-ROM drive's manufacturer and ask for their recommendation.

Headphones. For a tchotchke, a set of headphones is pretty darned handy. Most CD-ROM drives have a jack in the front of the unit for plugging in the headphones. Headphones are useful for playing audio CDs, and some music-based CD-ROMs also use them. And, when you accidentally step on your Walkman headphones, you can use the ones that came with your multimedia upgrade bundle.

Tools. A few upgrade kits I've seen came with little screwdrivers or pliers for installing the hardware. If yours did, keep these little tools nearby. You may need them later when something goes awry.

Miscellaneous spare cables, adapters, cable splitters, screws, nuts, and bolts. I've learned this through bitter experience: If your upgrade kit comes with extra stuff, even boring stuff such as cables, keep it.

"Why," you may ask, "do I need a spare ribbon cable?" You'll have to take my word for this, but I guarantee that if you throw this stuff out, you'll need it within a week. It's some sort of mystical law.

For example, I once discarded a cable splitter I didn't need, only to find two weeks later that I needed it to install a new hard drive. What did I do? Just what you'll have to do—I ran out to an electronics store and paid my hard-earned cash for a new one. It wasn't expensive, but it was a pain in the rear.

CD-ROMs. Now we're getting serious! Most multimedia systems and upgrade kits come with some multimedia CD-ROM titles. This paragraph is what's known in show biz as a segue-way to the next section. Read on. . . .

Installing CD-ROM Applications

Now it's time to get serious—let's install a multimedia CD-ROM application. Often, the most difficult part of this process is getting the shrink-wrap off the case that contains the disc. I can't help you much there—I tend to use my teeth. If you can restrain yourself, use a pocket knife or even a screwdriver to rip the plastic.

After you remove the shrink-wrap from the case, take out the disc. It is best to handle the disc by the edges to make sure that it stays pristine. Don't put your grimy fingerprints all over the flat surface of the disc. If your drive uses a disc caddy, put the disc in the caddy, and insert the caddy into the drive. If you don't use a caddy, just insert the plain disc in the drive.

At this point, read the documentation that came with the disc. Typically, you will run an installation program. If this is a DOS-based program, that means you must type a command to start the installation program at the DOS command prompt.

Typically, that command is *N*:SETUP.EXE or *N*:INSTALL.EXE. In this case, *N* represents the drive letter of your CD-ROM drive, which probably *isn't* N.

To install a CD-ROM program that runs through Windows, you first must select **File Run** from Program Manager's menu bar. Windows displays the Run dialog box.

The Run dialog box.

Depending on what the documentation for the disc says, type either **N:INSTALL** or **N:SETUP** in the Run dialog box. Press **Enter** and the installation process should start.

Why install a CD-ROM program on your hard drive when all the information you need is on the disc? Usually, the application places some data files on your hard disk that are needed to run the program. They should be on your hard disk because they are commonly used files, and your hard drive is faster than the CD-ROM drive. Also, sometimes, the application must install drivers, such as video or animation drivers, to make the multimedia application work correctly.

At any rate, follow the installation program's on-screen directions, if any, for installing the application. If you are installing a Windows application, the installation program leaves behind a new program group and icon for launching the application.

If you gather many multi-media applications, they will take significant chunks of hard disk space, and at some point, you must reclaim that space. To stay organized and to speed the process of deleting the multimedia files, create a directory called CDROM. If the multimedia application's installation program gives you the option, install all the multimedia files in a new subdirectory under the CDROM directory. For example, on my system, the files for my Myst game are in a subdirectory called E:\CDROM\MYST. When (and if) I finish the game, I won't have to search my entire hard disk for the files to delete.

As with other applications, you start the Windows multimedia application by double-clicking on its icon. If it's a DOS application, you'll need to read the documentation to learn what to type at the command prompt to launch the application.

Hello Out There! I'm Lost!

This keeps getting better and better. You've fired up your multimedia application and you're ready to go. You're looking at the first screen and maybe you've even heard a bit of introductory music.

The next chapter provides more details about navigating through multimedia applications, but I know you can't wait, so I'll give you the ten-cent tour now.

Let's Get Hyper(linked)

For the most part, finding your way through multimedia applications should be self-evident. A *hyperlink* is the key tool you'll use. Hyperlinks are on-screen cues for initiating an action. In most multimedia applications, clicking on a hyperlink performs one of two actions: Either it takes you to another section of the application action or it launches an action, like playing an audio clip. It may also display a window that contains additional information, such as a definition.

Often the section to which you jump is related to the section that you left. This enables you to find more information, see related information, or start on an entirely new track.

Hyperlinks make multimedia applications nonlinear. That is, they aren't like books in which you read a page, then read the next, one after the other. The ability to use hyperlinks to jump around from topic to topic and read, view, or watch items at will is one of the things that makes multimedia so exciting.

Hyperlinks can have different on-screen appearances, such as:

☛ **Differently colored text**. In a multimedia encyclopedia, for example, clicking on a word displayed with colored text typically takes you to another article, usually about or defining the colored word.

☛ **Buttons, icons, or tags**. These usually have either a graphic image or text to describe what they do. They either send you to another part of the application or launch something, such as a video clip.

☛ **Arrows.** Unlike the other on-screen hyperlink cues, which can deposit you somewhere else in the multimedia application, arrows take you to the next screen. Usually, clicking on an arrow is like turning a page.

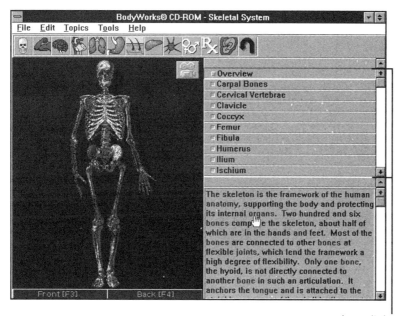

On-screen hyperlinks.

hyperlinks

Searching, Searching

Hyperlinks are cool, but they sometimes won't help you find what you're looking for. For example, you may be viewing a multimedia encyclopedia and want information about a specific subject, such as the human femur. Using only hyperlinks, it would be difficult to know where to find such information.

Fortunately, many multimedia applications, such as encyclopedias, include searching capabilities which enable you to type the item for which you are looking in a dialog box, then have the application find it wherever it is located. Then, if you want, you can follow hyperlinks from that item to other related items.

Usually, you start a search by clicking on a button or icon. This displays a search dialog box, such as the one shown in the following figure. You type the item for which you are searching, click a button, and the application should list all the instances of the item it finds. Then, you double-click on the item in the list to view it.

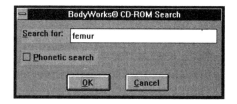

Searching for information.

Chapter 19 tells you more about searching capabilities.

You Need Help

A good multimedia application should be knucklehead-proof. That is, by combining good organization with hyperlinks and searching capabilities, anybody should be able to use a multimedia application.

There's that word again—*should*. The reality, of course, is that some multimedia applications take some getting used to and you may find them downright screwy to use.

That's why the multimedia gods invented help systems. Some, but certainly not all, multimedia applications include on-line help systems that are similar to those found in your regular applications, like your word processor.

If you're baffled and need an answer quickly, check the application's documentation to find out whether it has an on-line help system and how to access it. A common but not universal method is to press the F1 key. You can also use the Help menu on the menu bar.

The Least You Need to Know

We finally got to the fun stuff. This chapter provided a general overview of how to install, start, and navigate through multimedia applications. You learned:

- ☞ Disc caddies are useful for preventing damage caused by dust, but not all drives use them.

- ☞ Most CD-ROM multimedia applications require some hard disk space.

- ☞ Hyperlinks are a primary tool for navigating through a multimedia application. Hyperlinks often appear on-screen as buttons, icons, or arrows.

- ☞ Many applications enable you to search for specific topics of information.

You say, How much more blank could
a page be? And the answer is, None.
None more blank.

Chapter 19
Stuff . . . and *Good* Stuff

In This Chapter

- ☛ Balance is everything
- ☛ Advanced searching
- ☛ Balanced multimedia
- ☛ Getting output

I like computer trade shows because I can hang out with "them." These are the pundits, computer journalists, and other riffraff, the "they" of "they say . . ." fame.

You know what "they" are saying now? They say that multimedia will get less and less expensive as more people buy multimedia systems. They say that, before long, multimedia CD-ROM applications will cost about the same as audio CDs, which means that we'll all have many of them.

Multimedia already is easy to come by. It's all over; you can't avoid it. This stuff is inexpensive and getting more so all the time.

However, there's *stuff* and there's *good stuff*. The good stuff is rarer and sometimes more difficult to recognize. This chapter describes some of the elements that make for good multimedia. That, in turn, will help you make better multimedia buying decisions.

They Call It Shovelware

Remember what we said earlier in this book? CD-ROMs are, first and foremost, a storage medium, kind of like super floppy disks. Their chief advantage is their large storage capacity.

Many multimedia developers seem intoxicated with the large capacity of CD-ROMs. Others don't have the skills to make compelling multimedia applications. Both types of multimedia developers tend to simply shovel as much information onto a CD-ROM as can fit with minimal concern for finesse and organization.

The name that developed for these types of discs is *shovelware*. These discs may be long on data but are short on character. Worse still, if they are poorly organized, they may not even be particularly useful.

Don't get me wrong—not all shovelware is bad. For discs focused on a specific subject and aimed at researchers, shovelware is just fine, particularly if the disc has tools, such as retrieval capability, to find precisely the information you need.

One of my all-time favorite CD-ROMs is a classic shovelware application called Library of the Future. This disk contains about 1,700 separate book titles, ranging from literary classics to the great books of the various religions to plays and scientific works.

One reason I love this disc is that it *is* shovelware; with a single search, I can find all literary references to a specific subject in the great books of our civilization. It's not really a typical shovelware disc—it has hyperlinks and a little more character than most—but it's a good one to show you in a figure.

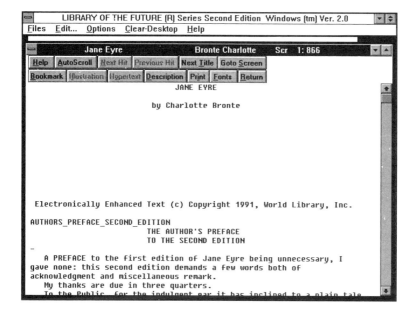

A good shovelware application.

Although it offers a wealth of information, Library of the Future is hardly compelling multimedia. Most people, myself included, prefer more refined applications that take advantage of different types of media to entertain and educate at the same time.

When shopping, you should probably try to avoid shovelware titles. There are many of them out there, and unless you need them for reference, you're unlikely to use them much after you buy them.

Keeping Your Balance

If you don't have good balance, you'll always be falling off things. Not much fun. Unbalanced multimedia isn't much fun either.

"Isn't balance an inner ear thing?" you're probably wondering. "What does it have to do with multimedia?" Thanks for asking; balance has a *lot* to do with multimedia.

Multimedia is composed of many elements: text, video, animation, sound, and still images. Multimedia applications that are too heavy in one of those areas are out of balance and are not likely to be very interesting.

It is particularly tempting for multimedia vendors to saturate an application with video. After all, video is the newest, greatest, snazziest thing around, right? However, using too much video has several drawbacks.

- ☞ Video taxes your computer system so that, unless you have a mega-rocket ship computer, you'll spend a lot of time waiting for videos to load and play. About the only benefit to this is that you will develop great finger-drumming skills.

- ☞ Video takes a lot of disk space, which can mean less room for other types of media that may be more appropriate.

I recently saw a "tour" disc of an exotic foreign country. Far and away, the most compelling parts of the disc were the relatively few still photos, accompanied by haunting music, that captured and froze in time the beauty of the land. However, the developer insisted on including too many videos, including some hard-to-see clips showing exciting (yawn) stuff, such as birds flying. To me, a beautiful close-up still image of the bird would have been more powerful.

In order to achieve balance in a multimedia application, developers need to use media appropriately. Multimedia vendors brag and shout about how many minutes of video and audio they have on their discs. However, if it's the *wrong* video and audio, they shouldn't be bragging. And, sometimes, good old boring text is the most appropriate medium.

Balance also refers to the on-screen appearance of the application. In magazines this is referred to as *layout*. Some vendors put too much stuff in each screen, forcing you to waste time figuring out what's important and what you should do next. The following figures show an example of a dense, crowded multimedia screen and one that has a nicely balanced layout.

A crowded multimedia screen.

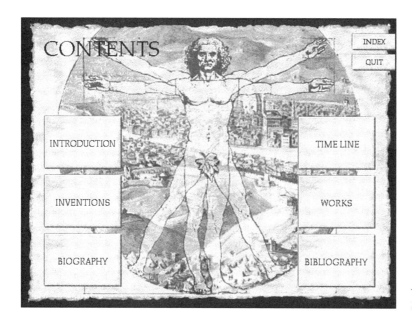

A well-balanced multimedia screen.

It doesn't matter how snazzy the media are, if you can't understand what the heck is going on, you won't enjoy and use the application. Balanced screen layout is essential in multimedia applications.

Jump In multimedia, a jump refers to the act of moving via hyperlinks from one piece of information to another.

Getting Hyper and Easy to Use

Remember hyperlinks from Chapter 18? These are the little on-screen cues you click with your mouse. When you do so, the application launches an action. Usually, that action is either playing a media clip or taking you to a related section of the application. Moving to another section of the application with a hyperlink is taking a *jump.*

Hyperlinks should be obvious. There shouldn't be any question about which on-screen element is a hyperlink or what kind of information you'll get if you click on the link.

Also, hyperlinks should be plentiful. The current crop of multimedia encyclopedias is a good example of applications with many hyperlinks. In fact, some encyclopedias blur the distinction between hyperlinks and searching capabilities (which we'll talk about later in the chapter).

Plentiful hyperlinks are critically important; they are, in some ways, the essence of many educational multimedia applications. They enable *serendipitous learning*, which is a powerful and fun way to learn. With this type of learning, you can start on one topic, and by following a series of hyperlinks, you can find information about other related topics that you wouldn't have otherwise found.

Hyperlinks started out in the pre-multimedia world as *hypertext.* In those days, hypertext was for jumping from one bit of text to another when you clicked on the marked text. Of course, text links still are common and the concept remains the same today. However, the name had to change because hyperlinks now also jump among video, animations, and images—not just text.

Here's an abbreviated example of serendipitous learning from well-done hyperlinking, in this case, from Microsoft's Encarta multimedia encyclopedia.

1. I started with a search for Bix Beiderbecke, the influential '20s jazz musician.

2. I read his biography, then clicked on an icon at the top of the screen. Encarta played some of his music.

3. I clicked on a button that said **See Also**. Encarta displayed a dialog box listing related articles. I clicked on the listing about Beiderbecke's contemporary, Louis Armstrong, and jumped to that article.

4. I read about Armstrong and listened to a bit of his music, then jumped to a general article about jazz.

5. From the general article about jazz, I jumped to a general article about African-American music, including the blues and ragtime.

6. From that article, I jumped to a general article about African-American people in America. From there, I could jump to all sorts of places.

When you can direct your own learning and exploring in this way, you're more likely to learn and explore. That's why hyperlinks are more than useful; they are *essential* to certain types of multimedia applications.

Another important hyperlinking tool is a way to backtrack through your travels in the application. In the previous example, I should be able to quickly return to the article about Louis Armstrong even if I'm reading an article about George Washington Carver. Many applications enable you to do this by clicking on a certain button, which displays a dialog box containing a list of all recently viewed articles. From there, you can click on the article you want and jump directly to it.

Still Searchin'

As I mentioned in Chapter 18, another way of finding information in many multimedia applications is with a searching capability. While hyperlinks started out many years ago as a way to move from one bit of text to another, searching remains primarily text-based, even in multimedia applications. That's because it is very difficult to search for the contents of a picture, audio, or video clip. Many applications let you search for those media, but you'll actually be searching for text descriptions of them.

Searching, of course, is particularly important for reference and educational applications. For example, a multimedia encyclopedia isn't very useful unless you can search for specific topics.

Searching for the Truth

Some searching capabilities are more powerful and thorough than others. Different multimedia applications have different search features. Here are some common types of searching capabilities.

- ☛ **Keyword searches** search only for specially designated words called *keywords*. Keywords are representative of broader topics and issues. The developer can assign keywords to each chunk of information (many developers don't).

  Keyword searches usually are faster than other types of searches, but they obviously don't search all text—only keywords. The result of a keyword search is usually a list of found keywords, or a list of articles containing the keywords. Double-clicking on an item in the list takes you to that item.

- ☛ **Topic searches** only search through a list of topics in the application. In most applications, chapter or section headings are considered to be topics. After a topic search, the application displays a list of topics that the application found.

- ☛ **Full-text searches** look through every word in the application. Depending on the size of the application and the technology used for full-text searching, these searches can be either lightning quick or frustratingly slow. The result of a full-text search is a list of articles or topics containing the word for which you are searching.

In most cases, you can click on a command from a Search menu, or click on some type of Search icon or button. You use a dialog box to define your search. After you type the search term into the dialog box, you click on a button to start the search. The following figure shows an example of a search dialog box from a popular multimedia encyclopedia.

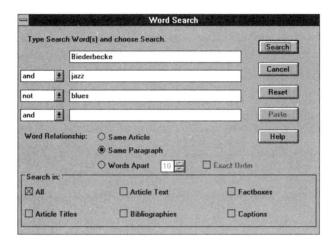

A search dialog box.

Get Output, or Get Put Out

A final capability to look for in a multimedia application is output. *Output* is whatever you need to get out of the application in the form in which you need it. Output can include:

☛ The ability to print specific portions of the application. For example, in a multimedia encyclopedia, you should be able to mark a specific section, then print out that section.

☛ The ability to copy material from the application and paste it into other applications. This ability doesn't just pertain to copying and pasting text. You may, for example, need to copy a picture from a picture collection and paste it into an annual report you create with your desktop publishing package.

You don't, of course, need output from all multimedia applications. A multimedia game is an example in which you don't need output to make the application useful. However, if you need to print or move information or multimedia clips to other applications, make sure the multimedia application has that capability before you buy it.

The Least You Need to Know

This chapter told you all about what makes up a good multimedia application. You learned that:

- ☞ Quantity is the easiest thing to add to multimedia applications, but quality is just as important.

- ☞ A good multimedia application uses the most effective media and balances its use of the various media.

- ☞ Well-designed and copious hyperlinks make it easy to navigate through multimedia applications and also to learn serendipitously.

- ☞ In many educational applications, text search capabilities are critically important.

- ☞ Depending on the multimedia application, you should be able to print or copy information to other applications.

Chapter 20
So Many Discs, So Little Time

In This Chapter

- Buying multimedia
- Keeping up with it all

In this chapter, we'll spend a little time reviewing where to buy multimedia CD-ROM titles, and the general nature of the titles that are available. In the next chapter, we'll get to the real payoff: my Top 10 List of CD-ROM titles. It's dirty work, but somebody's got to play with multimedia. It's just a job, though. Really. (Oh, Geez—I missed dinner again).

Where to Get 'Em (and What to Expect)

Like leaves in the autumn, multimedia discs are easy to find. Discount software stores like Egghead or Babbages stock them by the truckload. So do computer warehouse stores, office supply warehouse stores, discount stores, electronics stores, and many other outlets.

Perhaps the best deals on CD-ROMs are from mail-order vendors. To find mail-order vendors, simply open any computer trade magazine at random. The chances are pretty good that you'll open the magazine to an advertisement for a mail-order vendor.

As with most hardware and software products, mail order works best if you know precisely what you want to buy. However, if you want to take a multimedia title for a test drive before you plunk down your hard-earned cash, you'll have to go to a local retail store that will let you do that.

Mail-order vendors advertise a large number of multimedia titles. Prices can be as much as ten or fifteen bucks less than you'll pay even in a discount software store. That makes it worth price shopping, particularly if you buy many multimedia titles.

The price of CD-ROM multimedia titles is likely to drop in the near future. Some of the pundits I hang around with at computer trade shows insist that, before long, CD-ROM prices will be about the same as audio CD prices. That may be an exaggeration, but as more and more people get CD-ROM drives, particularly at home, the competition among multimedia developers will definitely heat up.

This trend will intensify because the monster-big software vendors, such as Microsoft, are into multimedia applications in a major way. These guys are remorseless about lowering prices. A cynic might say that they lower prices to push the little vendors out of the way, but the large vendors say they're doing it in the interests of the consumers. Who's to say?

As with so much in the hardware and software industry, price pressure and competition have an impact that goes beyond prices. Some say that as the big software companies have pushed the little guys out of the way, application software has become less innovative and more buggy. Right now this isn't a problem with multimedia—two of my ten favorite multimedia discs are from Microsoft; however, the danger certainly exists. As a matter of principle, I like to support smaller multimedia publishers whenever possible. That's my (unsolicited) opinion, anyway.

Hybrid discs A hybrid CD-ROM is one that works on both Macintosh and Windows machines.

At any rate, at this writing, multimedia CD-ROMs range from about twenty dollars to less than a hundred. Most discs fall in the middle of that range.

Besides decreasing prices, the other trend to look for is multimedia discs that work in both Windows and Macintosh. At this writing, this trend toward *hybrid* discs has gathered quite a bit of momentum; half or more of the discs that cross my desk are hybrids.

Finally, a word about quality. While there are many interesting and innovative multimedia applications available, there's also a lot of *dreck*. Dreck is another Yiddish word from my childhood, and to be blunt, it means junk, crapola, garbage. This is the sort of word that usually engenders additional body language for emphasis, like rolling eyes or a shaking head.

The best way to avoid dreck is to try a multimedia application before you buy it. If you are unable to do that, ask a friend who has used the application. Or subscribe to magazines that provide reviews of multimedia applications (and that employ talented hard working reviewers like yours truly.)

Multimedia is a new field and new consumers are easy to impress. Everybody is impressed with their first spinning logo accompanied by fakey MIDI music at the beginning of a multimedia application.

After you've used a few applications, though, this simple stuff loses its appeal. With so many new users, it's easier for vendors to sell dreck. I hope this will change as vendors and users become more sophisticated.

Like What, for Example?

Let's take a quick look at a few of the broad areas in which there are good multimedia titles available. These areas often are of interest only to particular segments of our world. As a result, the discs mentioned in this part of the chapter didn't make my Top 10 List, but that doesn't mean they aren't interesting applications.

Building Your Home

There are a surprising number of discs available for home builders and remodelers. I recently looked at one called Expert Home Design that was part multimedia clips providing building and decorating tips, part multimedia presentations of model homes, and part low-end drafting programs to rough out housing plans.

The most interesting section of this disc is the 3-D "walkthroughs" in which you view the home from the point of view of somebody walking through it. It also includes a little program for costing out the process of building and remodeling.

A 3-D home walkthrough.

Getting Goofy

There are goofy discs out there that some people may like. For example, I saw one based on that wretchedly popular show, *Lifestyles of the Rich and Famous*. That whiny guy—what's his name? oh, yeah, Robin Leach— narrates it.

This particular disc provided recipes from the rich and famous and, of course, had videos of their soirees and fabulous bashes. If your idea of a good time is eating what Elizabeth Taylor (or at least her publicist) eats, get this disc. If you don't like the idea of this disc, but have a yen for something else that's goofy and strange, don't worry—there are plenty of choices out there for you.

Traveling Around

Multimedia and travel applications are made for each other. If you have the travel bug but don't have the time to see the world, there are CD-ROMs aplenty to help you scratch your itch.

Some of these discs are both entertaining and educational, such as an imported disc I recently saw called Natural Argentina. This disc focuses on the natural aspects of this large and biologically diverse nation.

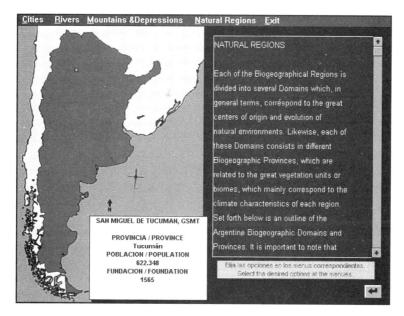

Learning About Argentina.

The still photos are stunning, and the Argentinean developers selected soulful music to accompany the photos. That, combined with the general wealth of information on the disc, makes it very satisfying.

I also recently saw and enjoyed two discs about Hawaii, one of which provided much more than the usual here-are-the-tourist-traps type of information. When I finished the disc, I was quite eager to go there.

Basic Training

One of the first popular applications for multimedia was training. The interactive nature of multimedia makes it a natural for training applications. That's because you learn more when you direct your own learning process. Initially, training titles were developed for specific industries, teaching, for example, how to use the XYZ Company's fabulous new widget. Now, however, we're starting to see a small glut of self-help training discs.

Typical of these discs is Connect for Success from Wilson Learning, a company with a lot of training experience. This is a surprisingly polished multimedia effort that teaches you how to communicate effectively to get what you want. It includes videos showing the right and wrong ways to communicate. It also provides games and other interactive opportunities to try out your newly learned skills.

Some people find these training discs strange—I confess, I'm not a big fan of this genre. But many people find multimedia training discs invaluable for improving various types of skills.

Training the Tykes

We threw a party when my son graduated from high school recently. When we asked him if he wanted to invite any teachers, he selected three; one was a teacher from his preschool years.

It is my belief that early childhood educators are often among the least appreciated and most underpaid professionals around. It was touching to see my son remember Miss Nora and understand how important she was to him. Miss Nora certainly appreciated being remembered.

Similarly, multimedia applications aimed at early learners don't usually get the attention accorded to other applications. Because the skills these applications teach are so basic, they tend to not be as much fun for older kids and parents.

Some early learning titles are well thought out and extremely useful for teaching the little ones basic skills, such as recognizing geometric shapes and simple counting. I was particularly impressed with a disc I recently saw from Bright Star called Early Math, which featured an amiable creature named Loid who leads youngsters through some basic learning exercises.

Loid teaches youngsters how to count.

Doing the Hobby Thing

Not surprisingly, there are many hobby-related discs. Obviously, these discs have narrow appeal but can be indispensable to those who are interested in the subject matter.

For example, I have a couple of car discs that were sent to me. Frankly, a disc about bicycle touring or the Tour de France would interest me more, but those discs probably wouldn't appeal to many others. That's the nature of these hobby discs. You either like 'em or you don't.

Multimedia at the Office

The office has been the hardest area for multimedia to crack. After all, multimedia is entertaining and educational, but it rarely is business-oriented. As a result, there still are relatively few commercially available multimedia business applications.

However, there are many CD-ROM applications available that don't qualify as multimedia. For example, a favorite disc of mine is Street Atlas USA, which has maps of every street and byway in America. This disc is a must-have for salespeople, but it has no media other than maps.

Examples of other common business discs include those that contain the contents of every phone book in the country, and discs listing filings with federal regulatory agencies. There also are tons of reference CD-ROMs for specific professions, such as the Physicians Desk Reference for doctors and discs of statutes and case law for lawyers.

At this point, business uses of multimedia tend to fall into these categories:

☞ **Annotating normal business documents.** Using a utility like Sound Recorder, which comes with Windows, with a standard Windows application like a word processor enables you to add voice annotations to business documents. Or you can import an image into a document. This isn't the most scintillating multimedia, but it *is* multimedia.

☞ **Kiosk applications.** A multimedia application in a public place is sometimes called a *kiosk application*. A typical kiosk application might be a computer set up in the lobby of a building. The application can greet visitors and provide on-screen hyperlinks to various options. For example, one hyperlink can lead to a list of employees and their phone extensions and another could lead to descriptions of the company's products.

☞ **Training.** We previously discussed self-help training applications. Before these generalized multimedia applications started appearing, there were many business-specific training applications available. An interesting application I once saw described all toxic substances used by a company and how to handle emergencies with those substances. Federal regulations required that this information be *readily* accessible to employees. Multimedia made sure that the information was *easily* accessible.

The Enclosed Disc

One of the great discs of all time is attached to this very book. Okay, so I'm (*very*) prejudiced. Still, I'm sure you'll find the disc interesting and useful. To find out what's on the disc and how to run the applications, turn to Chapter 31, "What's on the CD-ROM?"

The Least You Need to Know

Are we having fun yet? You bet we are! In this chapter:

- ☞ You learned that you can buy multimedia discs for less from mail-order vendors, but you won't be able to try them before you buy.

- ☞ Two important trends in multimedia titles are decreasing prices and hybrid discs that work on both Windows and Macintosh computers.

- ☞ There are CD-ROM titles for virtually any topic.

(zen text)

Chapter 21

Top 10 Countdown: My Favorite CD-ROMs

In This Chapter

- The buildup
- Ten cool CD-ROMs

Sure, people think I'm goofing off when I'm looking at multimedia titles. But it's my job. I review software, including multimedia applications, for a living. Twist my arm, though, and I'll (painfully) admit that my job is fun.

Out of all the CD-ROMs that have crossed my desk, this chapter describes my ten favorites. First, though, a few explanations are in order. Then, we can start the drum roll.

Setting the Stage

All the discs in this list are for Windows, and there's a good reason: I'm a Windows sort of guy. I love the Macintosh and the new PowerPCs, which arguably present a more elegant computing environment than Windows. At the very least, Apple was years ahead of Windows in defining ease of use. But, when the computing gods spat me out into the high-tech world, I landed on the Windows side of the fence.

Besides the Macintosh, Windows is the only platform in which there is consistently high-quality multimedia development occurring. As we discussed in Chapter 20, the good news is that most discs on my list are available for both platforms.

Here's another caveat: My list is entirely subjective, so your results may vary. I don't pretend to have seen every multimedia disc ever released, so I've undoubtedly missed some titles of high merit. There you have it—we live in an imperfect world and I'm a leading exemplar of that fact.

What does it take to get on my favorites list? There's no one answer to that question. Some of the discs, like Library of the Future, barely qualify as multimedia but tickled my fancy in some way. Other discs, like the JFK Assassination disc, don't cover topics that fascinate me, yet they make such superb use of multimedia that they are compelling. Others still are just plain fun and made the list on that basis. Hey, I get to be arbitrary—I'm the author here, after all.

Here's one final confession. I don't have a single favorite. Like a kid, I'm usually most enthusiastic about the most recent cool disc I've seen. That's why the following list is in alphabetical order, not in order of preference.

At any rate, here's my list. Drum roll, please.

Encarta

At this writing, there are three major players in the multimedia encyclopedia market: Compton's Interactive Encyclopedia (CIE), The New Grolier Multimedia Encyclopedia (NGME) and Microsoft Encarta. Each has its merits, but I like Encarta the best.

Of the three, the scholarship of the NGME is the soundest. However, this encyclopedia is largely text-based—the multimedia elements feel almost like afterthoughts. CIE makes good use of multimedia and is somewhat simpler to use than Encarta, but it doesn't compare well to Encarta's multimedia prowess.

Using Encarta is fun. The interface is attractive; Microsoft manages to get a lot on-screen without creating a cluttered appearance. And the multimedia elements are generally of higher quality and are more plentiful than in the competitors' products.

All three encyclopedias feature timelines, which list chronological events in history. Double-click on an event, and you jump to an article about the event. All three have text search capabilities, an area in which NGME clearly excels. However, Encarta's multimedia is simply put together better. Encarta could be a tad more thorough, but it is important multimedia because it proves that learning can be fun.

Microsoft Encarta.

Jazz: A Multimedia History

Compton's New Media is the publisher of one of my oldie-but-goodie sentimental favorites—Jazz: A Multimedia History. This title has been out a while, and its multimedia presentation is a bit dated. For example, the multimedia elements are segregated, requiring you to go to different parts of the interface to view videos or still images. Recent multimedia interfaces enable you to jump among these elements more effortlessly.

However, Jazz: A Multimedia History covers its subject thoroughly and with respect. It also includes some wonderful and rare video clips of several of the great jazz musicians. If you like music and want to know more about jazz, you'll enjoy learning from this disc. If you already are a jazz aficionado, you'll still appreciate the images and videos.

Jazz: A Multimedia History.

JFK Assassination: A Visual Investigation

The assassination of John F. Kennedy was one of the defining moments of my childhood. Like most people old enough to remember, I remember vividly where I was and how I learned the horrible news.

However, I'm not one of those who spends time trying to ferret out precisely who planned and carried out the assassination. So why is JFK Assassination: A Visual Investigation from Medio on my Top 10 List?

The answer is simple: This disc is superb multimedia. It takes a horrible moment in our history and the accumulated controversy about that moment and presents them with unflinching grace and drama.

I've seen another multimedia title about this subject that was dreck—pure shovelware. Medio's title, however, manages to be scholarly without losing the drama, horror, and ambiguity of this tragic event. In short, this disc is riveting, even if you aren't a conspiracy buff.

JFK Assassination: A Visual Investigation.

Leonardo The Inventor

Leonardo The Inventor is a fun disc that chronicles the inventions of that great Renaissance innovator, Leonardo da Vinci. While the disc contains some discussion of his great works of art, such as the Mona Lisa and The Last Supper, the focus is on Leonardo's notebooks in which he sketched many fabulous ideas. Many of Leonardo's inventions took centuries to become realities.

Part of the reason this disc makes my Top 10 List is the compelling nature of the information, but it also makes excellent use of multimedia to communicate that information. The disc shows pages from Leonardo's notebooks, plays voice narrations of the notebooks, and includes animations about how his inventions worked. You can interact with the inventions, getting them to work in on-screen animations. It also features one of the cleanest and easiest-to-navigate multimedia interfaces I've seen.

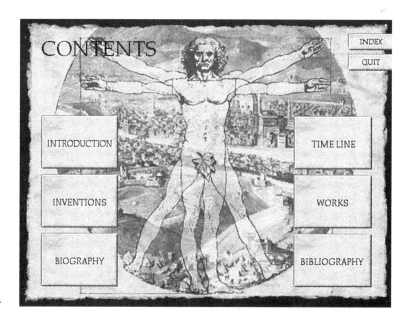

Leonardo The Inventor.

At times, the scholarship of the disc is a bit soft, but then the target audience is young people and their families, not Renaissance scholars. This is an excellent family disc that would also complement the libraries of elementary and middle schools.

Library of the Future

Even though this is one of my favorite discs, it barely squeaked into the Top 10 List. That's because it's barely multimedia. Rather, this disc contains the text of more than 1,700 literary and religious titles. Thankfully, the publisher, World Library, Inc., saw fit to add some videos (such as old movie clips) and some still images to the latest version. This qualifies Library of the Future as multimedia and enables me to put it on my list. I love this disc because it boggles my mind that so much of the world's great literature and knowledge can come in such a small package.

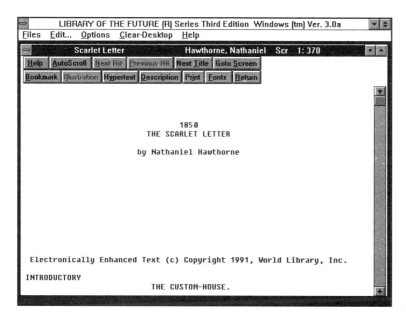

Library of the Future.

The enormity of the text is made accessible by the disc's powerful capabilities to search for specific text. This is a boon for speech writers looking for just the right quotation or pretentious people looking for impressive literary references.

Another interesting feature is the capability to have the application automatically scroll through the text so you can read it without having to use the mouse or keyboard. All this disc needs is the hardware necessary to hang your PC and monitor over your favorite reading sofa.

Multimedia Schubert

Microsoft's Multimedia Schubert is one in a series of titles that includes examinations of the works of Beethoven, Mozart, and Stravinsky, each of which is equally impressive. In addition to providing an excellent biography, Microsoft takes a single work by a composer and goes in-depth. You'll find this series to be enticing, addictive multimedia. Beginners to classical music will appreciate it as will those who have been fans for years.

Multimedia Schubert treats us to a close reading of Schubert's "Trout Quintet," in which an expert goes over each phrase of the work describing the effect for which Schubert is striving. It manages to be witty yet scholarly, and as dramatic as the musical work itself. Like a gripping movie or multimedia game, these discs have the propensity to keep you up late at night when prudence dictates that you should be getting your rest.

Hyperlinks from the close reading lead to related sections, such as those comparing the "Trout Quintet" to Mozart's "Eine Kleine Nachtmusik," another famous sonata. This is education at its entertaining best.

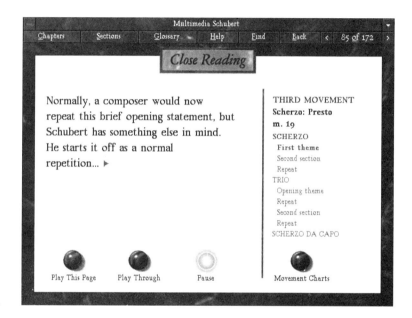

Multimedia Schubert.

Myst

Ah, Myst.

In the parlance, those who love games and play them frequently are *gamers*. I'm not a gamer, but I am a new Myst addict. As I write this, I'm a long way from finishing Myst, and deadlines prevent me from making the progress I want. However, I will finish, no matter how long it takes.

Myst.

Myst is difficult to describe. It's not a shoot-'em-up or even a game of high adventure. You don't run the risk of sudden, violent death in this game.

Rather, the game places you on an abandoned island in which something has gone dreadfully wrong. Through clues and hints, you track down the problem.

This sounds a bit mundane perhaps, but Myst is an unusually intelligent game, an inner game, with beautiful photo-realistic graphics and perfect mood music. This game is addictive. Sure, some people have allegiance to other games, but I'm in love with this elegant, multilayered joy.

Ocean Life: Hawaiian Islands

Like Multimedia Schubert and Ruff's Bone, this disc is one in a series, in this case, from a small publisher named Sumeria.

A disc about marine life runs the risk of being boring to everybody but marine biologists and scuba divers. Not this disc, though. This disc shows the power of properly selected and appropriate media.

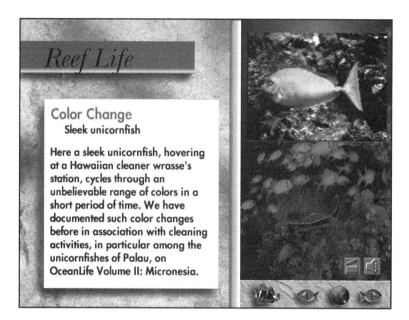

Ocean Life: Hawaiian Islands.

Ocean Life: Hawaiian Islands has several sections, the most fascinating of which is one showing life on the reefs around Hawaii. One reason this section is so powerful is the quality—and the rareness—of many of the videos. One clip, for example, follows a reef shark around in its journey for food. Another rare clip shows a sleek unicornfish changing through a variety of colors.

An hour with this disc is almost as much fun as a snorkeling expedition, but is more educational because of the expert presentation of the information.

Prehistoria

Prehistoria from Grolier is another top-notch *edutainment* disc. This disc tracks about 500 species of animals from the first life through relatively modern times.

Prehistoria is scholarly and fun. It doesn't provide so much information that you'll become bogged down, but it does provide enough so that you'll feel you understand the subject matter.

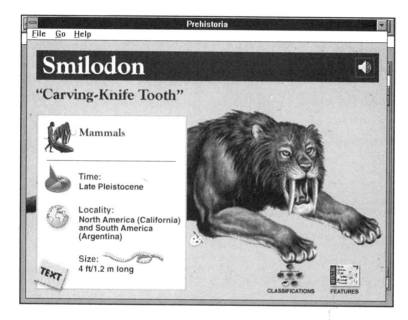

Prehistoria.

This disc fascinates me for a number of reasons. First, it reminds me what recent interlopers humans are in the overall scheme of things. Also, while it doesn't have much video, the video it does have is well selected. I was mesmerized by a series of video clips in which experts followed dinosaur tracks frozen in stone and explained what the dinosaurs were doing when they made the tracks.

Prehistoria is fun but its primary goal is education. This is a good title for home and school libraries.

Ruff's Bone

Here's my sniff test for what makes a good children's disc: If it makes me laugh like a child, it's a good children's disc. Do I enjoy Ruff's Bone, and all the titles in the Broderbund/Random House series? The answer is a no-brainer: yes. My kids like them, too, even though they're teenagers. More importantly, these discs bring the generations together. I've seen gatherings of children and adults crowded around the computer screen, giggling unselfconsciously at the discs in this series.

Ruff's Bone.

The premise of Ruff's Bone, based on the work of Eli Noyes, is simple: Ruff is a dog and his master throws a bone into the neighbor's yard. Ruff chases after the bone, leading to a hilarious series of adventures.

It's hard to pin down what makes the Living Books titles superlative. Part of the answer is that, like the best children's books, Ruff's Bone and the other titles in the series give children credit both for intelligence and their desire to explore and discover. On each of the twelve screens, if you click your mouse on various objects, you'll get a hilarious and unexpected series of responses.

If you have children, or even if you don't (who needs kids to have fun?), get Ruff's Bone and the other titles in this series. The other titles include works by Mercer Meyer and the superb Arthur's Teacher Trouble and Arthur's Birthday.

These are more than just children's multimedia titles. They are the best demonstrations I've seen of the power and potential of multimedia.

The Least You Need to Know

In this chapter, I gave you a list of CD-ROMs to aid in your Quest for Quality Multimedia. You learned:

- ☞ My list is entirely subjective. However, I've seen many CD-ROMs, and these programs made the top ten for good reasons.

- ☞ There are many types of multimedia applications out there. You may go to a store looking for one of these titles and come home with something completely different. That's okay. If you see something that looks really interesting, give it a whirl.

What are you lookin' at?

Part V
Multimedia Birds and Bees: Making Multimedia

"Daddy . . . where does multimedia come from?"

After you've been in the multimedia world for a while, you may start to wonder how it's made. How do you incorporate sound? How can you take a series of still images and transform them into a stunning presentation?

Making multimedia can be a ton of fun. Part V describes the process of making multimedia and the tools you use. It also tells you which tools are best for beginning and intermediate multimedia authors.

And I promise not to stammer and be embarrassed when I tell you.

Chapter 22
Multimedia Presentations That Say, "Wow!"

In This Chapter

- ☛ Multimedia word processing
- ☛ Presentations that sing and dance
- ☛ Making (electronic) books
- ☛ At the high end

With this chapter, we start our post-graduate work. As in graduate schools everywhere, those reading this section fall into one of two groups: those who are insatiably curious and those who don't have anything better to do.

In your earlier multimedia education, you learned what multimedia is and what capabilities are important in multimedia hardware and software. Then you learned what to look for in multimedia applications and how to install and navigate through them.

Your post-graduate education provides more information about multimedia objects like text, video, and images, and how to create your own multimedia applications. This chapter starts the ball rolling by discussing tools you can use to become a multimedia author. The other chapters in this section discuss the multimedia objects and the elements that make a good presentation.

If you only want to install and use commercially available multimedia applications, close this book, load a CD-ROM, and have some fun. If you want to become a true multimedia maven, keep reading.

Using the Right Tools

You create multimedia applications with *multimedia authoring tools*. This is a broad term which refers to any software program that you use to create multimedia applications.

The next four sections describe the common types of multimedia authoring tools: your normal Windows applications, presentation programs, electronic book programs, and professional authoring tools.

Making Your Windows Programs Sing and Dance

A word processor processes words. A database keeps track of data, and a spreadsheet lets you play with numbers. This isn't exactly supermarket tabloid material, but these seemingly practical programs have secret, hidden multimedia powers.

You can add multimedia elements to these programs so that they can display images, play videos and animations, and play sounds. True, the results won't be worthy of a commercial CD-ROM, but they will make your documents more interesting and useful if you distribute them to your work colleagues.

For example, to a memo you can add drawings of different packaging proposals for your newest product. Or a real estate office's database of available homes can include both pictures and vocal descriptions.

You can add multimedia elements to your other Windows applications in three ways:

- ☛ Cutting the multimedia from one application and pasting it into another using the Windows Clipboard.

- ☛ Importing multimedia elements directly into the application.

- ☛ Using a special Windows capability called OLE (pronounced like the bull fight cheer).

Like most of life, each of these capabilities has advantages and disadvantages.

Cut That Bale, Paste That Barge

Word processing users are undoubtedly familiar with the *Windows Clipboard.* The Clipboard enables you to cut text from one section of a document and place it into another.

You also can use the Windows Clipboard to copy information—including multimedia clips—from one file and paste it into another.

To use the Clipboard:

1. Select the information you want to transfer in the first application. Do this by highlighting it, or in the case of images, clicking on it.

2. From the Edit menu of the first application select either **Cut** or **Copy**. Cutting eliminates the information from the first application and places it into the Clipboard. Copying leaves the information in the first application and places a copy of it in the Clipboard.

3. Switch to the application into which you want to paste the information.

4. Place the cursor where you want to insert the information.

5. Select **Edit Paste**.

It's easy to cut and paste text and images. Depending on the applications, however, you may not be able to cut and paste sounds, videos, and animations. To do that you'll probably need one of the two other methods, which I, conveniently, describe next.

Like a bus station, life in the Windows Clipboard is quite transitory. Once you place something new into the Clipboard, the previous Clipboard contents disappear. This means that you must paste the new information into your application before you cut or copy additional information into the Clipboard.

The Import Business

Like many entrepreneurs, my father once tried his hand in the import/export business—a short-lived experiment to be sure. If only it was as easy as importing and exporting in Windows.

When you cut and paste, the selected material becomes an intrinsic part of the application. The same is true for *importing* information. A related action—but not one that you'll need often—is *exporting*.

Importing The process of bringing the contents of one computer file into another computer file. This differs from cutting and pasting because it brings in the entire contents of the external file (you don't have to select what you want).

Exporting The process of saving a file in a different file format.

If your application can directly import a particular file format, you need not worry about exporting. For example, most word processors can import commonly used graphic image file formats. However, if your application can't directly import a particular file format, you must go through the export process first (in the application the file was created in).

To do that, load the program that created the file you want to import. Load the file, then export it in a file format that your other program can import. Read the application's documentation for the exporting program to learn how to do that. The process is different in different programs.

OLE—and That's No Bull

The sovereign's lament is: "I'm powerful, but nobody *understands* me." The same is true with *object linking and embedding (OLE)*.

OLE enables you to embed a file in another file. Then, when you double-click on the item, Windows (behind the scenes) launches the application that created the object. If you double-clicked on a multimedia object, the source program plays or displays the object. You can also use the source program to edit the object.

OLE is a complex process. Fortunately, it usually is easy to use. Most mainstream Windows applications, such as word processors and databases, support OLE. This means, for example, that you can embed a sound file in a word processing document by making menu selections in the word processor. Then, when you click on an icon for the sound file, the sound player, like the Windows Media Player program, loads behind the scenes and plays the sound.

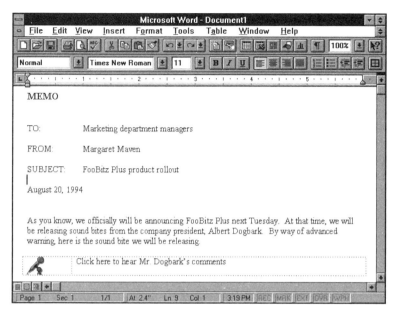

A Word file with embedded sound.

OLE is nifty and powerful, but it does have its drawbacks. Most notably, with all that behind-the-scenes loading going on, it is slow. It also requires a lot of RAM. If you don't have enough available RAM, OLE won't work.

Still, this is a good way to add multimedia to simple applications. Read your program's documentation to learn how to use OLE to add multimedia elements.

Now Presenting . . .

Multimedia applications you create with your mainline programs are kind of like a teenager's parents—they're okay if they stay in-house, but you wouldn't want to take them out in public.

Presentation programs
Originally designed to create text-and-graphics slide shows, this class of computer programs has evolved to make it easy to create multimedia presentations.

That's where business presentation programs come in. In the beginning, these programs—such as Lotus Freelance Graphics and Microsoft PowerPoint— were *presentation graphics programs*. The idea was to make it easy to create business presentations that you could show to customers, your board of directors, or other important people.

These presentations were made of "slides" created in the presentation program, and contained graphic images, such as logos or charts. Primarily, though, they included text as headlines and subheadlines, sometimes called *bullets*.

The first generation of business presentation programs wasn't very adept at adding multimedia. That's because most users converted presentations created with these programs into slides for old-fashioned slide projectors. And slide projectors can't play videos, animations, or music.

Some of the programs in this category have evolved into decent multimedia authoring tools, enabling you to create multimedia applications that offer on-screen video, animations, sound, text, and hyperlinks for interactivity. This software category is the best way nontechnical computer users have of creating professional-looking multimedia presentations, because it's relatively simple to use—usually easier than learning how to use a word processor. By contrast, high-end authoring tools, as discussed later in this chapter, usually require programming skills, but don't provide all that much more power.

One reason for the simplicity of presentation programs is that you can divide these programs' interfaces into three focused work areas:

- ☞ The **slide**, which is the on-screen view of what the multimedia presentation looks like, contains the text, images, and video or animation. Presentations consist of multiple slides. You format text and add animation, videos, and images directly to the slides.

- ☞ An **outliner** enables you to add text headlines and bullets, and to rearrange the order of the slides and text.

- ☞ The **slide sorter** allows you to view thumbnail images of each slide. Typically, you can change the order of slides by dragging and dropping them to another position in the slide sorter. You can also add items like sound to individual slides or to the entire presentation from the slide sorter.

Some of the best-selling presentation programs are not particularly adept at creating multimedia presentations, so, when you select a presentation package for creating multimedia applications, make sure it includes:

- ☞ **Its own built-in players for multimedia.** Many presentation programs, including some of the leading sellers, still rely on OLE to use external programs to play multimedia. This is clumsy to use and slows down presentations. Built-in media players enable you to finely tune how the media plays in your presentation.

Creating multimedia presentations.

☛ **Hyperlinking capabilities for creating interactive presentations.** You should be able to launch hyperlink jumps both from on-screen buttons and from individual text within the application. The hyperlinks should enable you to not only jump from one bit of text to another and from one slide to another, but also to launch multimedia items like video or audio clips.

☛ **On-screen animation capabilities.** This is different from the capability to play animation. Rather, it refers to the capability to animate on-screen elements so they move around. For example, you could bring text on-screen from the right side, and after ten seconds, have it disappear off the left side. Again, some of the best-selling presentation programs don't have this capability.

☛ **Extensive transition effects and backgrounds.** Transition effects are what appear on-screen as you switch to the next slide. Some effects, for example, look like window shades opening and closing and others look like little explosions. You should be able to control how fast these effects occur and where on the screen they start. The presentation program should also come with a large selection of stock backgrounds and make it easy to create your own.

Timelines   Timelines are a method for precisely setting the starting and ending points for each multimedia element in a presentation. Timelines usually are in dialog boxes that list each element.

☛ **The ability to fine tune the timing of multimedia elements.** For example, you should be able to start a slide with only a headline on-screen. Five seconds into the slide, you should be able to start the music, and then bring in a new bullet point every eight seconds after that. Then, at the end, you should be able to automatically start a video.

Presentation programs that support this capability typically make use of *timelines* for each slide. A timeline usually consists of a dialog box in which there is a list of each element in the slide, whether it is text or more complex multimedia elements. For each element, there is a slider bar and a scale showing the elapsed time for the slide. You use your mouse to drag the ends of each slider bar to set the starting and stopping times for each multimedia element.

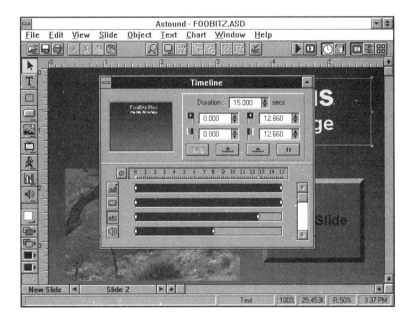

Timelines for setting timing.

One other item to look for if you plan to distribute your application widely is what's called a *run-time version* of the presentation program. A run-time version is, essentially, a stripped down version of the program that you distribute to others along with the application itself. Using the run-time version, the person who receives the application can view it but not alter it.

The run-time version should be royalty-free, meaning that you don't have to pay any royalties to the vendor of the multimedia authoring tool.

You wouldn't use a presentation program to create, say, a multimedia encyclopedia. Presentation programs simply don't have the horsepower or the features for that sort of application. However, you can use them to create all manner of multimedia business presentations or presentations you share with your family and friends. For example, this is a great way to create an entirely hip presentation of your family vacation.

Which presentation programs are best for multimedia presentations? This is changing every day, of course, but at this writing the best ones I've seen are Astound from Gold Disk, Compel from Asymetrix, and Action! from Macromedia.

Electronic Bookmakers

Electronic book authoring programs are another, although somewhat less commonly used, tool for creating multimedia. These tools originated as hypertext programs used to connect one bit of text to another. However, as multimedia became popular, they became known as *hypermedia* or *electronic publishing software.*

While presentation programs typically are slide-based and may have built-in media players, these two capabilities are rarely present in electronic book software. Instead, electronic book software tends to rely on OLE and other programs to play multimedia. As a result, these programs are best for text-heavy applications.

Examples of these programs are Folio Views and Lotus SmarText. Folio Views is probably the more powerful of the two programs, but SmarText has one significant advantage. It analyzes the words in your document and automatically creates hyperlinks. It doesn't do this perfectly, but it does perform this task well enough to save a lot of time.

This is a great advantage because creating a complex system of hyperlinks is ordinarily a time-consuming process in which you must create one link at a time. That explains why so many commercial multimedia applications are so poorly hyperlinked.

Unlike presentation programs, electronic book programs focus on documents and make relatively few concessions to on-screen appearance. This makes these tools best suited for in-house electronic documents, such as the electronic version of a policy and procedure manual.

Still, if your application is text-based but you want to add some basic multimedia, this type of program can be very useful.

At the High-End

Your meat-and-potato Windows applications are at the low end of the multimedia authoring spectrum, and presentation and electronic book programs are in the middle. At the high end, you find the authoring programs used by multimedia professionals, such as IconAuthor and Multimedia Toolbook.

Typically, these authoring programs have some pretty heavy-duty capabilities. For example, they usually include a programming language that you can use to engineer complex interactions between the user and the application.

If-then-else statement   An if-then-else statement is part of a programming language and tells the program what to do based on what the user decides.

The programming language used by high-end authoring tools uses if-then-else statements, sometimes called *branching statements*, to help the program determine what to do based on the user's actions. Here's a simple if-then-else statement that you're not likely to find in a multimedia application:

If I am hungry, I'll open the refrigerator.

If I'm not hungry, I'll keep working.

The keep working part is the "else" part of the if-then-else statement.

Why do you need these statements? In a multimedia training application, for example, an if-then-else statement might say something like, "If the user answers seven out of ten questions correctly, go on to the next lesson. If not, review the current lesson."

Many high-end authoring programs also have database capabilities. That is to say, they can collect information from users and keep it in a database file. This is handy, for example, for a kiosk presentation that is polling passersby about a particular issue.

Also, high-end authoring programs provide on-screen tools so that applications look like professionally created programs. For example, unlike presentation programs, a high-end authoring tool lets you display text in a box with scroll bars on the same screen as an image or video.

The Least You Need to Know

This chapter taught you about the tools available for creating multimedia presentations. You learned:

- ☛ You can create simple multimedia applications in your mainstream Windows programs. These applications are appropriate for spicing up documents that you share with colleagues and friends.

- ☛ Presentation programs have evolved so that they now are the best and simplest method for nontechnical users to create reasonably sophisticated multimedia applications.

- ☛ Electronic book programs are best for text-intensive applications to which you want to add some multimedia.

- ☛ High-end multimedia authoring tools provide for complex interactions with users and often have database capabilities.

Fix your eyes on the center of this page and wait for a 3-D image to appear. Be patient.

Chapter 23
Text: It's Everywhere, It's Everywhere!

In This Chapter

- ☞ ASCII text
- ☞ Proprietary formats
- ☞ Converting paper to computer files
- ☞ Text from on-line services

So . . . you have the bug and want to create your own multimedia presentations, huh? Many of us find this process to be fun; it needn't be difficult.

Before you start, you should know more about the multimedia elements that go into presentations. We'll begin that discussion in this chapter about text and continue it into the next several chapters, which are about images, sound, animation, and videos.

Say What?

Let's face it, text fans, the first medium was the graphic image. Cave drawings are more ancient than the oldest text we know about.

Of course, to use one of the great buzzwords of our time, that paradigm shifted with the printing of the Gutenberg Bible. Suddenly, printed words (or *woids*, as Uncle Louie would say) became the dominant method of communicating.

Many a doctoral thesis has been written about the social implications of text in today's society. For our purposes, though, suffice it to say that text still plays an important role. That's true about our society in general, and for multimedia.

It's Your ASCII

There are words on pages and there are words that your computer can use. For multimedia, you must use the latter. It doesn't take a rocket scientist or a doctoral candidate to know that.

As with any computer file, whether it's a graphic image or the word processing file containing this chapter, you must store the data in a form that your computer can read. With text, this typically is in one of two forms, *ASCII text* or *proprietary format*.

ASCII   A near-universal text file that has no special formatting, such as boldface type or different type sizes. Most applications can use it, and it usually comes with the file name extension .TXT or, sometimes, .ASC.

Proprietary format   A computer file that only the application that created it can read. Many other applications, however, can convert commonly used proprietary formats to their own proprietary format. Virtually every major application has its own proprietary format.

If you are creating text from scratch for a multimedia application, chances are you'll use your word processor or the multimedia authoring tool of your choice. A *multimedia authoring tool* is the program you use for creating multimedia applications. Often, these programs can create simple text, but rarely can you use them to add a lot of text to multimedia applications.

After you create the text, you import it into the multimedia authoring program. Some multimedia authoring programs let you import the text and maintain all the formatting you gave it in your word processor. Chapter 22 discusses multimedia authoring programs.

Scanning the Horizon

Oh, dear, you say (or words to that effect). I want to use text in multimedia applications, but all my text is on paper. Do I really have to manually enter all those words? Woe is me!

There, there, the author says, patting you condescendingly on the head. The technology readily exists to convert pages of text into text your computer can use. You need only two tools.

Scanners convert your page into an image of the page. In some ways, scanners are like photocopy machines. However, instead of printing a copy of the page on another sheet of paper, scanners save the page as a computerized file. Note, however, that scanners don't save the scanned page as text that you can edit in your word processor or other application. Rather, a scanner saves the page as an image.

Saving an image in an image file may often be useful, but if you need text, an image of a page is about as much good as a photograph of a printed page. You can't edit it or change the formatting. That's where *optical character recognition* software comes in. An OCR program can save scanned text as ASCII or, depending on the OCR program, in the format of most popular word processors.

This, of course, is useful for much more than just creating text you can use in multimedia applications. Attorneys, for example, can convert contracts to editable text without having to rekey them. College students can scan whole research papers written by their roommates, them add enough mistakes to convince their professors they really wrote them.

Optical character recognition (OCR) A process that converts the text in a computerized image file into text you can edit with your computer. Used in conjunction with a scanner, you can convert pages of text into computerized text that you can edit with your word processor.

Hanging On-Line

Besides creating your own text with a word processor or other application and scanning in text stored on paper pages, you also can gather text from *on-line services*. This is useful if you are creating a multimedia application about a research-related topic.

As I'm sure you know, one of the currently faddish buzz phrases is *information superhighway.* Like all buzz expressions, this can refer to almost anything. Our local newspaper, for example, seemingly has a policy of using this phrase once a week even if it's not warranted, including the use of a bad pun headline. For example, when cable rates went up, the headline predictably blared: "Tolls Increase on Information Superhighway."

In our case, though, this expression refers to any one of thousands of on-line services and bulletin boards that you can access with your modem. The largest of these services is the Internet, a barely organized global conglomeration of networked computers. However, there also are smaller international services, such as CompuServe, and tens of thousands of local bulletin board services.

On-line services On-line services provide a universe of information services and means of communicating. They also serve as an almost limitless source of text that you can collect and use in multimedia applications.

You can obtain almost anything from these on-line services, from the contents of books and magazines to debates among on-line users about virtually any topic. You are free to download this material for your own use. But beware—some information, such as the contents of magazines, is copyrighted and you cannot use that material for commercial gain.

When you download this information, it will often be in ASCII format. You can then import the text directly into the multimedia application you are creating.

The Least You Need to Know

Text is a basic building block of multimedia applications. But where do you get it? In this chapter, you learned you can obtain text by:

- ☞ Creating it in computer applications, such as your word processor.

- ☞ Scanning pages of text and converting them into a form your computer can use with an optical character recognition (OCR) program.

- ☞ Collecting it from on-line services.

Chapter 24
It's All Image

In This Chapter

- ☛ File formats galore
- ☛ Resolutions gone awry
- ☛ Color depth: a deep subject
- ☛ Free images

In the previous chapter, we talked about words. In this chapter, we talk about those things that are worth a thousand words. No, not a heavenly taste of dark Belgian chocolate, or a brisk bike ride on a beautiful summer day, but, as the cliché goes, pictures.

There's a practical reason for the widespread use of images in multimedia: current computer technology handles still images much better than flashier media like video and animation. The latter two media require significant computing horsepower to play smoothly, but most computers can display still images clearly and quickly.

So let's take a look at images, how to obtain them, and some of the problems you may encounter in using them in multimedia.

Image? What's an Image?

First things first. Let's use a simple definition for image: An *image* is a picture, drawing, or photograph that doesn't move or make a sound. If it moves or otherwise shakes its thing, it's either a video or animation. If you have to read it, it's text. If you can hear it, it's sound.

Images can be photos from your last family vacation or they can be diagrams of your company's latest whatamathingee. An image can be a company logo or an artistic rendering of a sunset. Images can be maps, flow charts, organizational charts, or a copy of your signature.

Sound simple? All you need to do is plop an image in your multimedia application and you can take the afternoon off, right? Ah, if only life were so simple. Read the next few sections to learn about some of the twists and turns you might encounter when using images.

Image Formats . . . and More Image Formats

In Chapter 23 we discussed how each word processor saves files in a proprietary format that only it can read. Usually, this isn't a problem because most of us only use one word processor. Graphic images, however, come in many different file formats.

Image format   The proprietary file format for an image. There are about forty different formats for images, although only a few of them are commonly used.

The following table lists the most common image formats and where they come from. It also lists the file name extensions used by the file formats. For example, if I have a PCX image of my cat, I might name the file MYCAT.PCX.

In some cases, the source column lists the specific program most often used to create images of those formats. In other cases, the table lists the context in which those image formats are found. For example, the Compu-Serve Information Service, a large on-line bulletin board, popularized the GIF file format.

Format Extension	Source
BMP	Windows Bitmap
GIF	CompuServe Information Service format (but used by many programs)
JPG	Various drawing programs
PCD	Photo CD
PCX	Windows Paintbrush program
TIF	Usually technical drawings, faxes, but they can be anything
WMF	Windows Metafile

So what do all these formats have to do with the tea in China? Often, not much. Especially for beginners, there's usually no reason to understand much about the differences between the formats.

Often is the key word, however. A common problem is that the programs used to create multimedia applications don't handle all file formats. That means that you can be ready to use the snazziest image you've ever seen to illustrate a point in your presentation, only to find out that your multimedia authoring tool says ix-nay.

There is help available for this problem, though, as the next section describes.

Undergoing a Conversion

Most software, including the multimedia authoring tools you use to create multimedia applications, can use images from several different file formats—but not all formats. If the authoring tool supports the file image format, you import the image into the application.

In this case, importing isn't what you do to bring something in from a foreign country, like Belgian chocolate or French wine. As described in Chapter 22, *importing* means the capability to bring into one program a file created by another.

Most programs can import at least several commonly used image formats. If your multimedia authoring program can't import at least three or four of the images listed in the preceding table, you're probably using the wrong authoring program.

Even the best programs are unlikely to be able to import all image formats. Say you're putting together a multimedia presentation to help sell your company's product: the renowned FooBitz Plus. When you try to import an image of the product, the multimedia authoring program displays a message saying, essentially, "You idiot, don't you know you can't use a picture with that format?"

What's an otherwise intelligent person to do? Well, we promised early on that this book would help prevent you from feeling like an idiot, so here's the solution: Use format conversion software to convert images from one format to another. Then import the image into your multimedia authoring program.

Some programs are specifically for converting image files from one format to another. Two popular programs for Windows are HiJaak Professional from Inset Systems and ImagePals from U-Lead Systems. These programs provide many tools for fine-tuning the conversion process.

Most image editing and drawing programs also can convert image files from one format to another, although typically they can't convert among as many formats as can products like HiJaak Professional.

TECHNO NERD TEACHES...

If you deal with a lot of different types of image formats, you'll probably be better off buying a program that specializes in converting file formats. These programs tend to support virtually all significant file formats. If you don't deal with a wide variety of image formats, the file conversion capabilities in a good image editor should be adequate for your needs.

Making A Resolution

Besides image format, you also need to keep in mind image resolution. In Chapter 6, we discussed monitors and how they have different resolutions. To review, *resolution* refers to the number of dots of light, called *pixels*, that are used in each square inch to make up the image.

Like monitors, images also have resolutions. Mixing and matching image resolutions can sometimes lead to some strange on-screen effects. Depending on the program you are using to create your multimedia application, you may not be able to mix and match resolutions.

For example, if you are creating a multimedia application while using 800 × 600 on-screen resolution and you use an image with 1024 × 768 resolution, the multimedia authoring tool may not be able to display it.

About the only thing you can do if you have problems in this area is convert the image resolution to one that works better with your application. This process is generally known as *sizing*. Many image conversion programs and image editing programs can convert between one resolution and another, or resize images.

If you convert image resolutions, you may distort the image's appearance. That's because the aspect ratio, or the ratio between the horizontal and vertical aspects of the image, changes when you resize the image. With some images, you may not notice. With others, however, you will notice some distortion. If you preserve the aspect ratio, the image usually resizes fine.

Out of Your Color Depth

Another thing that can create on-screen problems is when you try to use images that have a *color depth* that is different from that of your computer's video system. Color depth, in simple terms, refers to the number of colors that display on-screen at the same time.

The more on-screen colors, the more realistic images and photos appear. Photographic images, for example, will look weird on-screen unless you display at least 256 on-screen colors.

If your video system displays fewer colors on-screen than were used to capture or create the image, the on-screen image appears distorted. The next figure shows such an odd-looking image. In this case, it shows an image captured with 256 colors displayed with only 16 on-screen colors.

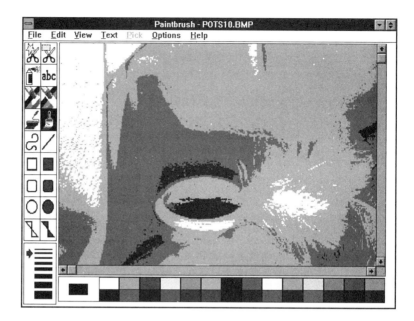

Mismatched color depth.

The next figure shows the same picture displayed with 256 on-screen colors. As you can tell, the image is of a Native American pot.

Correct color depth.

Most video adapters come with software that enables you to change on-screen color depth. If you are viewing multimedia presentations and the images are strange like the one in the preceding figure, increase the color depth. For example, if you are using 16 colors on-screen, switch your system to 256 colors. If that still doesn't work, increase it again until the image appears normal. (Keep in mind that you can only do this if your video adapter and monitor are agreeable. Some won't support these kinds of changes.) You won't notice any on-screen distortions if your on-screen color depth is greater than the color depth used to create or capture the image.

Color depth mismatches can be a big problem for multimedia authors. That's because higher-quality images have greater color depth. That means you must balance the need to use higher-quality images against the fact that some viewers may not have video systems that can display all those colors. The solution is to inform your users about the number of on-screen colors they should use in order to properly display your multimedia presentation. These days, most commercial multimedia applications come with such a recommendation.

TECHNO NERD TEACHES...

Before starting creation of a multimedia presentation, give long, hard thought to the computer capabilities of the people who will be viewing the presentation. If many of the users' computers are old, you may have to limit images to low resolutions (like 640 X 480) and low color depth (like 16 colors). Today, most commercial multimedia applications work best at 640 X 480, although more and more are requiring at least 256 on-screen colors. That is the minimum color depth for displaying photographic images.

I'm Compressed

One of the hard and sad lessons in life is that the good stuff costs more. The same is true with images. As you add more colors and greater resolution, the image files get larger and larger and will cost you more disc space. Put differently, quality images are disc hogs. It's not unusual for high-quality images to require several megabytes of disc space.

The sometimes-satisfactory answer is to use *compression*. Compression is the act of changing the makeup of the image file so that it takes less disc space. Compression is relatively easy to use for simple storage of image files that aren't part of your application. You can compress your image files to save space, then uncompress them to view them. There are many widely available utilities that compress files, but the most popular is PKZIP from PKWARE, Inc.

This compressing and uncompressing won't work, however, with images that must appear on-screen during a presentation. That's because the compressing and uncompressing take time and will bog down the presentation. That's why an image format called JPEG (.JPG extension) is slowly gaining in popularity. JPEG is a format that, by its nature, is compressed. When you go to view the image, the image uncompresses.

Note, however, that while JPEG has a lot of potential, it isn't yet widely accepted. That's because all that compressing and uncompressing requires a lot processing power from your computer. This will slow down the display of your application.

Because of this, there's a good chance that the program you use to create your multimedia application will not support JPEG. You also may have a difficult time finding JPEG files from other sources.

Where the Wild Images Are

Fortunately, high-quality images are easy to come by. You can either collect them ready-made or make your own. The next two sections provide more detail.

Let Somebody Else Do the Work

We all like our jobs, right? Well, even if you don't, there's one seemingly unbreakable rule for most jobs: Why do more work than necessary?

Often in multimedia applications, stock drawings or photographs will do quite nicely, thank you. This is a good deal—somebody else does the work to create the image and you borrow it. It's just that easy; find some clip media and plop it in the application. However, there are limits to what you can get cheap or for free.

In broad terms, two sources of images that you can use in your presentations are:

- ☞ **On-line services**, such as CompuServe, Prodigy, America Online, or the Internet. These are services you access with your modem. Some, such as CompuServe and Prodigy, you pay to join. Others, like some local bulletin board services (BBSs), you can access for free.

- ☞ **Clip media collections.** In the old days, clip art was commonly used by commercial artists for adding basic and generic art work to their efforts. These days, the computerized version is called *clip media* because it is more than just visual art.

Besides images, clip media collections often include sounds, animations, and videos. More and more clip media collections are appearing on CD-ROMs to ensure that you have a wide selection from which to choose.

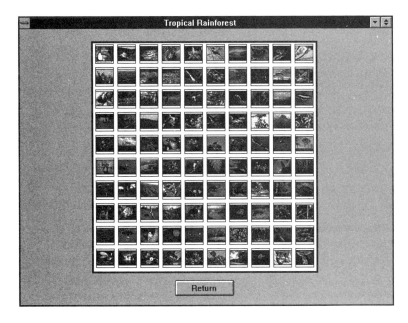

A clip media collection.

There is one significant caveat when using images or any other media developed by others. That caveat is that you must make sure what your legal rights are for using the media. That's because, often, clip media are copyrighted, which provide certain rights and protections for the clip media vendors.

Some clip media vendors will require that you pay royalties if you earn money from your multimedia application. Often, though, if you are just using the clip media for "internal" use, such as within a company, you won't have to pay royalties. Still other collections are completely royalty free, no matter how you use them.

At any rate, before you use any media developed by anybody else, make sure that you are using the media legally.

Photo Realism

There are times when you can use generic clip-art images, and there are times when you absolutely, positively must have your own. For example, if you are making a business multimedia presentation and want to show your office building, any old building won't do. You need an image of your actual office building.

For creating images of photos, you have two choices:

☛ Use a regular camera and develop the film into Photo CD format. You can then import the photos on the Photo CD disc into your multimedia application.

☛ Scan your photo using a scanner and save the photo image, then import the image into your application.

Image editing software
Image editing software enables you to fine tune the colors and on-screen appearance of photographs. It also enables you to add special effects to photos.

If you plan to use photographs in your multimedia application, you will need, at times, to touch them up. That's because, in simple terms, photographs sometimes will have colors that, on-screen, appear too vivid or too washed out. To correct this problem, you'll need *image editing* software.

Most good high-end drawing programs provide image editing capabilities. However, for professional results you may want to buy a dedicated image editing program.

Drawing on Experience

If you want to create an image that isn't a photograph, you must use a drawing program of some sort. There are programs available for all types of drawings and all levels of ability and complexity. For example, there are drawing programs that:

- ☞ Make it easy for even beginners to create simple charts, such as flow and organization charts. Examples of these programs are Visio from Shapeware and SnapGraphics from Micrografx.

- ☞ Enable beginners who will endure only a small learning curve to create complex charts and moderately complex technical drawings. An example of this kind of program is IntelliDraw from Aldus.

- ☞ Support a wide variety of complex effects. You can, for example, contour text around a shape. These programs, like CorelDraw and Micrografx Designer, are preferred by art professionals.

- ☞ Allow for advanced technical drawings—not for casual use.

There are two important things to look for in a drawing program:

- ☞ Is it easy to use? Particularly if you're not an artist by trade, you probably won't want to spend a lot of time learning how to use a drawing program.

- ☞ Can it save files in commonly used image formats? If it can't save files in common image formats, you'll have to buy a separate image file conversion program.

The Least You Need to Know

Image is everything. At least that's what the media tell us. In this chapter, you learned more about the images you use when creating multimedia applications. Specifically, you learned:

☛ Images come in many different formats. Depending on the program you use to create your multimedia applications, you may need special software to convert among the different formats.

☛ Like monitors, images come in different resolutions and with differing numbers of on-screen colors. If your system doesn't support the resolution and color depth of an image, you can get weird on-screen results.

☛ High-quality images take a lot of disc space. You may need to compress images when you aren't using them to save disc space.

☛ Good images are available on-line and from commercially available clip media collections.

☛ There is a wide range of programs for creating your own images and editing existing images.

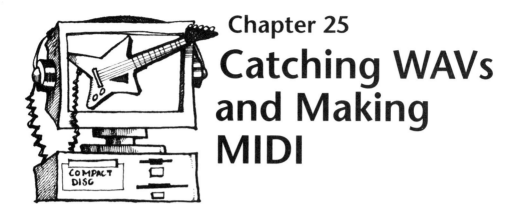

Chapter 25

Catching WAVs and Making MIDI

In This Chapter

- Making music easy
- MIDI and maxi
- Turning the wavetables

Take one from column A, two from column B . . . before long you have the sounds for your multimedia application. Audio is often the glue that holds together multimedia presentations, whether it is background music or narration or just weird sound effects.

Getting the right sounds, however, takes some time and effort. In this chapter, we'll discuss sound and where to get it. We'll also discuss the basics of how to create it and how to use it in multimedia presentations.

Let's Catch Up

As you might recall, there are three types of sounds you can use in multimedia presentations:

- **Audio CDs.** You probably know all about these. Most CD-ROM drives can play audio CDs.

☛ **Waveform files (also known as .WAV files).** These are computer-readable versions of recorded sounds.

☛ **MIDI files.** They contain musical data that a synthesizer, such as the one found on most sound cards, transforms into music.

Life is full of choices, but one choice you won't have to make is selecting the type of sound file to use. That's because each type of music file has its best uses and advantages. The following table lists the pros and cons of each type of sound and the best uses for the music.

Type	Best Uses	Pros/Cons
Audio CD	Background	Highest quality; hard to edit; copyright problems.
MIDI	Background	Dainty disk usage; simple edits are easy; sounds artificial with inexpensive sound cards; sound cards appropriate for professional level MIDI music are costly; copyright problems for commercial files.
WAV	Narrations; sound effects; brief musical clips	Easy to edit; mega-disc hog; copyright problems for commercial files.

The first step to collecting the music is to determine all the sounds you'll need for your presentation, such as:

☛ Introductory music. This may be a theme song or appropriately chosen music that captures the spirit of the presentation. Chances are, this will be MIDI music, perhaps even MIDI music created by a professional. While you may prefer tracks off your new audio CD, they are hard to fit into a presentation and also pose serious copyright infringement questions.

☛ Background music. After the dynamic introductory music, you may want background music that matches the mood of your regular presentation. This can by MIDI music or a .WAV file of music. It may be generic or, if you have the bucks, you can pay somebody to create it. In either case, you'll probably use your authoring tool's capability to "loop" the music file to play it continuously.

☞ Narrations. You will save these as .WAV files.

☞ Sound effects.

As described in Chapter 22, your multimedia authoring software should give you adequate tools for timing when each sound starts and finishes. That way, the exciting, dynamic introduction music can slowly fade away to an audio clip of the proud president of the company, which can be replaced by the generic background music.

Later in this chapter, you'll learn about the tools needed to manage your sounds. First, though, you must get the sounds. The following sections will get you started.

Sounds from Easy Street

Remember one of the prime directives of the working world: Don't do more work than you have to. Well, there are many sounds and music that are just waiting for you to use them in presentations.

Those sounds are MIDI and .WAV files that you can get from two places: on-line services or clip media collections. .WAV files are particularly common, but MIDI files are easy to find, too. For example, there's a forum (and associated library of files) on CompuServe

Not surprisingly, the quality of the music you can collect from on-line sources varies widely. I recently downloaded a version of one of my favorite songs from the rock group Dire Straits, which sounded like it was recorded by a ballpark organ gone berserk.

devoted to MIDI. This is not only a good source of free MIDI sounds, but also a good place to discuss problems and questions you have about MIDI with other users.

The best part about all this sound stuff is that after you get the basic sounds that others created, you can edit them so they more precisely meet your needs. Later sections of this chapter discuss editing .WAV and MIDI files.

There is one important thing to remember: You can get in big trouble if you use copyrighted material. Can you spell "copyright infringement?" Can you spell "lawyers?"

Copyright infringement is particularly a problem if you cop sounds from an audio CD. Typically, however, you can legally use the items you collect from on-line services and from clip media collections on your own PC. You may run into problems if you want to use the clips in multimedia presentations for others. The next figure shows a typical copyright notice from a clip media collection.

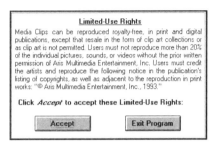

A copyright notice.

If you're not selling the presentation, you may not have to pay anybody anything. However, depending on the license agreement or terms of the copyright notice, if you are selling your presentation, you may have to pay royalties. Hey, composers (and authors) have to make a living, too.

Sometimes, the sound creators will treat the sounds like shareware, particularly if you get them from on-line services. That means, like shareware programs, you can try the sounds for free but if you use them you must pay the author a one-time fee.

Here's something I feel strongly about: people should be paid for their work, whether they're an author, a pipefitter, a pro-grammer, or a musician. While many people create MIDI files for fun and post them on bulletin boards with no profit motive, others create sounds for a living and deserve to be paid. If paying a fee for a clip media collection gives you the right to use that material without additional royalties, you're covered. But if the creator demands a fee and you don't pay, or if you use shareware and don't pay, you are ripping somebody off. You may get by with it, but it's wrong. End of editorial.

Whether you get the sound from a clip media collection or from an on-line service, carefully read the license agreement that comes with the files to learn your obligations to the author. If you didn't do that and the copyright police swoop down on you, I'll feel horrible. You, however, will feel worse.

As for using audio CDs, the copyright situation gets even stickier. That's why few multimedia authors, even those creating innocent little business presentations, use audio CDs for background music. Besides being hard to edit to fit precisely into your presentation, they typically have more lawyers protecting their rights than you even want to think about.

Making MIDI Music

Musicians glommed on to MIDI when it became practical in the early 1980s, and a strong subculture has existed ever since. As a result, there's a large range of MIDI hardware and software that you can acquire, and you can spend big bucks acquiring it.

Some of this stuff goes into your computer and some of it has nothing to do with your computer. In the hands of somebody who knows what they're doing, the results can be superbly artistic. You've undoubtedly heard the results frequently on the radio and on recordings.

Given the level of expertise required to create professional-level MIDI, it makes sense to (legally) borrow somebody else's MIDI creations either by downloading them from on-line services or using clip media disks. It certainly is possible, however, for beginners to create their own MIDI music from scratch.

At any rate, in simple terms, here's how MIDI works:

- ☛ MIDI files consist of a series of instructions that control how the music plays.

- ☛ MIDI music contains multiple tracks, each of which can play a different synthesized instrument. The composer assigns the instrument to each track.

- ☛ You can fine-tune the playing of each track, such as altering its volume and tempo.

Those are the basics. This isn't the place to go into great depth about MIDI—you can literally go to school to learn about that subject. If you want to create snazzy MIDI music, you'll need plenty of equipment, starting with a top-of-the-line sound card and maybe synthesizers (most sound cards have synthesizers built-in).

Sound cards are an important part of MIDI. For simply playing back MIDI sounds, a run-of-the-mill 16-bit sound card with FM synthesis is adequate. However, you can spend more and get better playback. This better quality includes cards that use WAVetable synthesis to play samples of real instruments instead of the normal, synthetic sounds that MIDI plays.

If you want to create MIDI music, your run-of-the-mill 16-bit sound card won't do. Instead, you'll need a sound card that can handle MIDI devices such as keyboards.

Whatever level you're working at, one MIDI tool you are likely to need if you're gathering music for presentations is a sequencer.

Out of Sequencers

A few pages ago, I mentioned that I downloaded a MIDI version of a rock song that sounded like it was recorded by a ballpark organ that was in a bad way. Real bad. Fortunately, however, there is software that you can use to edit MIDI files to make them sound better. This software is *sequencer* software.

There's a lot of other software—and hardware— out there for MIDI music. There are musical notation programs in which you work with an on-screen musical score. There is even a program that enables you to scan sheet music with a scanner to convert the paper music to MIDI music.

Most commonly, though, both experts and nonexperts use sequencer programs to create and fine tune MIDI music. The concept behind sequencers is simple. As stated previously, a MIDI piece has multiple tracks. You can assign a specific instrument to each track. With a sequencer, you can change all aspects of how each instrument plays, such as changing the tempo, pitch, and volume.

There are standards for MIDI sounds that enable MIDI devices, such as regular keyboards or MIDI software, to produce 128 general sounds and 46 percussion sounds. You can affix any of those sounds to a MIDI track.

A good MIDI sequencer will make each track obvious on-screen and provide interface elements for changing instruments and sound qualities. Beyond that, different sequencers have different capabilities aimed at different types of users ranging from beginners to professionals.

Sequencer Software that enables you to edit a MIDI file track by track. You can change the instrument played in the track, its tempo, volume, and many other aspects of the music.

In general, though, look for:

- ☞ The ability to make instrument assignments to individual tracks and to control their notes and chording without the use of an attached musical instrument.

- ☞ The ability, as stated previously, to change instruments in each track and all the characteristics of that instrument, such as volume, pitch, and special effects.

- ☞ An interface that makes these basic operations simple and obvious. This is what really sets apart the different sequencers.

Beyond those basics, sequencers can be pretty complex. This is one area in which computer novices with music experience can move quickly to the complex stuff. It is quite satisfying to go into deep detail about MIDI to nonmusical computer geeks; you will surely impress them.

Making (Wave) Music

If MIDI isn't your cup of tea, chances are, waveform (.WAV) files are the Earl Gray of your dreams. Creating waveform files is simple:

- ☞ Plug a microphone into your sound card.

- ☞ Load a program that can record the sound, such as the Sound Recorder program that comes with Windows.

- ☞ Start recording sounds.

If you're not too discerning, that's all it takes. You save the file (giving it the .WAV file extension name), and you're off to the races. You don't have to be a musician to deal with .WAV files.

Ah—how many times have we said the following in this book: *If it was only that easy.* The next few sections briefly discuss some of the things you should know for creating .WAV files.

Sound Cards—You'd Better Make This Good

The most obvious thing limiting the quality of the sound you create is the sound card. Here are two factors that impact on sound quality:

- ☛ The 8-bit sound cards don't produce good sound. That's because they literally are not recording or playing back as many sound samples per second as are 16-bit cards.

- ☛ Even most 16-bit cards are prone to background hiss and other unwanted sounds.

To review, to play a waveform file, the sound board replays digital *slices* (loosely termed *samples* here) of the sound many thousands of times per second. The more samples played per second, the greater the fidelity of the sound.

If you will be recording a lot of sounds, pay more for a high-quality sound card. Most vendors of 16-bit sound cards brag that the cards produce audio CD quality. That's because the top rate at which they play samples is the same rate as an audio CD player. However, since the quality of the electronics is unlikely to match that of a stereo system, the claim of audio CD quality is a bit of a stretch. Still, as with so much in life, you get what you pay for, so if quality is important, be prepared to pay for it.

There's a pretty good rule of thumb for recording sounds: for best quality, record them in stereo and at the highest sampling rate your system will support. With the current generation of sound cards, you can record at a minimum of 11KHz (kilohertz), which plays 11,000 samples per second. That sounds like a lot, but it isn't—you'll typically get muddy, incomplete sound. The maximum rate at which you can record (and play back) is 44.1KHz. This recommended rate is enough to create much richer sounds.

TECHNO NERD TEACHES...

There are many sounds around you when you are recording with your PC. Your sound board probably generates some low-level sounds. Then there's your computer's fan noise and perhaps even noise generated by your monitor, phones ringing, kids shouting, or whatever.

To eliminate as much noise as possible, use the correct microphone. If you are taking your laptop outside to record sounds of nature, use an omnidirectional mike, which, as the name implies, gathers sound from many directions. But if you are recording narrations indoors, use a microphone that accepts sound from a narrower range. If you want to be really discriminating, try to construct some sort of sound barrier. You can also get a long microphone cord and record in another room while someone else runs your computer.

In addition to paying for quality electronics with cold, hard cash, you'll pay for high-fidelity sounds with disk space. For example, a one-minute stereo recording with a 44.1KHz sampling rate can take 10MB of disk storage space. It's no wonder that CD-ROMs , with their large storage capacity, are the storage medium of choice for multimedia!

Another price you pay is in the demands high-fidelity sounds make on your computer's central processing unit (CPU). Playing back high-quality sounds can slow your system because it makes your CPU work harder. When your computer's CPU is busy processing .WAV files, it can't be doing other things efficiently.

The answer is either to use a more powerful computer or to use a sound card with a *digital signal processor (DSP) chip.* A DSP chip takes much of the processing burden off your computer's CPU. DSPs are becoming

SPEAK LIKE A GEEK

Digital signal processor (DSP)   A type of chip that can offload the processing of specific tasks, in this case complex sounds, from your computer's central processing unit. This prevents complex sounds from bogging down your computer.

commonly used for a variety of specialized computing functions—there's a fair chance, for example, that your modem uses a DSP. These days, more and more sound cards have DSPs.

Editing the Waves

Sometimes, simply recording .WAV files is enough. But when it isn't enough, you need a sound editing program, which will let you record sounds in stereo and at all the sampling rates your sound card supports. If you want to delete a portion of the file, you should be able to do that, too.

Sound editing software
Lets you record sounds at all possible sampling rates and in mono or stereo. It also lets you add additional sounds and enhance specific parts of the sound file.

Getting a bit more complex, you should be able to isolate specific sections of the .WAV file and enhance it with effects, such as reverb and fades. You also should be able to add additional sound files to create complex sound effects.

Besides enhancing the qualities of sounds, sound editing software is useful for matching sounds to videos. For casual users, these capabilities aren't very important. But for multimedia producers, they are the staff of life.

There is a sound editing program included in the disc that comes with this book. Turn to Chapter 31 to learn how to start it up.

The Least You Need to Know

In this chapter, you learned the basics of collecting music to use in your multimedia presentations. You learned:

- ☛ The easy way to get music is to get it from on-line services or from clip media.

- ☛ You should honor all copyrights for music you collect.

- ☛ Recording .WAV files is easy, requiring only that you connect your microphone to your sound board.

- ☛ MIDI music is flexible but can be complex to create, requiring knowledge not just of the hardware and the software, but also of music.

- ☛ You use a MIDI sequencer to edit each track in a piece of MIDI music.

Get some crayons and draw a nice picture with some trees and mountains and birds and flowers on this page. It'll make you feel good, I bet.

Chapter 26
Making Movies

In This Chapter

- ☞ Capturing video
- ☞ Editing video
- ☞ Making video teeny-tiny

I admit it . . . when I was a kid, I was glued to the TV. But I turned out just fine, didn't I? DIDN'T I??

In "The more things change, the more they stay the same" department, movies and cartoons (we'll call them videos and animations) are a staple of multimedia. As a result, now that we're adults, we can watch them and not even have to argue with our parents about doing our homework. I love progress.

Videos and *animations*—two similar-but-different media—are the focus of this chapter and the next. In this chapter, we'll briefly discuss the differences between video and animation, but we'll focus on video. You'll learn the ins and outs of video and find out what tools you need to capture and edit it.

So . . . on with the show.

They're the Same . . . Kinda

At a very basic level, videos and animation are similar. That is to say, both consist of a series of frames, each of which is almost, but not quite, the same as the frame before it and after it. When played back in rapid succession, the pictures give the illusion of motion. In this way, they are like traditional movies and cartoons.

The rate at which the frames are played back is measured in *frames per second (fps)*. This also is sometimes called the *frame rate*. Like traditional movies and cartoons, the more frames per second, the smoother the moving image will be.

Frames per second (fps) Also called the frame rate, frames per second is the rate at which videos and animations are played. The higher the frame rate, the smoother the playback.

Typically, the fastest frame rate used in multimedia is thirty frames per second, which is the same frame rate as standard video movies and cartoons. Often, though, you can play back multimedia videos at a slower rate.

Another similarity between multimedia videos and animations is that they both take a lot of computing horsepower. More RAM, a faster central processing unit, better and faster video display, and a bigger and faster hard drive all contribute to playing back videos and animations more smoothly and without delays.

Beyond those similarities, however, these media are different. Video is life captured, so it begins with a device, such as a camcorder. Animation, on the other hand, usually is made from drawings in motion. You use different software tools to create videos and animations. Also, video requires special hardware.

The rest of this chapter discusses the hardware and software needed to create multimedia videos.

Why This Is Post-Graduate Work

Virtually any PC sold these days comes with the power needed to play videos. Sure, the faster and more powerful the PC, the better videos play. However, most PCs will play videos without any special added equipment, but they do need special software drivers.

Creating videos, however, is another matter. You'll need special hardware and software to do that. While this hardware and software are getting cheaper and easier to use, at this writing, it's still not exactly mainstream stuff. Rather, it is designed to solve several special problems you must overcome before you can create your own videos for multimedia presentations. The next few sections describe those problems.

You Say Analog, I Say Digital

The first problem you'll encounter when creating multimedia video is that the video you capture on your handy camcorder isn't in a form that your computer can use. Remember, your computer is a *digital* device. That means, in grossly simple terms, that it understands one of two states: 0 or 1 or, if you prefer, on or off.

Your prized video tape collection, however, is *analog*. Also in grossly simple terms, analog is a representation of precisely what happened, in this case a representation of real images as captured on a video tape.

The first trick of multimedia video is converting analog video to digital so you can use it on your computer. This process requires a *video capture board*. The good news is that video capture boards are getting more powerful and less expensive. We'll discuss video capture boards and analog-to-digital conversion a bit later, but first, another section to help set the stage.

This Is Big . . . Really Big

Here's the truth about video: It's big stuff. Not necessarily big as in important. Big as in . . . well, big.

I wish I had a more precise statistic, but here's an approximation. If you put the movie *Terminator* (or any other movie) on CD-ROMs, it would fill up a zillion discs, maybe more.

Okay—I can just see my editor wincing, so I'll get a bit more specific. Take a single video frame in VGA (640 X 480 on-screen resolution) with the highest color depth (called 24-bit color). Each of those frames requires a bit less than 1MB for storage. Remember that good video is 30 frames per second. I'm sure you don't need your pocket calculator to figure out that one second of this quality video requires the better part of 30MB of storage capacity.

This is a problem. At a bit less than 30MB per second of video, a video producer is going to have to be remarkably concise. Even a CD-ROM devoted entirely to video will fill up with less than thirty seconds of video (assuming the image and file aren't compressed).

Besides hogging disc storage space, there's another problem with file sizes this big; they can take forever to play on your computer. A reasonably fast hard drive has a data transfer rate of about 1MB per second and a double-spin CD-ROM drive has a data transfer time of about 300KB per second. Data transfer times, as discussed in Chapter 10, refer to the amount of data you can move from a drive to your computer in one second. The bottom line: Big files take longer for your computer to process.

Fortunately, there are several solutions to these problems; you can:

☞ Make the on-screen video image smaller than full-screen VGA. That's why a typical video size is 160 x 120 (or something similar).

☞ Decrease the color depth. Instead of 24-bit color, which displays deep rich colors, you can go as low as 8-bit color. This displays 256 colors on-screen and, while minimal for video, often is adequate.

☞ Reduce the frames per second. While standard video is thirty frames per second, you could cut that in half.

Voilà! Just using these three techniques reduces a second of video to about 1MB. Before you heave a sigh of relief, however, remember that you've reduced the video quality, and even at 1MB per second, you'll still need a lot of storage space. In other words, we ain't done yet.

I'm mentioning all this now to give you an idea of the problems related to creating computerized video. Not to worry, though; there are even more solutions available to you.

I Have My Standards!

The solutions to these video problems start with *standards*. With standards, it becomes cost effective for vendors to create generally accepted solutions to problems. And what's cost effective to vendors is, often, cost effective to consumers.

Far and away, the most important standard for the average PC user is Microsoft's Video for Windows. Introduced in 1992, this quickly accepted standard created, among other things, the audio/video interleave format; the format used in the majority of videos. These videos have the file extension .AVI.

As with any good standard, the result of Video for Windows was that vendors got busy. Real busy. Now, the market is full of hardware products that let you capture video from standard video tapes and edit the video.

Another standard that is quickly being accepted in the Windows world is QuickTime for Windows. While new in Windows, QuickTime has been around for a while on the Macintosh.

Video for Windows Developed by Microsoft, the Video for Windows standard sets guidelines for how Windows and Windows applications deal with video. It was important because it spurred development of standardized and readily available video hardware and software for Windows.

Audio/video interleave (AVI) The format for video files created by the Microsoft Video for Windows standard.

The major advantage of QuickTime for Windows is that the same videos can run both in Windows and on the Macintosh, a claim that Video for Windows can't make. That makes QuickTime for Windows increasingly popular with multimedia developers who want their product to work on both platforms.

If you use many commercially available multimedia applications, you'll soon encounter products based on QuickTime for Windows. As an end user, however, there's no need to worry about the difference. The application automatically loads the necessary files for running QuickTime for Windows and it doesn't conflict with Video for Windows.

Despite the fact that they are competing standards, there isn't much of a battle between Video for Windows and QuickTime for Windows for market dominance. While QuickTime is gaining popularity among dual-platform developers, QuickTime development (and the appropriate hardware and software) occurs on the Macintosh. Development using the Video for Windows standard, of course, is done entirely in Windows. So far, there seems to be plenty of room for both standards.

The upshot of these standards—particularly the Video for Windows standard—is that software video products that even a year ago were both rare and expensive are now common and (relatively) inexpensive. You can buy a decent video capture board for under $500, and good video editing software also costs only a few hundred dollars.

If you need to, of course, you could spend much more to get professional-level hardware and software. However, for most basic multimedia applications, the lower-cost stuff is good enough. The next two sections discuss these types of products and why they are useful to you.

Capturing the Wild Video

The first step in creating your multimedia video is easy; get your video camera and make like Steven Spielberg. If you only want to play your masterpiece on television, plop the darn thing into your VCR, pop some popcorn, and enjoy.

However,—this is getting repetitious—*if it was only that easy to create multimedia videos*. We'll talk about the software and hardware you'll need in the next few sections.

The Nitty-Gritty: Video Capture Boards

Say you're creating a multimedia application to distribute to sales personnel. They, in turn, will use it to wow their sales prospects. You have your masterpiece tape of the president of your company sitting behind her desk extolling the virtues of your products.

The question, of course, is how to get it from here to there, or in this case, from video tape to the computer. The first step is to install a *video capture board* to convert analog video to digital video.

Video capture cards are subject to some of the same failings as the other expansion cards, such as IRQ conflicts and base I/O address conflicts. However, you're no idiot; after reading Part III of this book, you should know all about these sorts of problems.

Video capture board An expansion card you plug into your computer's motherboard. It captures video by converting standard analog videos from sources, such as a VCR, to digital videos you can use in multimedia presentations.

At any rate, video capture cards should:

☞ Have connectors for your VHS video-cassette recorder and accept input from other devices, such as Hi-8 camcorders. You should also be able to capture video directly from a television.

☞ Convert videos from analog to digital at rates as high as thirty frames per second or capture video with high-color depth (known as 24-bit color) at fifteen frames per second. The board does this in "real time," meaning the conversion occurs as the board accepts the video signal from the source. (Most lower-end boards don't create videos in real time.)

If your video board and computer can't handle the video in real time, they will *drop frames*. Dropping frames is exactly what it sounds like; your system simply won't play all the frames in the video. The result is a herky-jerky video. You need a video card that is powerful enough to not drop frames as it does the analog-to-digital conversion.

☞ In some cases, the video capture boards have hardware-based compression capabilities. This speeds things up dramatically, but will cost you some extra bucks. Otherwise software must handle the compression, which is cheaper but slower.

The video you captured has sounds attached, and you're probably wondering where they go when you capture the video. Not to fear; remember that the standard is *audio/video* interleave. *Interleaving* refers to the process of mixing two media. In this case, audio mixes with video. You'll need a sound card, of course, but the main thing to remember is that, like your videotapes, the audio stays with the video after you capture it to your computer.

When you finish this process, you'll have video saved on disk. Of course, it won't be precisely the video you want. After all, even Steven Spielberg must do more than just shoot a few hours of film before releasing his latest blockbuster to the neighborhood multi-mega-cineplex. Just like Steven, to make that video into a masterpiece you'll have to edit it.

Video editing software
This is the software that enables you to cut videos to the proper length, add special effects like fades, and mix in additional videos and add titles.

Making It Pretty

With the help of your video capture board, you've converted your video from analog to digital, and it's just waiting for you to make something great out of it. That's where *video editing software* comes in.

You'll probably start using your video editing software during the capture phase, because it controls the capture as it comes through the video board, enabling you to control factors such as the type of compression and the frame rate and size.

That's just the first step. Video editing software enables you to:

☞ Tighten up videos by cutting out extraneous stuff. This is a benefit both because tightly edited videos are more interesting and because shorter videos require less storage space and computing resources.

☞ Mix in the contents of animations, still images, and other videos.

☞ Add transitions between video sequences. We talked about transitions between slides or sections of presentations in Chapter 22. The principle is the same here.

☞ Use filters to add special effects to frames. Examples of effects can include blurring or inverting colors.

☞ Add titles, like "Margaret M. Maven, President."

Your video editing software should be able to:

☞ Support common sound formats, like WAV files. Remember, sounds and videos are combined.

☞ Support commonly used still image formats so you can insert still frames into your video.

☞ Simplify the process of interspersing all these different elements.

☞ Save all this into an .AVI file that you can incorporate into your multimedia presentation.

Like creating music using MIDI (as discussed in Chapter 25), video editing is a skill that people often go to school to learn. Still, those of us who grew up in the television generation have acquired a surprising number of skills through osmosis.

A good video editing program has an interface that makes sense even to people who think of themselves as idiots. One common interface element, for example, is VCR-like controls for running the video. (And you know precisely how to use every element of your VCR, don't you?)

Good video editing programs also use timelines. As discussed in Chapter 22, which told you about multimedia authoring tools, timelines are adjustable on-screen lines that allow you to precisely control the starting and stopping points of all elements in a frame. The frame can be the on-screen part of your presentation, or when talking about video, the frame refers to the actual video frame.

Beyond that, the rest is gravy. You want special effects, the better video editing programs have 'em. You want to fine-tune on-screen colors? Yup, that too. As with so much in life, however, the more you want, the more you'll pay. While you can buy decent video editing software for hundreds of dollars, you can, if you want, also spend thousands. Isn't that just the way life is?

Tightening It Up with Compression

You've shot your video and converted it to digital format. You've tightly edited it and added special effects and titles. You may have decreased the amount of disc storage space it uses by reducing the size of the on-screen video image, decreasing the color depth and/or reducing the frames per second. With the monster size of these videos we're dealing with, though, that's not enough.

Codec   Stands for compression/decompression. The various codec schemes provide methods for compressing videos to a smaller size for storage and uncompressing them when you want to play them.

That's where compression comes in. In the computer video biz, there are several *codecs* used to squeeze videos. Codec stands for *co*mpression/*dec*ompression.

Codecs are complicated, and there's no need to go into the guts of how they work. Here are some basics you should know, though:

First, they are not perfect. Because they are doing an incredible amount of work in an incredibly short period of time—compressing and uncompressing on the fly as you need the video—there will be some loss of video quality. Fortunately, this quality loss usually is minor—that is, "minor" if the codec was chosen well by the person creating the video.

Second, because codecs are such hard workers, they require a lot of computing horsepower. The bottom line: The more powerful your computer, the more quickly codecs operate, and the more smoothly videos will play.

TECHNO NERD TEACHES...

The compression we're talking about here specifically deals with video files. Perhaps, though, you've heard of other types of compression. For example, there are programs, such as PKWARE's PKZIP, that compress and uncompress ordinary computer files. There also are programs like Stac Electronics' Stacker that compress everything on your hard disk and uncompress it when you need it. This, actually, is roughly similar to the video codecs discussed in this section. Some of the basic concepts of all types of compression are the same, but the video codecs won't work with other types of files.

Microsoft's Video for Windows standard includes support for two codecs called Indeo and Cinepak. These newer codecs join other supported codecs, including ones called Video 1 and RLE.

Video producers must choose the right codec. Codecs each have their strengths and weaknesses. We won't get techie here, so suffice it to say that:

☞ Cinepak compresses tightly, and it works well with clips with a lot of motion. It also works well with clips that have a lot of color depth.

☞ Indeo works well for static clips, such as someone sitting behind a desk. It works particularly well when used with Intel video capture boards. Intel is the company that developed Indeo.

☞ RLE is an old codec that is best for animations, not videos.

☞ Video 1 is an old codec that is becoming less commonly used.

TECHNO NERD TEACHES...

If your multimedia application is for both Windows and the Macintosh, you must be careful to use codecs supported by both Video for Windows and QuickTime for Windows. The two codecs with such support are Cinepak and Indeo.

In addition, MPEG (which stands for the group that created this standard, the Motion Pictures Experts Group) is looming on the horizon. While the other codecs use only software to achieve compression, MPEG is a hardware-based compression scheme. This means that it requires hardware, such as a dedicated expansion card.

MPEG results in faster, larger videos that require less storage space. At this writing, though, MPEG still isn't widely accepted, but that should change as hardware prices decrease. It is becoming increasingly popular with CD-ROM games.

So what kind of compression can you expect from these codecs? Depending on the file and the codec, you can expect anywhere from between a 5% reduction in file size to more than 40%.

These codecs require special drivers to work in Windows. The good news is that the drivers are easy to come by. If you use a commercially available multimedia application that uses these codecs, chances are the application installed the driver for you. That's why most end users will never know which codec is at work.

The easy way to tell whether the codec driver is installed is to look in the Drivers dialog box, which you access from the Windows control panel. The next figure shows my Drivers dialog box. As you can see, every type of multimedia driver and its brother is installed on my system, including a number of video codecs.

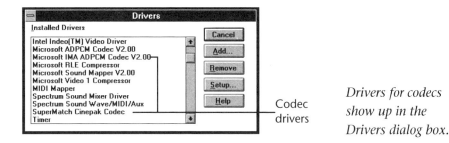

Codec
drivers

*Drivers for codecs
show up in the
Drivers dialog box.*

Not If . . . When

Your video editing software should enable you to select a codec for your
videos. There is one rule, however, that you must obey: compress a video
only once, otherwise you'll lose image quality.

That makes the issue of *when* to apply the codec extremely important. In
simple terms, you have two choices. You can:

- Apply the compression when you first capture the video.

- Apply the compression when you finish editing the video.

If you are simply removing entire frames during the editing process, you
can compress the video file at the start—if your video capture board
supports this capability. However, if you'll be doing things like changing
the frame rate or making changes *within* frames, such as cropping the
frame, wait until you finish your editing before applying the codec.

Note that some video capture cards will only capture uncompressed
video. Others can compress during the capture process. Obviously, this is
good information to know before you purchase your video capture board.

The Least You Need to Know

Video is often the star of multimedia. However, in this chapter, you learned that it can be complex to create. Specifically, you learned:

☛ Video capture boards capture analog video from televisions and VCRs and turn it into digital video your computer can use.

☛ Video files are huge and require the use of codecs to compress and decompress video files.

☛ Codecs sometimes are built into video capture boards, but you often apply them from the video editing software.

☛ Video editing software enables you to create tight video productions with all kinds of effects and transitions.

☛ You can buy a video capture board for under $500, and video editing software is even less expensive. For professional level products, however, you must spend much more.

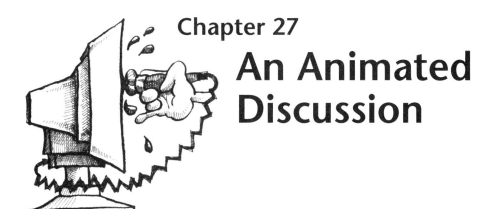

Chapter 27

An Animated Discussion

In This Chapter

- ☛ Adults watching animations
- ☛ Simple path-based animations
- ☛ Morphing and warping
- ☛ Twisting text
- ☛ Complex animations

George of the Jungle was my favorite cartoon as a kid, although these days, hardly anybody remembers it. I liked Rocky and Bullwinkle, too. You'd think, then, that I'd enjoy animation used in multimedia presentations since I have such a long history with animation.

Well, I do. The truth is, multimedia animation usually isn't as entertaining as George of the Jungle. While I recently saw an entertainment CD-ROM featuring Toons, such as those in the movie, *Who Killed Roger Rabbit*, most multimedia animations are more ordinary and business-like. That doesn't make them uninteresting or unimportant. This chapter describes some potential applications for animations and describes the tools you use for creating them.

If Not Cartoons, Then What?

Animation is important in a number of multimedia situations, such as:

☞ Simple animations that, for example, emphasize text by giving it the appearance of bulging in and out, or by changing the color and size of the text. These animations are both amusing and help make a point.

☞ Introducing logos and other drawn items. If you're a movie fan, you've seen these business animations just before the movie starts. The animations typically tell you which company produced or distributed the movie. More and more, multimedia CD-ROMs start out with animations just like the movies. Similarly, commercial multimedia applications often begin with a presentation of the logo.

☞ Controlled demonstrations of products or processes. You can, for example, animate a blow-apart diagram to show how to assemble the internal whatchamathingee in your product.

☞ Walkthroughs, drivethroughs, and flyovers. These animations give you the point of view of a person walking, driving, or flying through or over an object or location. This is useful, for example, for illustrating home floor plans or showing how that new subdivision nestles into the (former) countryside.

What's This—Standards *Again*?

As with other media, standards for animation file formats have emerged. Also as with other media, these standards mean that most multimedia authoring tools can easily make use of animations.

Specifically, most animations these days are saved in either the FLI or related FLC formats. Most people don't need to understand much about the FLI/FLC formats, but you do need to know whether your multimedia authoring tools support these formats. And, of course, the program you use to create animations also must support these formats. These days, it would be difficult to find a program that doesn't.

You also need to know that, unlike the video formats, there are no built-in sound capabilities in the FLI/FLC formats. In most cases, this isn't a horrendous problem; your multimedia authoring tool should allow you to add sound to accompany an animation. However, it does mean there's an extra step that doesn't exist when creating videos. It also explains why there are a number of proprietary animation formats available, some of which support interleaved sound.

Ready, Set, Animate

Now to start animating. As you'll learn in the next several sections, some animations are extremely uncomplicated while others are very complex. First you should understand the different types of animations and the tools used to create them.

Starting Simply

Some animations are simple, requiring only that text, an image, or some other medium move from one place on-screen to another. For example, Gold Disk's Astound lets you pick your object, then plot its trajectory across the screen. This easy path-based animation is different from other animations because it isn't based on a series of frames played in rapid succession. Rather, the program merely moves the location of the item on-screen.

Some programs even let you add special effects to the movement, such as rotating the object or, more simply, making it stop in a certain way. For example, one of my favorite effects is the bounce stop. You bring text in from one corner of the screen, and when it settles into its position, it bounces a little bit. Sure, I'm easy to please, but basic effects like this can add to a multimedia presentation.

Simple path-based animations let you, for example, start a presentation by animating the company logo as it traverses the screen. Time this bit of animation to work with some music, and you have a professional-looking start to your application.

Capture Those Screens

A relatively new type of simple animation program captures the contents of your computer screen, or at least a portion of the screen. For example, you could draw a small item, capture the item with the screen animation program, then add something to the item, and capture it again. When you finish this process, the animation program creates an animation file.

To be blunt, you won't win any awards with this type of animation, but capturing programs do have their uses. By showing an animation made up of captured screens, you can teach other people how to use a program.

For example, say the famous XYZ Company standardizes on WordWhiz 5.5. Due to an unforeseen design flaw, nobody at XYZ Company knows how to perform a particular function with WordWhiz 5.5. The XYZ Company employee assigned to help the other employees use computers can fire up WordWhiz 5.5 on his computer. Then, saving screens for each step in the operation, he can create a little animation that explains how to properly use WordWhiz 5.5. Then, he can either incorporate the animation into a larger presentation about using WordWhiz 5.5 or simply distribute the animation to those who need it. These animation programs typically come with a run-time version for playing back the animations.

Animations Mean Business

There are a few animation programs aimed at spicing up standard business documents and presentations that are easy to use, and provide a surprisingly sophisticated range of capabilities. For example, you can make a headline in a standard word processing document jump up or down for emphasis, or you can take a drawing of a logo and move or rotate it through space.

These programs typically support both path-based animation and more sophisticated animation techniques. Along with text animation and morphing programs discussed later, they are the most accessible and useful animation programs for nontechnical users.

Animating Text?

At first glance, animating text seems like a goofy idea. However, like morphing, described in the next section, the capability to animate text is often highly useful. You can use a text animation program to create a spinning logo, for example. Besides giving motion to text, these programs can make text grow, shrink, change shape and color—or do just about anything you want. You also can add backgrounds to these animations. Like business animation and morphing programs, text animation programs are relatively uncomplicated for nontechnoids to use.

Do the Morph

You've seen morphing; it became popular a couple of years ago in the Michael Jackson video in which people's faces changed on-screen into other faces. Since then, morphing has become a staple in television commercials and movies.

Morphing Morphing is an effect in which one thing changes on-screen into another. The object can be changing one person's face into another or a dog into a cat.

There are an astounding number of inexpensive morphing products available these days, and for the most part, they are easy to use. The general drill with morphing products is:

☞ You load two or more image files. One is the starting image and the others are the intermediary and ending images into which you want the starting image to morph. For example, if you morph a dog into a cat or a man into a woman, you load images of both. It sounds strange, but it's only make-believe on computers, so don't worry.

☞ You outline the key areas in each image that are similar. For example, you can mark the mouths, eyes, chins, and foreheads of the people in both the starting and ending images. Simply click your mouse in the key areas. Then, the morph software pays particular attention to those areas to make sure that the morph proceeds smoothly.

☛ You set the frame rate. As with video, the higher the frame rate, the smoother the animation. Also, however, the higher the frame rate, the more resources the animation demands from your computer.

☛ The morphing program compiles the morph. The program creates the images between the starting image and the ending image, making one frame slightly different from the frame before.

The capability to automatically generate the images between the starting point and the ending point is one of the powerful things that computerized animation offers. In the "olden" days of creating film animations by hand, artists had to create each of the in-between drawings manually.

☛ You save the morph as an animation file, typically with either the .FLI, .FLC, or .AVI file name extension.

A related effect that several morphing programs offer is *warping*. As the name implies, warping simply warps a single image. Typically, a grid overlays the image you want to warp. You can drag any line in the grid with your mouse, and the part of the image underneath the line warps to fit the new grid line.

Warping and morphing are way-cool effects, but what are the applications? Well, there are plenty. You can create amusing warps or morphs to break up an otherwise dull multimedia presentation. More importantly, it's fun to apply your imagination to these products. Say, for example, your company changes its name from the XYZ Company to the ABC Company. You can use a morphing product to create an animation in which the name literally changes from the old name to the new name on-screen.

Best of all, besides being inexpensive, morphing programs are easy to use. This combination makes them indispensable tools for those who don't have the experience and expertise to use the high-end products discussed in the next section.

And at the High End

The most sophisticated action in animation occurs at the high end of the product spectrum. These specialized programs usually require a significant learning curve, although some are friendlier.

3-D rendering programs are becoming popular. These enable you to draw three-dimensional objects and then move those objects through space. This is useful for displaying new products and showing how they work.

These programs have as much in common with CAD programs as with other animation programs. They typically provide reasonably sophisticated tools for creating three-dimensional drawings, but they depart from CAD programs in that they provide sophisticated methods for animating the drawings.

TECHNO NERD TEACHES...

Autodesk, best known for its high-end CAD programs, leveraged their CAD expertise to become a leading vendor of high-end animation programs. This, in turn, led to their development of the FLI/FLC file format for animations, the de facto file format standard.

One clever feature of good 3-D rendering programs is the capability to situate a "camera" at any point in or around the animation path. This enables the animation to take the point of view of the camera. The results of these animations can range from a walkthrough of a house or a drive-through of a subdivision to a flyover of the same subdivision. This is powerful stuff, indeed, but it requires a fair amount of technical drawing skill.

There also are a slew of high-end programs with more traditional anima-tion skills. You've seen the results of these types of computerized anima-tions in movies, television commercials, and even animated film festivals.

These programs include drawing capabilities coupled with traditional animation techniques to create animations. For example, most use *cels*, which are overlays over a frame. The frame can contain the static images— the stuff in that frame that doesn't move—or the parts of the images that do move. As with 3-D rendering programs, these high-end animation programs typically require a steep learning curve and drawing skills.

The Least You Need to Know

Animation is an important part of multimedia. Except for high-end applications, animations are relatively easy to create. In this chapter, you learned the following about animation:

- ☛ The most common file formats for animation are the related FLI and FLC formats.

- ☛ Path-based animations simply move an object from one place to another.

- ☛ You can create simple path-based animations in many multimedia-oriented presentation programs.

- ☛ Morph, business animation, and text animation programs provide reasonably thorough animation capabilities but don't require a steep learning curve. This makes them accessible to nontechnical users who don't have extensive drawing skills.

- ☛ High-end animation programs can create powerful effects but are complex to use.

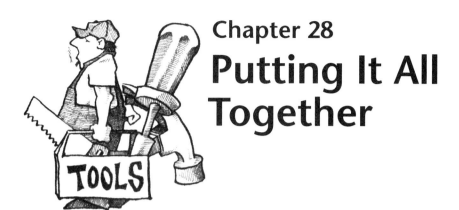

Chapter 28
Putting It All Together

In This Chapter

- Thinking it through
- Using the right tools
- Elements of style

Just because somebody collects bricks and mortar, doesn't mean she has the skills to build a beautiful house. It's the same with multimedia. Owning a multimedia authoring tool and acquiring the media, as described in the previous chapters of this section, are only the beginning.

You also must learn how to weave your application together to achieve the greatest effect. That takes both practice and some basic knowledge. The practice is up to you, but this chapter provides some basic knowledge about how best to create multimedia applications.

Your Roadmap to Success

Here's an earth-shattering concept: Think through your multimedia application before you start it. Here's an even more radical thought: Take a low-tech pen and paper and write down the most important aspects of your presentation.

Let's say, for example, that the multimedia application is about WordWhiz 5.5, the amazing word processor your company manufactures. Is this a training presentation? A sales presentation?

On your handy piece of paper, write the main goal and the subgoals of the application. Think of it this way: when the user finishes the application, what is the information you want him or her to have?

Next, who is the audience for the application? Is it an internal audience, such as sales personnel, or a critical external audience, such as customers?

Third, what physical medium will you use? Are you pressing this presentation onto CD-ROMs or distributing it on floppy disks?

You might have a lot of ideas about your multimedia application, but unless you organize those ideas, you could come out with a mash. Getting your thoughts together *before* you start creating your application will save you time, money, and a lot of frustration.

Pandering to the Audience

If you ask me, pandering gets a bad rap in our society. What's wrong with a little pandering?

For example, if you create a training application, you should pander to those being trained. The application needs to reflect their needs. A typical training application will:

- ☞ Be highly structured in a series of learning steps.
- ☞ Make heavy use of hyperlinks to move to other lessons.
- ☞ Have plenty of background material explaining the subject matter.

Or say you are creating a sales presentation for customers. Such a presentation will:

- ☞ Have flashy, tight production.

☛ Include a wider variety of media, focusing on video and animation.

☛ Be uplifting and bright with appropriate theme music to match.

What if you're creating a reference work? Sure, this can be an encyclopedia, but it also can be a policy and procedure manual or a user's guide. Such presentations will:

☛ Be text-heavy.

☛ Require retrieval tools to find specific text.

☛ Use media besides text only for illustrative purposes.

Perhaps you're starting to get the idea: By considering the nature of the application and the audience before you start, you can pick the right tools and media beforehand. This will save you a lot of time and trouble down the road.

See—pandering isn't so bad after all. Just because every politician does it doesn't mean it has no value.

Use the Right Tools

Let's expand a bit on this pandering stuff. Specifically, let's discuss how to determine which authoring tools to use. Using the wrong tools will cost you time and money, and will make your application less effective.

Let's face it: for in-house use, you usually won't create the most highly polished multimedia. That's because highly polished multimedia is expensive to create. Using high-end tools for in-house multimedia is like dressing up for dinner with your family; it's a nice thought, but you aren't going to do it often.

As a result, you're unlikely to use a high-end multimedia authoring tool. You're more likely to use a presentation program, such as Gold Disk's Astound; an electronic book authoring program, such as Folio Views; or even a meat-and-potatoes application, such as your word processor.

TECHNO NERD TEACHES...

On balance, I think that multimedia presentation programs, such as Astound, are useful for all but the flashiest and most text-heavy applications. That's because they are relatively easy to use and can create highly attractive presentations with a fair amount of interactivity. They're not plug-ugly like electronic book authoring tools, and they don't require an advanced degree, as do most high-end authoring tools.

Similarly, for text-heavy reference documents, chances are that you'll use an electronic book authoring program. That's because content is more important than style and appearance. Besides, most other multimedia authoring tools can't handle large amounts of text, but this is what electronic book authoring tools do best.

On the other hand, since sales and kiosk presentations are best-foot-forward types of things, you may want to use high-end authoring tools to create the most professional-looking presentations possible. However, you also can do a pretty good job creating attractive multimedia applications with multimedia presentation programs.

Dave's best-use concept
This isn't an official concept that you'll find in a book (other than this one). It does, however, reflect my rather (un)startling idea that you'll create the most effective presentations by using the appropriate authoring tools and media.

By now, you're probably getting the idea that I believe in a "best-use" concept. The idea is simple: use the right tool for the job. Whether you are constructing a backyard patio or a multimedia presentation, this will save you time and trouble.

I'll be the first to admit that this is an elementary concept. Amazingly, many new multimedia authors ignore it. Somebody gets his hands on a great new authoring tool and some hot video, and he's off to the races. A year later, there's still no multimedia application but, boy, is that guy having a great time.

Use the Right Medium

Dave's best-use concept doesn't apply only to selecting authoring tools. It also applies to selecting the media you use in the presentation. Especially for beginners, there's a great temptation to use the flashy stuff, such as video and animation, at the expense of more ordinary media like text.

In most cases there are three guiding lights for media selection:

☞ **Use the most appropriate medium.** When defining concepts, for example, text is still the best medium. Some multimedia applications I've seen, however, use audio of somebody reading a definition. Ix-nay. Put it on the screen and let people read it. On the other hand, after you've defined something, you can best show how it works with video or animation.

☞ **Match the media to the level of your end user's PCs.** If you are creating an in-house application and most of your users have old door-stop PCs, don't fill the application with videos. That's because you need a fair amount of horsepower to run videos. Even more obviously, if your end users don't have sound cards and speakers, don't use audio. Or if they have junky, old video systems, don't use many fancy graphics.

☞ **When possible, use one medium to support another.** This is an old concept, kind of like how a dictionary uses an illustration for a definition.

One of the great things about multimedia is that you can mix media. You can have text or audio describing the feeding habits of sharks, then show a video of the shark actually feeding. Since some people learn best by seeing and others learn best by hearing, mixing media not only reinforces your message but also makes sure that everybody can learn from your application.

The Final Step (Almost)

Now that you have a good idea of the goals of your application and the right authoring tools and mix of media, it's time for more concrete planning.

Specifically, it's time to think through the application on a screen-by-screen basis. It's time to:

☞ Determine the logical flow of the application from beginning to end. True, multimedia users don't always use applications from beginning to end. But they often do, particularly for training applications. Keeping things linear and well-structured makes application development easier.

☞ Determine the sections and subsections of the application. Each section and subsection should have a logical flow.

☞ Determine the subject of each screen. This is easiest to do after determining the logical flow of the entire application and of each section. It's best to have one primary subject per screen.

☞ Map out the navigation basics. Will you have many hyperlinks or a few? Will there be a specific section, such as an index or glossary, that will serve as a common launching point or destination for links? Whatever you decide will have an impact on the application's structure.

☞ Decide where you want to focus the various media. Some applications have a single screen for launching specific types of media, such as videos. Others launch videos directly from related topics. Again, this decision has an impact on the shape of the application.

If you are using a presentation program, you're really in luck. That's because presentation programs usually have an outliner in which you can organize the presentation setup for each screen in one fell swoop. If you are using another type of authoring tool, however, you'll need to keep using the old pen and paper.

The Elements of Multimedia Style

So here's where we're at: You've thought through your multimedia application and determined the right authoring tools and the right balance of media. You've thought through the structure of the application and, using the other chapters in this section, you've already created or selected your media.

Now we're ready to rock and roll. The next several sections discuss the various media and factors that can make them either effective or ineffective.

The Last Word on Text

In writing school (of which I am a gradu-wit), they teach you this: keep it bright, keep it tight. That means make the writing style fit the subject, and use as few words as possible.

This is particularly true in multimedia. That's because, in general, people prefer not to read many words on-screen. Some applications, like multimedia encyclopedias or electronic books, are by definition focused around words. But most applications need not be as word-heavy.

Well-balanced text.

When you do use text, don't crunch it together or use too much in a screen. Thick blocks of text appear impenetrable and can discourage use of the application. The figure above is a good example of how to present text on-screen.

Besides using few words on each screen, don't hesitate to use bullets. Bullets are succinct, and they visually break up blocks of text. It's no surprise, for example, that this book makes regular use of bullets.

Next, make sure your writing is well-edited and free of spelling errors. I recently came across a commercial multimedia application with misspelled words, which immediately caused me to lose respect for the application. It's like a manager getting a cover letter for a job application that contains misspelled words—they jump out at you and lessen the candidate's credibility.

Another important element with text is to use easy-to-read fonts. Avoid frilly, decorative fonts except for occasional use in headlines. Multimedia applications are visual feasts. Difficult-to-read fonts can result in the multimedia equivalent of indigestion.

Getting Your Image

As with all media, using images appropriately is very important. An appropriate image is one that serves the goals of the presentation. For example, a technical training presentation might need a blow-apart diagram of a part while a sales presentation would include a photo of the product.

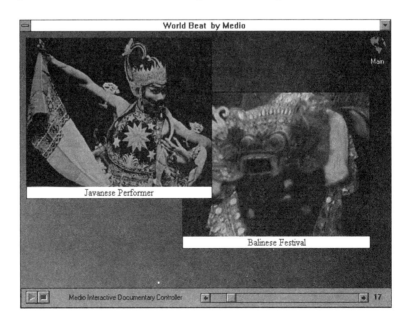

Well-used images show you rather than tell you.

Here's another one of those little rules: A well-selected and well-done image is a more effective storyteller than a poorly selected or poorly done video or animation.

Finally, as with all media, make sure the quality of your images is high. This is particularly important for applications you will show outside your organization, for example, to customers. Fuzzy, out-of-focus photos or poorly drawn artwork will detract from the credibility of the application in the same way as misspelled words.

Sounds Like . . .

Audio in multimedia presentations usually serves two purposes: music or narration. While it is easy to provide a balanced on-screen appearance for visual multimedia objects, it is harder to balance audio because you can't see it. But unbalanced audio detracts from an application.

For example, one of my Top 10 multimedia applications (as discussed in Chapter 21) is Leonardo The Inventor. The developers of this disc did a superb job making every screen visually attractive. However, the disc overrelies on audio. Most new screens start with a music clip, and each new section starts with a narration about the section's contents. If you just want to hop to a new section, you must first listen to the music and audio. After extended use of the disc, this can be a bit exasperating.

An important rule of audio is to not use it unless it bears repeating. The corollary of this rule is don't use narration unless it adds something to the application that other media, particularly text, can't add. When you do use narration, don't use it in opening screens of sections. It's better to use it on the informational screens within sections.

Music is an excellent way to set the tone for the application, but appropriateness is vital. An application about a somber topic shouldn't have lilting reggae music in the background. Well-selected music can intensify the power of a video or a slide show of still images.

Here comes another of my multimedia application buzzwords: the music should be *consistent*. Don't be afraid to use the same music in different sections if the prevailing tone of the sections is the same.

TECHNO NERD TEACHES...

Consistency is one of those things that is most powerful at a subliminal level. Users of your applications are unlikely to think, "Hmmm . . . that music isn't consistent with the music in the other section." But if the music and other elements are consistent, the user will feel at ease with the application and is likely to stay with it longer and get more out of it.

Makin' It Move

You probably have the idea by now that I feel strongly that you should use media appropriately. So, as they say in my old neighborhood, I won't beat that dead horse to death again regarding videos and animations.

Instead, let's talk about *quality*. Obviously, quality is important for all media, but since creating quality video and animations is generally more difficult than the other media, it's worth focusing on a bit.

First, let's remember Dave's Rule of Working: Don't do more work than you need to. Creating high-quality video is difficult, so if you have the budget and if the video or animation is critical to the application, hire a professional to create the video for you.

If you create your own video, however, here are some things that can improve video quality:

- ☛ Remember that video and animation are, by definition, about motion. If you must have the president, Margaret Maven, talking about WordWhiz 5.5, get her away from the desk and have her speak while walking, say, down the WordWhiz assembly line. However, don't get carried away with the motion thing and create frenetic videos.

TECHNO NERD TEACHES...

Motion is an important concept when editing videos. A good video often consists of several separate video clips spliced together, which gives the video a dynamic feel. This requires editing skill and a good sense of pacing. A common error is to overedit and create a frenetic video in which you switch clips every second or two. It is better to pace the video so that it is consistent with the overall tone of the application.

☞ Use solid production techniques. This includes framing each shot so the most important part is most prominent. It also includes the proper use of lighting.

☞ Keep the camera still by using a tripod. The jittery camera effect is useful occasionally for adding a sense of on-the-scene urgency, but mostly, it gives viewers headaches.

☞ In the application itself, make sure that the video doesn't get lost on the screen amidst other media. That doesn't mean you should devote an entire screen to the video. It just means that you should balance a video with something else, such as on-screen text.

Appearance Is (Almost) Everything

A visually beautiful multimedia application is a feast for the eyes. Still, it is impossible to describe the ideal on-screen appearance of a multimedia presentation. However, there are some general guidelines. To wit:

☞ Empty space is good. Keep each screen simple, leaving plenty of empty space. This is more attractive and makes using the application easier (see the following figure).

☞ Make sure you physically balance each screen. For example, if you have an image in the upper left corner, place something in the lower right corner to balance it. Don't bunch all your media together.

☞ Select an appropriate background. Most authoring tools let you create your own background or choose a stock background.

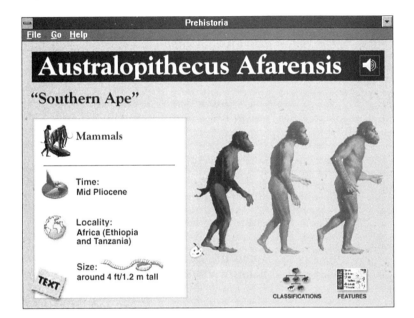

Lots of information kept simple with lots of empty space.

☞ Make screens consistent. Make sure that important on-screen elements are in the same place in every screen. This is particularly important with navigation tools, such as buttons, for going to the next, previous, or opening screen.

Navigating by the Stars

One of the reasons that books are so comforting is that they are predictable. There's a table of contents, the contents itself, and an index. The contents divide into chapters and sections. No matter what the subject matter is, nearly every book follows the same basic format.

By definition, with multimedia you usually hop around from place to place and don't necessarily start at the beginning and finish at the end.

That doesn't mean, however, that you can't provide both structure and navigation tools to make multimedia applications as comforting as books.

We've already talked about creating an overall structure for your application. Don't hesitate to make that structure obvious on-screen. For example, you can have an opening screen listing all the sections of the application with hyperlinks leading to an opening screen for each section.

This type of structure gives users comforting anchor points and prevents them from becoming disoriented when using the application. Common parts of even the best multimedia applications are:

☞ The opening screen. From the opening screen you can jump to any of the sections.

☞ An index listing all the important topics in the application. You can jump from a topic to the specific section in which it is located.

As you might guess, *hyperlinks* are the way users move through a multimedia application. The most effective hyperlinks take advantage of the application's structure. Ideally, minimal hyperlinking will include:

☞ A button on every screen on which the user can click to take him or her to the opening screen. From there, the user can move to other sections of the application.

☞ A button on every screen on which the user can click to get to an index. From the index, the user can select a topic and jump to it.

☞ In applications that are more linear in nature, such as an on-line user's guide, buttons on every screen for moving to the next and previous screens.

To repeat an important point, *these basic navigation capabilities should be in the same place on every screen.* The previous figure shows a well-designed screen. Notice that it has obvious buttons for navigation. Take my word for it: Those buttons are in the same place in every screen in each of those applications.

Beyond that, creating hyperlinks is as much an art as a science. It requires both a sound knowledge of the contents of the application and a sense of which topics are most important to users.

Depending on the application, you can make individual words or media the starting point of jumps to related information. Or in text-oriented applications, you can place a "See Also" section at the bottom of articles for jumps to related articles.

Don't forget that hyperlinks can jump from one medium to another. In a multimedia encyclopedia, for example, you might see a button beside a text article that you can click on to view a video about that topic.

The Least You Need to Know

This chapter provided the basics for putting together effective multimedia presentations. There are a number of words that summarize this process:

☛ **Appropriateness.** Use media that is appropriate for the point you are making. Don't use media just because it's snazzy.

☛ **Balance.** Balance pertains to the mix of media throughout an application. It also means that you should balance and not overcrowd the on-screen appearance.

☛ **Simplicity.** Clutter is hard to navigate and understand and discourages use of the application. Keep each screen simple.

☛ **Consistency.** Consistency leads to predictability, which is a good thing when navigating through a multimedia application. Put important interface elements in the same place on each screen. Keep music consistent from section to section. This makes people more comfortable with the application.

☛ **Credibility.** Credibility is related to accuracy. Obviously, the information in your application should be accurate. But it also should be professional, and properly spelled and edited.

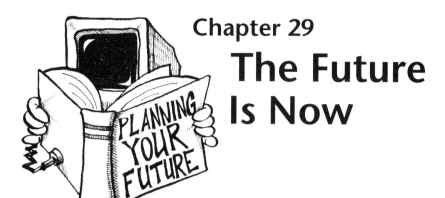

Chapter 29
The Future Is Now

In This Chapter

- ☞ Better and faster sound, video, and drives
- ☞ Multimedia: beam me up!
- ☞ Virtual reality hits multimedia
- ☞ Surfin' the net

If there was an Understatement of the Decade Contest, one of the leading contenders would be this: Computer stuff changes quickly.

We hear this idea repeated so often that it is verging on attaining clichè status. Although I think of myself as clichè-averse, I utter this chestnut frequently. The rapidity of the changes sometimes baffles me even though it's part of my job to keep up with them all.

Nowhere in the computer business is change occurring more rapidly than in multimedia. In this chapter, we'll scan the horizon for the trends that are unfolding now and those that will unfold in the not-too-distant future. These trends will change the way you use and create multimedia.

What Are You Waiting For?

First, let's chronicle some recent changes in the multimedia world. Technologically, these changes are already here but, in most cases, they are still gathering momentum. Put differently, we haven't yet felt the impact of these changes, but we will soon.

CD-ROM Drives for Everybody

This topic fits into the "Technology Marches Ever Forward" category. You long have been able to purchase multimedia-ready computers that come with CD-ROM drives. However, with the growing acceptance of PCs based on the Pentium chip, more and more computers are coming with CD-ROM drives as standard. In many cases, CD-ROM drives are replacing the old 5.25-inch floppy drives.

There are several reasons for this trend. First, the Pentium chip is so powerful that it greatly enhances the playback of multimedia applications. More practically, however, software vendors are increasingly distributing standard applications, such as word processors and databases, on CD-ROMs instead of on floppies. That's because these applications keep getting larger, and installing them from CD-ROMs is simpler and faster.

For multimedia mavens, this trend has some potentially important ramifications. Using basic supply-and-demand, it is logical to expect that if there are a lot of CD-ROM drives out there, demand for multimedia titles will increase. This will result in more multimedia titles and lower prices, perhaps as low as audio CD levels.

Of course, we all know that increased quantity and lowered price have nothing to do with increased quality. As multimedia CD-ROMs become more popular, we can expect more discs that pander to the lowest common denominator. However, if the market works as it should, there also should be more high-quality discs. We can always hope.

Pressing Matters: Creating Your Own CD-ROMs

It's getting cheaper and cheaper to master your own CD-ROMs, a trend that will have significant impact on business applications. Mastering is the process you must go through before you duplicate the discs in large quantities.

No, the hardware and software for mastering CD-ROMs aren't inexpensive enough for average Josephines—at this writing, the hardware alone still costs thousands of dollars. Nor are prices likely to become low enough for those of us without trust funds to afford.

However, the hardware and software *are* becoming inexpensive enough to entice many corporate users. With CD-ROM drives becoming standard equipment, this trend points to a time when it will be common to distribute in-house multimedia applications and electronic books on CD-ROMs.

This has bigger social implications. Can you say "paperless office?" Actually, this trend alone isn't enough to move us toward the mythical paperless office. Yet, it is one of the trends that will nudge us in that direction.

Sound Advances

We talked in previous chapters about the advances in digital audio technology. Many of the advances are here already—they're just a bit expensive for the time being. Those advances include:

- ☛ Wavetable synthesis, which will greatly increase the quality of MIDI music.

- ☛ The ability to create MIDI music with more musical tracks.

- ☛ Use of digital signal processors (DSPs) to add power to sound boards. Besides enabling sound boards to have more capabilities, DSPs also offload processing demands from your computer's central processing unit. This, in turn, means you'll be able to listen to more complex sounds without bogging down your system.

TECHNO NERD TEACHES...

Improved sound capabilities should be accompanied by increased quality and decreased prices for PC speakers. Unlike speakers for your stereo, most people consider PC speakers to be a peripheral, not an essential part of their computer system. As a result, it's hard to get people to fork over the dough for good PC speakers. Good speakers, however, are essential to appreciate the advances in sound technology.

Even as you read this, the prices of this new generation of audio technology are tumbling. Yes, there is better sound in your future.

Mumbly MPEG

Let's be blunt: For most of us, multimedia video is a mixed blessing. Unless your PC is a real rocket ship, videos are small and often jerky; and they can take forever to load. The MPEG codec offers hope. MPEG compresses videos tightly and uncompresses them quickly. It enables larger, full-screen videos as opposed to the tiny video windows that still are common.

The problem, however, has been that MPEG is a hardware-based solution requiring a special expansion card. This has made MPEG too expensive and too clumsy for most users. There are, however, some potential solutions to this problem that could make MPEG easier to deal with and less expensive. For example, there already are expansion cards that combine the functions of a video accelerator and an MPEG expansion card.

MPEG, or something like it, is critical if acceptance of multimedia is going to continue to grow. The multimedia industry is aware of this fact, and so are hardware vendors, who are expected to come up with MPEG solutions in the not-to-distant future.

A special programming note: Read the section later in this chapter about the new version of Windows for some encouraging news about MPEG.

The Multimedia Road Show

Multimedia presentations have become a popular tool for sales personnel and others who travel. Until recently, however, it's been messy to use multimedia on the road. Portable CD-ROM drives have been available for a couple of years. They have carved out an important niche among traveling multimedia warriors.

Of greater interest is the direction in which notebook computers are going. Not only are these babies getting smaller and lighter, but they're also starting to have greater multimedia capabilities. For example, notebooks with color displays, built-in CD-ROM drives, and sound capabilities are now common, if somewhat expensive.

Look for notebook computers to get even more sophisticated and useful for multimedia presentations. In the corporate world, this will greatly increase the acceptance of multimedia as a business tool. It also will help sales and marketing types collect some really major frequent flier miles.

Coming Real Soon Now (RSN)

Software, as the cliché goes, is like sausage: You may like the result, but you don't want to know how they do it. Software development is, to say the least, an imprecise process, and it is extremely difficult to put a precise date on the release of a product.

When I was a product manager for a software company, however, we always had customers and the media badgering us about when we'd be releasing a new version. It was my job to deal with these people.

Like most product managers, I quickly began responding with the phrase, "Real Soon Now." Internally, we abbreviated this to RSN. Real Soon Now can mean anything from tomorrow morning to sometime before interstellar space travel becomes common and inexpensive. It's the marketeer's version of "the check is in the mail."

The next several sections discuss stuff that isn't quite here yet, but will be RSN. Really.

Pluggin' and Playin' in Chicago

Microsoft, the software company that lots of people love to hate, may well have blessed us with the new version of Windows by the time you read this. Code-named Chicago (remember when code names were supposed to be secret, not generated by the marketing department?), this Windows upgrade will clean up the Windows interface and the hundreds of annoyances that plague Windows users. In the ideal Windows world, anyway.

TECHNO NERD TEACHES...

One of the important things about the new Windows is that it isn't a shell that works with DOS, but rather is an operating system in its own right that replaces DOS. DOS is a creaky senior citizen that didn't keep up with technical advances. However, hundreds of utilities and environments, such as Windows, have covered up many of DOS' shortcomings, such as its inabilities to deal well with multimedia or to use lots of memory. As its own operating system, the new Windows will simplify and speed up many computing operations because it doesn't have to work along with the ancient DOS.

There are several things in the new Windows that will appeal to multimedia mavens. First, it is a 32-bit operating system compared to the current 16-bit Windows.

In simple terms, this means that Windows applications, including multimedia applications, will run much faster because Windows can handle data more quickly. This in itself should speed up sluggish multimedia applications—at least those developed with authoring tools specifically designed for this new technology.

Second, the new Windows will support the *Plug and Play* standard. In Section Three of this book, we spent a lot of time discussing how hard it can be to install multimedia boards. You learned that there can be IRQ, DMA, and base I/O address conflicts with other boards that can cause a host of problems.

Plug and Play should solve many of those problems. Plug and Play enables your computer (assuming your expansion cards support Plug and Play) and Windows to automatically detect the IRQs, DMA channels, and base I/O addresses of newly added boards and to adjust for them automatically. This will greatly reduce the time and complexity of installing these items.

In the more speculative realm, the new Windows also will have direct support for MPEG decompression. At this writing, it looks like this MPEG support will still require some hardware. However, this hardware assistance can be built into your PC's motherboard, which should make it less expensive than current MPEG boards.

> **SPEAK LIKE A GEEK**
>
> **32-bit operating system**
> A 32-bit operating system, such as the new version of Windows, can handle more information more quickly than can older 16-bit systems like Windows 3.1. Applications developed to run in a 32-bit environment, including multimedia applications, will run much faster than you're used to.

Bigger, Better, Faster

As with so much in the computing world, in the future we can expect storage media to store more, be easier to install, and operate more quickly. There are some prospects on the horizon that could dramatically change the way we store multimedia.

What's unclear is which technology the marketplace (that's us) will embrace. Two alternative types of optical drives, WORM (write-once, read-many) and MO (magneto-optical) drives have been around for many years and remain leading candidates.

Fully rewritable optical disks, sometimes called *flopticals*, also have been around for a while. However, they never caught on, probably because they are slower than other magnetic media, and they're expensive. Of course, this places flopticals in the same catch-22 situation: if they became popular, they'd be less expensive.

There are standards evolving for floptical disks. Adherents of flopticals claim that prices will fall, and they will catch on. We'll see.

There also are schemes floating around to dramatically increase the storage capacity of CD-ROM drives. One idea that could catch on is the capability to compress and decompress the contents of CD-ROM drives invisibly as you use them.

This already is a popular technique on hard drives, but proved to be a tricky technical problem to solve for CD-ROMs. Supposedly, however, the problem is now solved and could serve to double the capacity of CD-ROMs.

Let's face it: CD-ROM capacities, which used to seem unspeakably large, don't seem so large any more. These schemes should unfold in the next year or two and perhaps one of them will catch on.

TECHNO NERD TEACHES...

I can't predict which storage technology will finally become king of the hill. However, I do predict this: Within a few years, our current CD-ROM drives will be like the old 5.25-inch floppy drives. That is to say, we'll be able to obtain CD-ROMs that work in our current drives, but they will be on their way out in terms of market acceptance. That, of course, is good news and bad news.

One thing is certain, however: CD-ROM drives will continue to get faster. Single-spin drives are rarely sold any more and double-spin drives are now the norm. Triple-spin and quadruple drives are now readily available and their prices are decreasing as we inevitably move toward even faster drives.

Give It a Voice

We've moved in this chapter from currently accepted technology to Real Soon Now technology. Now, we move into what-if technology by discussing *voice recognition*. Anybody who's watched Star Trek knows what voice recognition is, and like most of the other technology discussed in this chapter, voice recognition is already with us. There are many cute, little utilities for issuing commands for navigating through Windows. All you need to do with these utilities is plug a microphone into your sound card.

There also are some more advanced programs that enable you to dictate into your applications rather than type. I just used one that enabled me to accurately dictate at forty words per minute—the speed of an average typist.

However, you-had-to-talk-like-this, putting a fraction of a second pause between each word. Also, you can't yet use speech recognition to ask your computer questions, such as "Where on the ship is Mr. Data?"

Voice recognition The ability to interact with computers with our voices instead of with keyboards and mice. Hopefully, we won't have to wait until the Starship Enterprise flies before voice recognition becomes practical.

The problem is that we all know the eventual end point of voice recognition—Star Trek-level recognition. That means the current generation of voice recognition software already seems out of date while we wait for Voice Recognition: The Next Generation.

However, voice recognition with those capabilities takes a lot of computing power and some software technology that doesn't yet exist. It's coming and it's coming quickly.

This potentially means a lot for multimedia. After all, multimedia is interactive. Wouldn't it be great to play Myst or any other interactive game with your voice instead of with clumsy keyboards, mice, and joysticks? I thought you'd agree.

The Virtual Reality Information Superhighway

This is the ultra-mega buzzword section. The idea is to cover some of the currently popular buzzwords that we haven't yet discussed and to apply them to multimedia. Here goes.

Virtual reality is, by definition, multimedia. By using special hardware and software, it places you in the middle of the action. For example, instead of just playing a game on-screen in which you fly a jet, with virtual reality you actually feel like you are flying the jet. For you Star Trek fans, virtual reality is a primitive version of a holodeck.

Besides playing games, there are many business-like applications for virtual reality. For example, instead of creating a 3-D animation of a home floor plan, you can use virtual reality to literally walk through a life-size representation of the house. Pilots can practice with virtual reality-enhanced simulators and heart surgeons can practice experimental procedures before actually doing them—a terrific idea from the patient's point of view.

Virtual reality Virtual reality uses special hardware and software to make you feel you are in the midst of the action. Still a novelty, over the next few years, virtual reality should become more realistic and more accessible.

Virtual reality still is something of a novelty. There are virtual reality arcade games and some specialized serious virtual reality applications. However, the graphics still are relatively primitive, and the hardware, such as gloves and visors you wear to create the virtual reality effect, are still clumsy.

Not surprisingly, you can expect all of these shortcomings to be addressed in the coming months and years. When they are addressed, expect virtual reality to become a part of your multimedia life—perhaps even a big part. This is because virtual reality is part of the information superhighway, which is the mythical method by which we have access, through our computers, televisions, or both, to all the information in the universe. This information can range from the total contents of every library to reruns of "Leave It To Beaver," which we can view whenever we want.

At this writing, the reality of the information superhighway consists of the Internet: an international, chaotic, relatively ungoverned computer network composed of thousands of other interconnected computer networks. Being on the Internet is, indeed, an awesome experience. While difficult to navigate, its sheer size and the volume and variety of the information on the "net" are staggering.

What does this have to do with multimedia? Right now, you can *net surf* to find multimedia files like videos and sound files, but that isn't particularly special. Net surfing refers to the act of hopping willy-nilly from one part of the Internet to another. (Techies like to call it "exploring." For most beginners, though, it's more like hopping willy-nilly.) Net surfing is the information superhighway version of channel surfing on television and is a real hot buzzword, with a lot of people claiming that they do it.

The eventual goal is to make multimedia available directly through the Internet or whatever we call the information superhighway in the future. This means, for example, you could log onto a computer run by a multimedia company and experience their multimedia first-hand instead of loading a CD-ROM.

This is a wonderful dream, and I have no doubt it someday will come true. Here's the short-term problem: think about how slow multimedia can be on your current CD-ROM drive. Then think about using multimedia over the Internet, in which communications can be many times slower and more error-prone than your CD-ROM drive. The speed at which we communicate with the net will have to increase many times over before this can happen.

SPEAK LIKE A GEEK

Internet (a.k.a the net) The Internet is a chaotic, loosely governed international computer network. The sheer size, volume, and variety of information on the net is incredible.

SPEAK LIKE A GEEK

Net surfing The act of exploring different parts of the global Internet. Net surfing has a lot of status in the Yuppie world and, thankfully, is a heck of a lot cheaper than a BMW.

TECHNO NERD TEACHES...

Actually, the thought of unlimited multimedia on the information superhighway gives me the all-overs. I have nightmares about buckling myself into my chair in front of my monitor, plugging the IV into my hand, and getting lost for days and weeks at a time. All told, a scary fantasy.

The Least You Need to Know

Technology marches on. In this chapter, we discussed many of the trends to look for in multimedia in both the short term and the long term. Specifically, you learned:

- ☛ CD-ROM drives are becoming standard equipment in the new generation of PCs, which should increase the number of multimedia titles available and decrease prices.

- ☛ Creating a CD-ROM is a more attainable goal for companies.

- ☛ Sound and video will improve with advances in sound boards and with tighter and faster video compression.

- ☛ Voice recognition will eventually improve the way we interact with multimedia applications.

- ☛ Virtual reality and the information superhighway will impact on multimedia, but not for a few years.

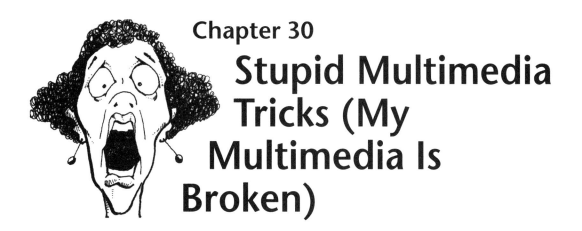

Chapter 30

Stupid Multimedia Tricks (My Multimedia Is Broken)

In This Chapter

- ☞ Those *&^% IRQs again
- ☞ MIDI won't play
- ☞ Things that look bad

It's not always that easy. I've used that expression several times in this book, and it seems to fit when it comes to making multimedia work on your PC.

Multimedia requires a complex set of software and hardware to work together in synch. There are add-in boards for your CD-ROM drive and for sound. There are software drivers for your drive and for sound plus a wide variety of other items, such as for playing video. All of these must not only co-exist among themselves, but also must work with other boards and software that have nothing to do with multimedia. That's why it's not always easy.

In this chapter, we discuss some of the common problems that occur when playing multimedia and provide some help with solving them. This isn't a comprehensive list of problems, but you'll be surprised at how frequently the things we discuss in this chapter crop up.

We'll start with the worst, first: Either your whole *&^% computer doesn't work, or a specific element of multimedia doesn't work.

Crash and Go Boom

I hate it when this happens: Either my computer doesn't start, or if it does start, it crashes when I try to do something. Or one part of the system doesn't work, like the CD-ROM drive or the sound board.

Chances are that the problem has one of four causes:

☞ Your expansion card isn't firmly seated in its slot in your computer.

☞ An IRQ conflict.

☞ A DMA channel conflict.

☞ A base I/O address conflict.

If your expansion card wasn't seated properly, chances are that you didn't tighten it down. Before you insert a card into a slot for the first time, you must remove a little metal plate that covers the back of your computer where the slot is. If you use the same screw that tightened down the plate to tighten down the expansion board, you shouldn't have to reseat the board.

This list assumes, of course, that there's not something more dramatically wrong with your computer, such as can occur when you accidentally spill your coffee into the computer when you install your CD-ROM drive.

It's good news if your expansion card isn't firmly seated in your computer. Turn the computer off, pop the top, and firmly press down on each card. If one pops into place, you've found your problem. Since this is such an easy solution, when something goes wrong, try it first.

The bad news is that the other three problems can be frustrating to solve. Here, though, are a few hints.

☞ IRQ conflicts can cause crashes at most any time. And, of course, they can prevent your expansion cards from functioning. If you crash soon after starting your computer, or if you crash when you first try to use an expansion card, check for IRQ conflicts first.

☞ DMA conflicts tend to be the least serious. That is, they can result in an expansion card not functioning correctly, but they usually don't cause start-up malfunctions or total crashes. Usually.

☞ Base I/O address conflicts also typically result in expansion cards that don't work. However, they also can result in a computer that, after starting up, suddenly shuts down and begins the start-up process again.

The basic drill for resolving these conflicts is to use a diagnostic utility, such as Microsoft Diagnostics, to determine which IRQs and base I/O addresses are in use. Then read the user's manual for your expansion cards to determine how to change settings.

Ah, if it were only that easy. Refer to Chapters 13, 14 and 15 for more information about installing your hardware and dealing with these three types of conflicts.

This Sounds Bad

Newcomers to multimedia who are on a tight budget often make the mistake of buying 8-bit sound cards. While these cards aren't widely sold any more, the fact that they are dirt cheap makes them very tempting.

Well, there's a reason why 8-bit sound cards are so cheap—they're outdated technology. While 8-bit sound cards sound okay for voice narrations, they sound like—oops, I almost said a bad word—they sound bad for music. So if you have an 8-bit sound card and don't like the music, there's not much you can do about it except upgrade to a 16-bit card.

If you have a 16-bit sound card and music still sounds bad, the leading suspect (other than a malfunction on your sound card) is your speakers. PC speakers are an area in which it is particularly easy to be a cheapskate. It's easy to imagine spending hundreds or even thousands of dollars for speakers for your stereo system, but it's hard to imagine spending much money for PC speakers.

TECHNO NERD TEACHES...

True confession: I'm still using my first PC speakers and they are something less than stellar. When I first upgraded my PC to a multimedia system, I succumbed to the cheapskate bug when it came to speakers. My speakers are okay with synthesized MIDI music, but for every other type of music, they are poor. The extra fifty bucks I would have spent for better speakers would be long forgotten by now, but I am reminded of my bad decision every time I listen to music.

The solution to this problem is obvious: Save your pennies and buy a good set of PC speakers.

Don't Give Me Any Static

Another frustrating problem regarding sound quality is static. Chances are that one of the following is to blame:

☞ A faulty recording. The obvious solution is to try another sound file. If the other file works fine, the problem was with the first file.

☞ The speakers aren't firmly plugged into the back of your sound card. This is an easy problem to check for and correct.

☞ The speaker wires are frayed. This is a hard problem to check for because the wires are hidden by their plastic casing. Try headphones and see if you still hear static. If not, you'll have to install new speaker wires.

☞ Other electronic devices inside your PC, such as your video adapter, are interfering with your sound card. Try moving your sound card as far away from other expansion cards, particularly your video adapter, as possible.

☞ You have a faulty sound card. If this is the case, you're likely to get static on every MIDI and WAV file that plays; you may also hear humming or other inappropriate electronic sounds.

One Works, the Other Doesn't

Here's a frustrating problem: Your Windows system plays WAV files just fine, but it either doesn't play MIDI at all, or it plays MIDI sometimes and not other times. This latter problem had me stumped for months before somebody offhandedly suggested the simple solution, which I'll tell you about shortly.

In either case, open your Windows Control Panel and click on the Drivers icon. The drivers dialog box, discussed in several sections of this book, appears.

First, make sure that you have a MIDI driver loaded. The name of your MIDI driver is hard to predict, but chances are it includes one of the following words:

- ☛ MIDI. Note, however, that you must not delete the driver called MIDI Mapper. This serves another purpose, which we will discuss a bit later.

- ☛ Voyetra, which is the name of a company that does a lot of sound-related stuff.

- ☛ FM Synthesis, which describes the process of creating MIDI music.

- ☛ OPL-3 or OPL-4. These are the trade names of two commonly used FM synthesis chips used by sound cards.

If you don't have a MIDI driver loaded and don't know where to get one, contact your sound card vendor's technical support department. They should take care of you.

If you have two MIDI drivers loaded, they may be conflicting with each other. That was the problem I encountered when MIDI worked sometimes, but not other times.

To solve this problem, delete one of the MIDI sound drivers by following these two easy steps:

1. Highlight the driver you want to delete in the Drivers dialog box.

2. Click on the **Remove** button.

The difficulty with this solution is that it often is difficult to know where each MIDI driver came from, particularly if you do a lot of work with multimedia. As a result, it's hard to know which MIDI driver you should keep. Sorry, but you'll have to make your best guess.

Even after deleting the extra driver, MIDI still might not work. If that's the case, it's time to become acquainted with MIDI Mapper, a dialog box you access from the Windows Control Panel. In simple terms, MIDI Mapper sets the rules for how Windows interacts with MIDI. You can have multiple setups for different types of MIDI usage, which, for our purposes, means that, if MIDI still doesn't work after deleting a duplicate MIDI driver, your current MIDI setup probably refers to the deleted driver. If the driver your MIDI setup file expects to use isn't there, it can't play MIDI.

Midi Mapper.

To solve this problem:

1. Activate the **Setups** radio button in the MIDI Mapper if it isn't already activated.

2. In the Name drop-down list, make a selection other than the currently loaded set up.

3. Click on **Close** and try playing a MIDI file.

If your MIDI file plays correctly, then we can assume that we have successfully replaced the setup that reflected the deleted MIDI driver with one that reflects the MIDI driver you still are using. Problem solved.

If it doesn't play correctly:

1. If possible, select a setup that is similar to the name of your remaining MIDI driver.

2. Click on the **Edit** button. You will see the MIDI Setup dialog box for the setup you selected. Notice that there is a column named Port Name. A good guess is that the item listed in this row for all MIDI channels refers to the driver you deleted.

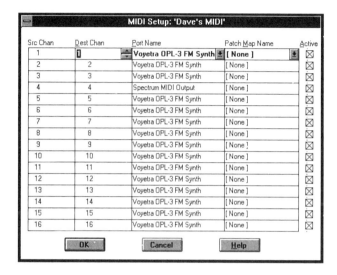

The MIDI Setup dialog box.

3. For each channel, click on the **Port Name** box, which turns into a drop-down list. From the drop-down list, select the name that resembles the name of the MIDI driver you kept.

4. Make sure you've activated the **Active** check box for each channel.

5. Click the **OK** button, then the **Close** button in the MIDI Mapper dialog box.

Losing That CD-ROM Spin

Your CD-ROM drive should be spinning away happily. If it's not, chances are it's suffering from one of two maladies:

☛ The drive is broken.

☛ You've been visited by the Terrible Trio: DMA channel, IRQ, or base I/O address conflicts.

If the drive is broken, holler at the vendor or the person who sold it to you. If the problem is one of the Terrible Trio, read the documentation for the CD-ROM interface, and Chapters 13, 14, and 15 of this book.

Sometimes, however, the drive will stop working or work sporadically, and the problem won't be a conflict or a broken drive. The problem may be that the drive isn't properly connected to its power source. You could also have a problem with bad cables.

This is easy to solve for external drives since they plug into a standard electrical socket. Simply make sure the power cable is firmly seated at both ends. For internal drives, you'll have to pop the top of your PC and go rooting around. Chapter 15 described plugging internal drives into your computer's power supply. Make sure all connections are firm.

You Call This a Video?

This section discusses common problems for video, animations, and still images. Video and animations first.

Most multimedia applications install the drivers needed to show videos and animations contained in the application. Since this happens automatically behind the scenes, chances are that you will be able to play video and animations without difficulties. If they don't play, reinstall your application; that should take care of the problem.

However, that doesn't mean you'll like what you see. That's because many PCs simply aren't powerful enough to play video and animation well.

Common problems resulting from running video and animation on underpowered PCs include clips that:

- Are herky-jerky.
- Have blotchy colors that make it hard to see.
- Take a long time to load, and pause from time to time.

If these problems irritate you, join the club. As you'll recall from Chapter 10, the Multimedia PC Standard supposedly provides guidance about what type of PC you should buy in order to effectively run multimedia applications, but the reality is that PCs adhering to this standard are inadequate for playing video and animation the way they should be played.

If you're stuck with a too-slow-for-video PC, there still are some things you can do to improve video performance. They'll cost you some money, but they won't cost you as much as a new PC. These include:

- ☞ Adding RAM to your system. When I increased the RAM from 8MB to 16MB on my old 33MHz 486, video performance improved dramatically. Adding enough RAM to make a difference, however, can be expensive.

- ☞ Opening the Windows Control Panel, opening the Drivers dialog box, and selecting **[MCI] Microsoft Video for Windows**. If you uncheck **Skip video frames if behind**, you may get choppy audio, but you may see improved video playback.

- ☞ If you have a video card with 1MB of on-board RAM, add another megabyte.

- ☞ If you have an old, clunky video card, get a new rocket-ship video card. Upgrading your video card is the most effective way to eliminate blotchiness and make videos run smoother.

- ☞ Use a disk cache for your CD-ROM drive. If you already use a disk cache, see if you can make the cache larger. Read Chapter 8 for more information about disk caches.

A Bad Image

Junky-looking images aren't pleasant, but they often are easy to correct. True, upgrading your video adapter will help in many cases. However, typically the problem is that the conditions in which the image was captured were different from the conditions in which you are viewing it.

Specifically, images will look bad if:

☛ The image has more color depth than you currently are displaying on-screen. For example, you may be displaying only 16 colors
on-screen, but the image was captured with 256 or more colors.

With this problem, the image contains colors that your system, as
you've currently configured it, can't display. If that's the case,
you'll barely be able to make out what the image is.

☛ The image was captured at a higher resolution than you currently
are displaying. If that's the case, and if you have enough color
depth, you should get a decent idea of what the image is, but it
will look blotchy and won't be pleasant to view.

Most recent video adapters come with software than enables you to
change on-screen resolution and color depth. (Many less-expensive adapters do not have any such software.) Using this utility should solve your
problem. Read the documentation that came with your video adapter for
more information about how to do this.

The Least You Need to Know

☞ DMA channel, IRQ, or base I/O address conflicts are prime suspects in any malfunction involving an expansion board. This includes faulty video or audio, or a nonfunctional CD-ROM drive.

☞ Another prime suspect is that the board isn't properly seated in your PC's motherboard.

☞ Many computers—even MPC Level 2 computers— simply aren't powerful enough to play video and animation well. Common problems include herky-jerky videos and sporadic pauses.

☞ Short of buying a new PC, you can improve the display of videos and animations by adding RAM, using a larger disk cache or upgrading your video card.

☞ If still images don't appear clearly, you may be displaying them at either a lower color depth or a lower resolution than those in which the images were captured. Correct that problem by increasing your on-screen resolution or color depth with the utility that came with your video adapter.

OK people, move it along. Nothing to see here.

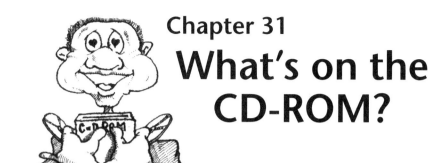

Chapter 31
What's on the CD-ROM?

In This Chapter

- ☛ How to see what's on the disc
- ☛ Installing the applications
- ☛ Playing, playing, playing

The CD-ROM that comes with this book is packed with all sorts of cool multimedia applications, files, and games. There is so much on the disc that you'll very likely feel overwhelmed if you try to figure it out for yourself. Read this chapter and you'll reduce your level of frustration to the minimum.

First, I'll tell you how to look at the disc's contents in Windows File Manager. (That's right, *Windows*. The disc doesn't work on a Mac.) Then, we'll run through each program, one at a time. I'll tell you what the application does and how to install it. I'll also tell you the name of the *readme file* that will help you figure out how to use the application.

Readme file   A *readme file* is just what it sounds like: it's a data file you should read to get important information. Usually, the file will have an obvious name, like README.TXT or even README.1ST. You can open the file in a word processor, read it, and even print it out for future reference.

Ready? Let's begin by setting up. Carefully remove the disc from the back of the book, then insert it in the CD-ROM drive (as described in Chapter 18). If you know how to use Windows File Manager, start it up, and skip to the next section. If you're a Windows novice, read the next section before you read the rest of the chapter.

Using Windows File Manager

To start File Manager from Program Manager, follow these steps:

1. Double-click on the **Main** program group icon. It opens into a window.

2. Double-click on the **File Manager** program icon. File Manager starts, and the window shown in the following figure appears on-screen.

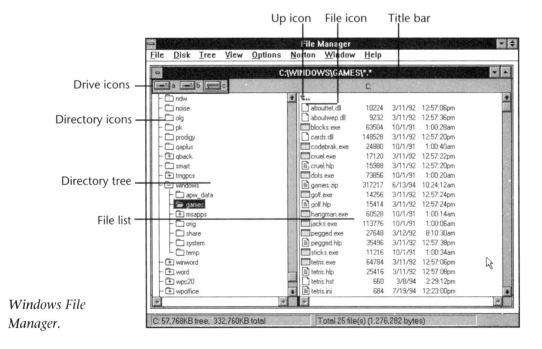

Windows File Manager.

As you can see, the File Manager window has many parts. You should familiarize yourself with the following elements:

Drive icons   The icons in the top left corner of the window which represent your hard drive, floppy drives, and CD-ROM drive (if you have one). The selected drive has an outline around it.

Directory tree   The list of directories that runs down the left side of the window. The selected directory appears highlighted.

Directory icons   The small pictures that look like folders next to each directory name. If a directory icon includes a plus sign (+), that means it contains subdirectories. If the icon includes a minus sign (–), that means you can see its subdirectories in the directory list.

File list   The right-hand section of the window lists all the files in the current directory (the one that's selected in the directory tree). Selected files appear highlighted.

File icons   The small pictures next to the file names. An icon that looks like a program group (a rectangular icon) means the file is executable. An icon that looks like a dog-eared document means the file is a data file that's used by a program.

Up icon   Located in the file list, you click on this icon to go to the parent directory.

Window title bar   This tells you the drive and directory of the current window.

Selecting Drives, Directories, and Files

When you first open File Manager, the window displays the contents of the root directory of your hard drive. (You can tell it's your hard drive by looking at the window's title bar.) However, your root directory may not be the one you want to look at. You need to tell File Manager which drive, directories, and files you want to work with by *selecting* them.

Changing Drives

To see a list of the CD-ROM's contents, you have to *select* the drive. To do this, click on the appropriate drive icon. (You can also hold down **Ctrl** and press the letter of the drive.) The current window changes to display the contents of the new drive.

If you want to show the contents of the CD-ROM in an additional window—in other words, have two windows on-screen at once—double-click on the appropriate drive icon. The new window will cover up part of the original window; select **Tile** from the **Window** menu so you can see them both. The following figure shows an example of tiled windows.

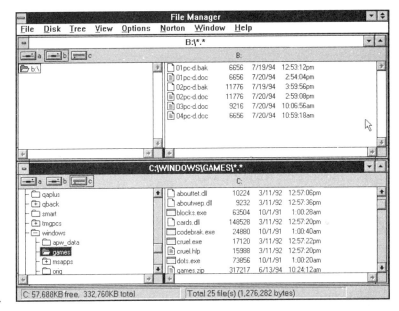

Two windows are open, displaying the contents of two drives.

Selecting Directories and Files

Once you have the right drive window open, you need to select the directory you want to work with. If it is not showing in the directory tree on the left side of the window, use the scroll bars to scroll down to it. When you see the directory you want, click on it. The selected directory's files appear in the file list on the right side of the window.

If you're looking for a subdirectory and you don't see it in the directory tree, it is probably hidden under its parent directory. To *expand* a directory, double-click on the parent directory's icon. Its subdirectories will appear (as shown in the preceding figure). Click on the subdirectory you want, and its file appears in the file list.

If subdirectories appear in the directory tree and you don't want them to, double-click on the parent directory again. This action *collapses* the directory and hides the subdirectories.

To select a file, just click on its icon. If you *double-click* on an executable file's icon, File Manager will run the program. If you double-click on a file that is *associated* with a certain program, File Manager will start that program and open the file you double-clicked on.

To select multiple files, you use a combination of the mouse and the keyboard. To select contiguous files (files that are next to each other), click on the first file, then hold down the **Shift** key and click on the last file. The two files you clicked on and all the files in between will be highlighted.

To select noncontiguous multiple files (files that are not next to each other in the file list), hold down the **Ctrl** key while clicking each file you want.

You can also use a combination of the Ctrl and Shift keys to select files. For example, say you want to select six files. Four of them are next to each other, but two of them are in a different part of the file list. You click on the first file in the group of four, then hold down the Shift key and click on the last file in that group. Then, with the group of four highlighted, you hold down the Ctrl key and click on the remaining two files. You have selected all six files.

A **file association** is a special link between files with a certain extension and the program that runs them. For example, my .DOC files are associated with Microsoft Word for Windows. If I double-clicked on MYPAPER.DOC in File Manager, Word for Windows would start, and MYPAPER.DOC would automatically open.

Creating a New Directory

Before you create a new directory, you need to decide where you want it. File Manager will create the new directory under the directory that's selected in the directory tree. For example, if you want to create a subdirectory called MYWORK and put it under your 1-2-3 for Windows directory, you select the 1-2-3 for Windows directory in the directory tree. If you want to create a new directory under the root directory, select the root directory at the top of the list.

Once you have the right directory selected in the directory tree, pull down the **File** menu and select **Create Directory**. The Create Directory dialog box appears, enabling you to enter the name of the new directory. (Remember that directory names can be up to eight characters long and must follow DOS naming rules.) Click **OK** after you enter the name, and the new directory appears in the directory tree.

Moving and Copying Files and Directories

When moving and copying files, it's a good idea to have two windows open on-screen. You can scroll the contents of the first screen to find the files you want to move or copy, then you can scroll the contents of the second screen to find the destination directory. (Refer to the "Changing Drives" section for information on opening additional windows.)

Select the files you want to move, then hold down the **Alt** key and drag the files to the new directory in the directory tree (see the following figure). A warning box appears on-screen, asking you if you are sure you want to move the selected files. Click on the **Yes** button to move the files.

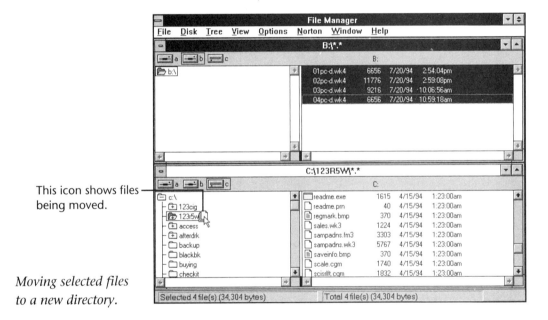

This icon shows files being moved.

Moving selected files to a new directory.

If you want to copy some files to a different directory, select them, then hold down the **Ctrl** key and drag the files to the new directory in the directory tree. A warning box appears on-screen, asking you if you're sure you want to copy the files. Click on the **Yes** button.

For example, say you want to copy the files in the JAZZ subdirectory of the GAMEDEMO directory on the CD-ROM to your hard drive. With both drives' contents showing on-screen, select the files in the JAZZ subdirectory, and then hold down the **Ctrl** key and drag the file to the **C:** icon in the directory tree of your hard drive. A dialog box appears, asking if you want to copy the file. Click **Yes**, and the file is copied.

When moving and copying files, your changes may not appear on-screen right away. If you don't see your files, press the **F5** key. File Manager *refreshes* (updates) the current window.

Now that you know your way around File Manager and can select directories and files and run programs, let's dig into the good stuff.

Cranking Up the Sound

There are tons of cool waveform and MIDI files on this CD-ROM (they're in the SOUNDS directory). You can listen to them with a program called BoomBox, or with Media Player, the multimedia applet that came with Windows. If you want, you can edit the .WAV files and even create your own with the Cool Waveform Editor. We'll discuss all of them in this section.

BoomBox

BoomBox is a great little program for listening to .WAV files and assigning them to Windows events. To run the program, first double-click on the **PLAYERS** directory icon to expand the directory, then double-click on the **BOOMBOX** subdirectory. Its files will appear in the file list. Double-click on **BOOMBOX.EXE**.

If you just want to hear a .WAV file, search through the directories in the lower left corner of the window for the .WAV file you want. (There are many .WAV files in the CD-ROM's WAV directory.) Then, select the file (from the Wave Files list from the upper right corner of the window), and click the **Play** button. If your sound card and drivers are configured correctly, BoomBox plays the file. You can assign sounds to Windows events by selecting the event in the upper left box and selecting the sound you want in the upper right box. To get help for BoomBox, use the on-line help. You can also look at the BOOMBOX.TXT file in a word processor. To exit BoomBox, click on the **Exit** button.

Cool WaveForm Editor

This is a more powerful program than BoomBox. Not only can you play files, you can edit them and record them. You can play any of the .WAV or .MID files (if you have a sound card) on the CD-ROM with this program. There are many little gizmos and doodads in this program; your best bet is to use the on-line help to figure it out. I can't go into all the details here.

To run the Cool WaveForm Editor, first open the **PLAYERS** directory, then copy the **COOL** subdirectory to your hard drive. Then switch to your hard drive and double-click on **COOL.EXE**. The program starts, and you can open a .WAV file (from the WAV subdirectory) or record your own (provided that you have the proper equipment). Play around in the program a little while. If you get stuck, use the on-line help. When you're ready to quit, select **Exit** from the **File** menu.

Media Player

If you just want a simple program to listen to sound files, use Windows Media Player. It's easy. Exit File Manager if necessary (by selecting **File Exit**), then open the **Accessories** group window. Double-click on the **Media Player** icon. A small window displays on-screen. You can open a file and play it, or you can record your own sounds. For help with Media Player, see your Windows documentation or use the on-line help.

Make sure you have the VBRUN300.DLL file in your Windows directory or this program won't run. If you look in the Windows directory and it isn't there, don't panic. It's on the CD-ROM; you can copy it to your Windows directory.

Surf's Up!

There's a fabulous program in the SURFSUP subdirectory of the SOUNDS directory called Surf's Up! With it, you can attach sounds (.WAV files) to *icons.*

Before you can run the program, you have to set it up right. First, copy the SURFSUP.EXE file to its own directory (call it SURFSUP) in the root directory of your hard drive. Then, copy all the other files to your C:\WINDOWS directory. To run the program from File Manager, double-click on

SURFSUP.EXE in the **SURFSUP** directory on your hard drive. Double-click on the Surf's Up! icon that appears.

If you need help with the program, read the documentation in the SURFSUP4.WRI file. To exit the program, double-click the **Control-menu box**, then click.

Video Killed the Radio Star

Surely you want more than plain old sounds on your CD-ROM. You want action, you want to be wowed, you want *video*. What you need are .AVI files (movies made with a video camera), .FLI files (animation), and .GIF files (awesome still images). This disc has loads of video files on it (in directories cleverly labeled AVI, FLI, and GIF), and several programs you can use to look at the video files.

AAPlay

AAPlay stands for Autodesk Animation PLAYer. You can play .FLI (animation) files with this program. You must run it from the DOS prompt, so exit File Manager and Windows. At the DOS prompt, switch to the CD-ROM drive and the **AAPLAY** subdirectory of the **PLAYERS** directory. Type **AAPLAY**, and you're all set. If you need help, use the AAPLAY.DOC file.

.FLI files in the AUTODESK subdirectory appear Courtesy of Autodesk.

CMORPH

This is a pretty powerful program. You basically give the program two images, and it changes one into the other. (It's much more complicated than that, but that's the gist.) You must install this program to your hard drive to run, so (in File Manager), find the CMORPH directory on the CD-ROM. Copy the whole CMORPH directory to your hard drive. To run the program, switch to your hard drive, then switch to the **CMORPH** directory and double-click on **CMORPH.EXE**. If you just want to see a demo of how the morphing works, double-click on **DEMO.BAT**. Check out the README file for help.

Microsoft Video for Windows

This is a great program for viewing video files. You should copy this to your hard drive so you have it available at all times. When you're ready to install the program, double-click on **SETUP.EXE** in the **MSVIDEO** directory. The program installs, and you'll be able to run it. Double-click on any .AVI file in the AVI directory to see the video. You can use the on-line help to figure out how to use the program.

Vidvue*

You can look at GIF files with Vidvue. Install Vidvue on your hard drive by using the SETUP.EXE file in the VIDVUE24 subdirectory of the PLAYERS directory. Then, double-click on the VIDVUE2.4 icon in the VIDVUE 2.4 program group. When the program starts, you can view a file from the GIF directory on the CD-ROM. To view the file, just double-click on the file name. When you want to return to the main window, select View Home, or click the icon that's farthest left on the icon bar. To close the program, double-click the **Control-menu box**. If you need help with this software, check the on-line help.

Would You Like to Play a Game?

There are some fabulous shareware games in the GAMEDEMO directory. You can play the games and shoot the bad guys, but you are limited to one or two levels. If you want to get the other levels of the game (and I know you will), order the real game from the owner and get a registered copy.

TECHNO NERD TEACHES...

Only use the shareware demos to try the games. If you want to play a game regularly, order a registered copy of the game from the owner/author. The people who wrote these programs spent a good deal of their time on them—if you enjoy playing them, then they deserve your money. 'Nuff said.

If you find a game you like a lot, buy it. None of the games are expensive. Here's a rundown of the games on the disc.

DOOM

Ah, DOOM. What a game. With this shareware version, you can play the entire "Knee Deep in the Dead" mission, and even access the hidden level. To play DOOM, you need to install it on your hard drive. Do that by changing to the **DOOM12** subdirectory of the **GAMEDEMO** directory in File Manager, then double-clicking the **INSTALL.BAT** file. The install program will create a directory on your hard drive called DOOMSW. You should play the game from DOS, so exit Windows and switch to the **DOOMSW** directory. Type **DOOM** and then press **Enter**; the terror begins.

For help with DOOM, use the README.EXE file in the DOOMSW directory, or use the on-line help. If you select Read This! in the opening screen, you'll get a screen full of marketing information. You don't want that, so press **Enter**, and you'll go to a new screen. It has all sorts of information about which keys to press and how to get different weapons. To exit DOOM, select **Quit Game** from the opening screen, or press **Esc**.

You might also notice a subdirectory called DOOMADON in the GAMEDEMO directory. Those are advanced levels of the game. You can't use them until you get a registered version of DOOM, so do that right away. There's a screen that shows up when you quit the game that tells you where you can get a registered copy. When you want to add the advanced levels, use the LBINST.EXE program to install the files.

There's a great book called *DOOM: Totally Unauthorized Tips & Secrets* by Robert Waring (published by Brady). You can pick it up at your local bookstore if you want to learn all the secret ins and outs of DOOM.

Jazz Jackrabbit

Jazz is a cool rabbit. He shoots turtles and flies and he eats carrots. To install Jazz Jackrabbit from File Manager, switch to the **JAZZ** subdirectory of the **GAMEDEMO** directory and double-click on **INSTALL.EXE**. (From DOS, switch to the **JAZZ** subdirectory, type **INSTALL**, and press **Enter**.) The install program will ask you which program you want to install. You just have one choice, so press **Enter** to accept it. Select the drive to install to (probably C:), and then press **Enter**. Choose the directory to install to, and then press **Enter**. If the directory does not exist, press **Y** (for Yes) when prompted to create the directory. The install program unzips the JAZZ.ZIP file and copies the files to the drive and directory you specified.

This game should be played from the DOS prompt. If you simply must play from Windows, double-click on **JAZZ.PIF** instead of JAZZ.EXE. You may still run into problems; check the HELPME.DOC file if you need help.

When you install the program, it asks if you want to read the instructions. You can press **Y**, or you can press **N** and read the instructions later. Exit the installation program and exit Windows if you haven't already. In DOS, switch to the **JAZZ** directory, type **JAZZ**, and then press **Enter**. The first time you run the game, you might need to configure your sound card with the setup program.

To play the game, choose the difficulty and the level you want (you can only choose the first one because this is shareware), and then press **Enter**. Run around and shoot things by pressing the **Spacebar**. To jump, use the **Alt** key. Read the instructions in the HELPME.DOC file for the low-down on how to play. When you're finished, press **Esc**, then select the **Quit Game** command from the menu that appears.

Epic Games

There are two different games you can install from the EPIC subdirectory of the GAMEDEMO directory. The first, OverKill, is a space mission-type of game where you shoot at aliens and other bad things. The second game is called Pinball, and it is just what it sounds like: a computerized pinball game.

These programs install similarly and have similar help systems. Let's run through it quickly. From File Manager, double-click on the **INSTALL.EXE** file in the **EPIC** subdirectory. (From DOS, switch to the **EPIC** subdirectory, type **INSTALL**, and press **Enter**.) You see an opening screen, and the install program asks you to make a choice. Since the first game is already highlighted, press **Enter**. The installation for OverKill begins.

Choose the drive to install to (probably drive C:), then press **Enter**. Choose the directory to install to, then press **Enter**. If the directory does not exist, the Epic install program asks you if you want to create it. Press **Y** for Yes. Wait a few seconds while the game installs on your hard drive. When finished, it asks if you want to look at the instructions. For now, press **N** for No. You can read the instructions in the help system later.

To install the other game (Pinball), press **2** and then press **Enter**. Choose the drive and directory like you did earlier. When finished, it asks if you want to read the instructions. Press **N** for No; you can read the instructions later if you want. Exit the install program when you finish installing. Before you try to play the games, go to the DOS prompt. (These games will probably run under Windows, but bad things can happen. You're better off just running them from DOS.)

To play OverKill, switch to the **OVERKILL** directory (if that's what you named it when you installed the game), and type **OVERKILL**. Press **Enter**, and away you go. Notice when you're making your pre-game selections that you can only choose planets 1 and 2. That's because this is shareware; to get the whole game, send away for a registered copy.

To play the game with the keyboard, use the arrow keys to move around and the **Spacebar** to fire. Just fly around and shoot everything. Run over the little red and gray pods that appear when you take out aliens. They'll give you fuel or ammo or something else that you need. To quit the game, press **Esc**. If you need help or instructions, type **HELPME** at the DOS prompt (while you're in the OVERKILL directory). Epic supplies great on-line help.

To play Pinball, switch to the **EPICPIN** directory (or whatever you named it), type **PINBALL**, and press **ENTER**. Notice that there are many different pinball machines to choose from, but you can only select **AN-DROID** in this shareware version. Buy a registered copy to get the other games. (You can see what the other games look like by selecting them, but you can't play them.) This game makes *ding-ding* and *ping* sounds like a real pinball machine.

To start the game, hold the **Spacebar** down for a couple of seconds, and then let it go. The ball shoots into the machine and the action begins. To use the flippers, press the **Spacebar** and the arrow keys. To quit the game, press **Esc**. If you need help with this game, type **HELPME** at the DOS prompt (from within the **EPICPIN** directory).

If you are having memory problems and can't run the games, check the help system for solutions. The nice people at Epic included some good suggestions under the Troubleshooting category in the help system.

I Don't Know What I'm Doing

If you try to run a program and a message appears telling you that it needs to run at the DOS prompt, exit to the DOS prompt and try running it from there. If a program doesn't start when you try to run the .EXE file, that probably means you need to install it or you need to set up a configuration. Look for a file called INSTALL.EXE or SETUP.EXE. Run one of those files to install or set up a program.

If you're having trouble running a program off the CD-ROM, try copying the program to your hard drive. If you run out of memory on your hard drive, you're on your own. I can't really help you unless I know your system. I can tell you that sometimes it helps to restart your computer, sometimes you can delete some things off your system, and sometimes you can run MEMMAKER or a similar memory maximizing program. Check your DOS documentation for more details, or get a book about memory.

Good luck!

---

*The price paid for the book and CD-ROM purchases the right to try the Shareware contained; payment to the original author is required if Shareware is used beyond the specified trial period.

VIDVUE is distributed "AS IS." Any expressed or implied warranties, including, but not limited to, warranties of merchantability and fitness for ANY use or purpose are specifically disclaimed. In no event shall the author be liable for ANY loss of profit or damage including, but not limited to special, consequential, incidental, or other damages.

Speak Like a Geek: The Complete Archive

Everybody's talking about computers and multimedia these days, but few people really know what they're talking about. This archive contains a complete glossary of important multimedia terms. So if you take this to your next party as a cheat sheet for small talk, you'll be immensely popular and admired.

32-bit operating system   A 32-bit operating system, such as the new version of Windows, can handle more information more quickly than older 16-bit systems, such as Windows 3.1. Applications developed to run in a 32-bit environment, including multimedia applications, will run much faster than you're used to.

access time   Refers to the average amount of time a drive (whether it is a floppy drive, hard drive or CD-ROM drive) takes to find data and start reading it from a disc. The lower the disc access time, the faster the disc responds to your requests to read data.

animation   A series of still images, such as drawings and other nonphotographic images, shown in rapid succession to create the sense of motion. Animations can be like coyotes chasing roadrunners or they can be more mundane.

ASCII   A near-universal text file; a text file that has no special formatting like boldface type or different type sizes.

Audio/Video Interleave (AVI)   The format for video files created by the Microsoft Video for Windows standard.

buffer   A section of memory that temporarily stores information until your PC can process it. Many different applications use buffers, but for our purposes, we're talking about buffers built into CD-ROM drives. An adequate buffer is important to keep information flowing smoothly from the drive to the computer.

bundle   Refers to the vendor's practice of enabling you to buy multiple items at the same time. In a multimedia upgrade bundle, for example, you get at least a CD-ROM drive and a sound card. You also might get a CD-ROM interface, discs, and all sorts of other goodies.

CD-ROM drive   The drive in which you use CD-ROMs. This is similar to using floppy drives that use floppy disks.

CD-ROM interface   Plugs into your computer's motherboard. You connect your CD-ROM drive to the interface and the interface, in turn, allows the computer to read and understand data from a CD-ROM. Like other items you plug into your computer's motherboard, CD-ROM interfaces are sometimes referred to as adapters or cards.

CD-ROM XA   Stands for CD-ROM Extended Architecture. A format that makes it easy for multimedia developers to combine more than one medium, such as still images and sound, relatively seamlessly. However, it requires a special CD-ROM adapter card that's rare right now.

CD-ROMs   CD-ROMs look and, in many ways, act like audio CDs. However, CD-ROMs store computerized information. Because of their relatively large storage capacity, CD-ROMs have become the most popular medium for storing multimedia applications.

central processing unit (CPU)   The main computing chip in your computer. It is involved in virtually every computing operation from calculating numbers to displaying information on-screen.

clip media   Refers to the multimedia version of clip art. Clip media are images (and also animation, video, and sound) that you acquire from various sources that you can insert in your multimedia presentations.

codec   Stands for compression/decompression. The various codec schemes provide methods for compressing videos for storage and uncompressing them when they are played.

color depth   Refers to the number of colors that can appear on-screen or in an image at the same time.

compression   Changes an image file so that it takes less disk space. Usually, you need a special utility to compress and decompress files, although there are some image formats that do this automatically.

daisychain   Several SCSI devices that are connected by cables to each other and to your computer.

data transfer rate   The amount of information that a CD-ROM drive can read and send on to the computer for processing in a second. The data transfer rate is measured in kilobytes per second.

Dave's best-use concept   This isn't an official concept that you'll find in a book (other than this one). It does, however, reflect my rather (un)startling idea that you create the most effective presentations by using the appropriate authoring tools and media.

digital signal processor (DSP)   A DSP is a type of chip that can offload the processing of specific tasks, such as processing complex sounds, from your computer's central processing unit. This prevents complex sounds from bogging down your computer.

digitized and analog sounds   Normally, sounds are *analog*—they consist of sound waves. The different tones are, essentially, peaks and valleys in the wave. However, computers can't understand and play sound waves. Digitized sounds, then, are sounds contained in files that computers can read and play back.

DIP switches   A series of on-off switches you use to change settings for things, such as IRQs and DMAs. Typically, you use a small device like a pen point to move the switches.

disk cache   A utility program that stores recently-used information in your computer's random-access memory (RAM). This speeds up drives because accessing data from RAM is faster than accessing it from a mechanical device, such as a CD-ROM drive. Not all disk cache utilities work with CD-ROM drives, but those that do also speed up your hard drive.

disc caddy   A disc caddy is a plastic housing that holds the CD-ROM. You place the disc in the caddy, then place the caddy into the drive.

DMA   Stands for direct memory address. It is the channel through which information moves from devices, such as your CD-ROM interface to your computer's random-access memory (RAM). As with IRQs, you should avoid having more than one device accessing a single DMA channel.

dot pitch   Refers to the distance between on-screen pixels. The tighter the dot pitch, the crisper the image. It isn't advisable to buy a monitor with a dot pitch of more than .28mm.

dreck   Junk, crapola, garbage. Or more politely, something of inferior quality.

drive bay   An area in your PC into which you insert a drive. You can insert a floppy drive, hard drive, or internal CD-ROM drive into a drive bay.

driver   A program that tells your computer how to communicate with a peripheral, such as a CD-ROM drive. There are many mentions of drivers in this book since multimedia requires extensive use of drivers in order to work properly.

dropping frames   When your video card and PC can't handle the demands of video, they drop frames, or simply refuse to play some frames. The result is herky-jerky video. This can occur during capture, but also during playback if, for example, your video system isn't fast enough.

edutainment   An overused word that describes multimedia applications that are both fun and educational.

electronic books   Electronic versions of books. Electronic books are most popular in business, where they replace formerly paper-bound books, such as policy and procedure manuals and other books that gather dust on office bookshelves.

expansion slot   A slot on your computer's motherboard into which you insert add-in cards, such as a sound card or a CD-ROM interface. Once inserted, the cards can work along with other components of your computer.

exporting   The process of saving a file in a different file format.

floptical   A "floptical" disc is a rewritable optical disc. They never caught on as a substitute for magnetic media because they are slower and more expensive.

frames per second (fps)   Also sometimes called the frame rate, frames per second is the rate at which videos and animations are played. The higher the frame rate, the smoother the playback.

graphical user interface   Also called a GUI and pronounced "GOO-ey"; uses things, such as icons and dialog boxes, for navigation. This is easier than issuing text-based commands, as DOS programs require.

hybrid discs   A hybrid CD-ROM that works on both Macintosh and Windows machines.

hyperlinks   A method of linking one bit of information to related information. When you select a hyperlink, typically by clicking on it, you immediately go to the related information. Hyperlinks are particularly useful for educational and reference works because they enable you to follow a train of thought or to explore information serendipitously.

I/O port address   The I/O port address is the specific segment of memory that a device, such as a CD-ROM interface, uses. Conflicts and system crashes occur when more than one device tries to use the same I/O port address.

if-then-else statement   An if-then-else statement is the part of a programming language that tells the program what to do based on what the user decides.

image conversion software   Converts image files in one format to other formats. This is essential if your multimedia authoring tool can't import the image in its original format.

image editing software   Enables you to fine-tune the colors and on-screen appearance of photographs and other images. It also enables you to add special effects to images.

image format   The proprietary file format for an image. There are about forty different formats for images, although only a few of them are commonly used.

image   Image refers to a nonmoving picture. In multimedia, that picture can be anything from a full-color photograph to blow-apart technical diagrams, or even stick figures and line drawings.

importing   The process of bringing the contents of one computer file into another computer file of a different format.

information superhighway   A mythical mega-network that will give us access, through our computers, televisions, or both, to all the information in the universe. It's also a case in which everybody's talking, but few know what they're talking about.

interactive multimedia   Lets you interact with the application or presentation to get the specific information you want. A simple example is a multimedia training program that asks you to click your mouse on one of several buttons, each of which takes you to a different topic.

Internet (a.k.a. the net)   The Internet is a chaotic, loosely governed international computer network. The sheer size, volume, and variety of information on the net are incredible.

IRQ   Stands for *interrupt request*. It is a method of briefly interrupting other computer processes so that information can flow from your CD-ROM interface, sound card, or from any other adapter to other parts of your computer system. If two devices have the same IRQ address, your system can crash.

ISO 9660   The ISO 9660 standard was one of the first standards set for the format of CD-ROMs. It helps determine the way information is placed on a disc and provides standardized tools that enable the CD-ROM drive to find that information. Since virtually all CD-ROMs for PCs support this standard, it is essential that your CD-ROM drive support it also.

jump   In multimedia, a jump refers to the act of moving via hypermedia links from one piece of information to another.

jumpers   Little devices on your expansion boards that you use to change settings for things like IRQs and DMA channels. They consist of a row of pins that is usually two pins wide, and plastic/metal coverings for the pins. The order in which pin pairs are covered or not covered determines the setting.

keyword searches   Keyword searches are text searches that only examine specially designated words called keywords. Keywords are words that represent entire topics.

kilohertz (KHz)   The number of actions per second a device takes, measured in thousands. In this case, it refers to the number of sound samples a sound board uses per second. The more sound samples used, the more realistic the sound quality.

kiosk presentation   A multimedia presentation placed in a public place, such as an office lobby. An example of a kiosk presentation in a lobby would contain information about your organization, its products, and employees.

mail-order vendor   Buying "mail order" usually means purchasing an item over the phone and having it delivered to your home address or business.

Media Player   A utility that comes with Windows which enables you to play virtually all types of multimedia clips. You load it by double-clicking on its icon in the Accessories program group in Windows Program Manager.

media   Refers to the method used to deliver information. Media is plural; medium is the singular form. Types of media described in this book include text, video, still images, sound, and animation.

megahertz (MHz)   Measures how frequently something happens. However, this isn't like once a week, or annually. Rather, megahertz refers to how many millions of times per second something happens. With computers, it refers to how many millions of instructions, or tidbits of your computer program, the system can process per second.

MIDI   Stands for Musical Instrument Digital Interface. It is a type of music data file created with a computer that you can play through virtually all PC sound cards.

morphing   An effect in which one thing changes on-screen into another. The effect can be changing one person's face into another, or a dog into a cat.

motherboard   The motherboard is the technical hub for your computer. It contains the basic hardware and software needed to run your computer. For example, located on the motherboard are random-access memory (RAM) chips and your computer's central processing unit, which is the main chip that runs your computer.

MPC   Stands for Multimedia Personal Computer, which is a series of informal standards stating the minimum hardware and software requirements for a PC running multimedia applications. Developed by a group of vendors called the Multimedia Marketing Council, the first MPC standard was inadequate for many multimedia applications. The most recent MPC standard, called MPC Level 2, more accurately provides guidance about the sort of equipment you need for multimedia, but still is underpowered for some applications.

MSCDEX   MSCDEX stands for Microsoft CD Extensions. This is a program that comes with DOS and is required to integrate your CD-ROM drive into your DOS system. Usually, you will load MSCDEX automatically from your AUTOEXEC.BAT file.

multimedia authoring tools   Programs you use to create multimedia applications. They can be as simple as your normal word processor. However, when multimedia mavens talk about authoring tools, they usually are referring to programs that specialize in creating multimedia.

multimedia upgrade kit   A collection of the multimedia components needed to create a multimedia PC. Upgrade kits always include a CD-ROM drive and a sound board. They often also include a CD-ROM interface and speakers.

net surfing   The act of exploring different parts of the global Internet. Net surfing has a lot of status in the Yuppie world and, thankfully, is a heck of a lot cheaper than a BMW.

object linking and embedding (OLE)   OLE is a Windows capability that enables you to embed one file, such as a multimedia file, within another file. When you click on the embedded object, Windows loads the program that created the object behind the scenes. It then plays or displays the object.

on-line services   Provide a universe of information services and means of communicating. They also serve as an almost limitless source of text that you can collect and use in multimedia applications. Beware of copyright infringements, however.

optical character recognition (OCR)   A process that converts the text in a computerized image file into text you can edit with your computer. Used in conjunction with a scanner, you can convert pages of text into computerized text that you can edit with your word processor.

output   The ability to move information from a multimedia application to other sources. Output can be printing or it can be the ability to cut and paste data from the multimedia application to other applications.

photo CD format   Photo CD format, developed by Kodak, is a means of placing high-resolution photographs on CD-ROMs. It is steadily gaining in popularity as a computerized format for photos used in multimedia presentations and by desktop publishers. Before you buy a CD-ROM drive, make sure that it supports the Photo CD format and also multiple Photo CD sessions.

pointing device   Something you manipulate with your hand to help make on-screen selections. The most common type of pointing device is a mouse, but others include trackballs and joysticks.

presentation programs   Originally designed to create text-and-graphics slide shows, this class of computer programs has evolved to make it easy to create multimedia presentations.

proprietary format   A computer file that can only be read by the application that created it. Many other applications, however, can convert commonly used proprietary formats to their own proprietary format. Virtually every major application has its own proprietary format.

proprietary interface One that is designed only to work with a specific CD-ROM drive. Often a variation of the SCSI standard, these interfaces often simplify installation but sometimes make for a slightly slower system.

QuickTime for Windows Another standard program, along with Video for Windows, for handling videos. QuickTime for Windows is closely related to QuickTime for the Macintosh.

random-access memory (RAM) The place that your applications store much of the information needed to run on a moment-to-moment basis. RAM is comprised of a series of chips. The more RAM you have, the more quickly and efficiently your multimedia applications operate.

Real Soon Now (RSN) The high-tech marketeer's version of "the check's in the mail." It is used to describe when a company will release its next, greatest product. It can mean any time from now to the indefinite future.

refresh rate Refers to the frequency with which a monitor replaces lines of electrons that appear on-screen. The electrons activate red, green, and blue phosphors that make up the image on the screen. Higher refresh rates create steadier images, are easier on the eyes, and also display multimedia elements better.

resolution Refers to the number of dots, called pixels, that appear on-screen. The higher the resolution, the greater the amount of detail you see on-screen. Standard VGA resolution, which has 640 pixels per inch by 480 pixels, is adequate for most current multimedia applications but is quickly becoming out of date.

ribbon cable A flat, plastic piece of cable that connects an internal CD-ROM drive to the CD-ROM interface. You must make sure that the edge of the cable that is red (or possibly has a dotted line) connects to pin 1 of the connector located on the interface card.

run-time version A stripped-down version of the multimedia authoring tool. In enables those who receive the multimedia application to play it but not to alter it.

samples Just like it sounds, a sample is a snippet of a sound played back by your sound card. The more samples your sound card can play back, the better the sound quality.

scanner   An input device that reads printed information such as pictures or text and, with the right software, converts images into digital data the computer can understand.

SCSI ID   A number you give to each SCSI device in a daisychain. Each device must have a unique SCSI ID number. Usually, you set the SCSI device number with a switch on the device itself.

SCSI   Stands for Small Computer System Interface (pronounced "SCUZzy"); a common type of CD-ROM interface. It has the advantage of being usable by many other types of devices besides CD-ROM drives. You also can daisychain multiple devices to a single interface. However, they can be complex to install.

self-cleaning lens   A self-cleaning lens refers to the capability of a CD-ROM drive to automatically clean the lens that focuses the laser beam on the CD-ROM. This ensures that the drive accurately finds data. While a good feature, you can always buy an inexpensive add-in kit to clean your drive's lens if the drive doesn't come with this capability.

sequencer   Software that enables you to edit a MIDI file track by track. You can change the instrument played in the track, its tempo and volume, and many other aspects of the music.

shovelware   A derogatory term for multimedia CD-ROMs that contain a lot of information but aren't easy or entertaining to use. Vendors who create shovelware often are intoxicated by the amount of data they can store on CD-ROMs, but don't have the skills or time to create compelling multimedia presentations.

sound card   A sound card plugs into your computer's motherboard. It analyzes the contents of sound files—most typically WAV or MIDI files—and plays them through speakers or headphones.

sound editing software   Lets you record sounds at all possible sampling rates and in mono or stereo. It also lets you do things such as add other sounds and enhance specific parts of a sound file.

Sound Recorder   A utility included with Windows that enables you to record sounds as WAV files and to perform some minor editing functions on the files.

SoundBlaster-compatible   This refers to the capability of any sound card to act like a SoundBlaster sound card. The SoundBlaster was one of the first best-selling cards and many multimedia applications require that your sound card act like a SoundBlaster card.

standards   Generally agreed-upon ways of doing things. Standards exist for items ranging from nuts and bolts to virtually all sorts of computer equipment. There are several international organizations that focus on creating standards.

switches and parameters   You use switches and parameters to modify a command so that it executes in a certain way. A well-known switch is **DIR/W**, which tells DOS to display the results of the DIR command in wide mode.

tchotchke   A gimcrack or doodad. For some, a tchotchke is an ashtray bought at a roadside rest stop commemorating a state or tourist trap. In my house, a tchotchke was something like a pitcher in the shape of a parrot. In the multimedia world, tchotchkes can include CD-ROM driver cleaners and headphones.

terminator   A plug that you attach to the last device in a chain of SCSI devices. This plug closes the loop—without it, your SCSI devices may not work.

text retrieval   A set of software tools built into many multimedia presentations. It enables you to find specific instances of text wherever it is located in the application. This is particularly useful in multimedia reference works because, like an index, it speeds the process of homing in on the precise information you want.

text   Written words. While these days text shares the limelight with other media, it remains one of the key elements of communication—and of multimedia.

timelines   Timelines are a method for precisely setting the starting and ending points for each multimedia element in a presentation. Timelines usually are in dialog boxes that list each element. For each element, there is a slider bar. You drag the ends of the slider bar with your mouse to set the starting and ending points.

video   Refers to live-moving images captured by a video camera. It can show real-life situations, while animation shows, in simple terms, drawings in motion.

video adapter   The video adapter plugs into the motherboard of your PC. It analyzes instructions from your applications, and then passes instructions to your monitor, telling it how to display items on-screen. A fast video adapter with a lot of attached memory helps make multimedia appear crisp and fluid on-screen.

video capture board   A video capture board is an expansion card you plug into your computer's motherboard. It captures video by converting standard analog videos from sources, such as a VCR, to digital videos that you can use in multimedia presentations.

video editing software   This is the software that enables you to cut videos to the proper length, add special effects like fades, mix in additional videos, and add titles.

Video for Windows   Developed by Microsoft, the Video for Windows standard sets guidelines for how Windows and Windows applications deal with video. It was important because it spurred development of standardized and readily available video hardware and software for Windows.

virtual reality   Makes use of special hardware and software to make you feel you are in the midst of the action. Still something of a novelty, over the next few years, virtual reality should become more realistic and more accessible.

voice annotation   A recording of your voice that you can embed in applications, such as word processing documents and spreadsheets. You can use voice annotations to explain or expand on points in your document.

voice recognition   The ability to interact with computers with our voices instead of with keyboards and mice. Hopefully, we won't have to wait until the Starship Enterprise flies before voice recognition becomes practical.

waveform files   Waveform files, often called WAV ("wave") files, are files that store digitized sounds. They are a frequently used type of sound for multimedia and are called WAV files because the files containing these sounds often have the .WAV file extension name. WAV files can contain music, but typically they contain sound effects.

WIN.INI and SYSTEM.INI   These are the two basic Windows startup files. Just like your computer reads the AUTOEXEC.BAT and CONFIG.SYS files when you start your computer and executes the commands located in those files, Windows does the same with WIN.INI and SYSTEM.INI. These two Windows startup files contain many commands needed to run Windows, including commands for multimedia.

Windows Clipboard   You use the Windows Clipboard as an intermediate resting spot when moving or copying information from one document into another. You use the Cut or Copy command in the first application to place the information in the Clipboard, and the Paste command in the second application to insert the information into the new document.

Windows Control Panel   Windows Control Panel is a collection of icons. When you double-click on the icons, you see dialog boxes for adjusting various aspects of Windows. Among the dialog boxes you access from Control Panel is the Drivers dialog box for adding, deleting, and fine-tuning various multimedia software drivers.

Windows Multimedia Extensions   First added to Windows 3.1, Windows multimedia extensions are the software pieces needed for Windows to play multimedia and work with multimedia hardware and software.

Index

Also Available!

The Complete Idiot's Guide
to 1-2-3, New Edition
ISBN: 1-56761-404-3
Softbound, $14.95 USA

The Complete Idiot's Guide to
1-2-3 for Windows
ISBN: 1-56761-400-0
Softbound, $14.95 USA

The Complete Idiot's Guide
to Ami Pro
ISBN: 1-56761-453-1
Softbound, $14.95 USA

The Complete Idiot's Guide to
Buying & Upgrading PCs
ISBN: 1-56761-274-1
Softbound, $14.95 USA

The Complete Idiot's Guide to
Computer Terms
ISBN: 1-56761-266-0
Softbound, $9.95 USA

The Complete Idiot's Guide
to Excel
ISBN: 1-56761-318-7
Softbound, $14.95 USA

The Complete Idiot's Guide
to Internet
ISBN: 1-56761-414-0
Softbound, $19.95 USA

The Complete Idiot's Guide
to The Mac
ISBN: 1-56761-395-0
Softbound, $14.95 USA

The Complete Idiot's Guide
to VCRs
ISBN: 1-56761-294-6
Softbound, $9.95 USA

The Complete Idiot's Guide
to WordPerfect
ISBN: 1-56761-187-7
Softbound, $14.95 USA

The Complete Idiot's Guide to
WordPerfect for Windows
ISBN: 1-56761-282-2
Softbound, $14.95 USA

The Complete Idiot's Guide
to Word for Windows
ISBN: 1-56761-355-1
Softbound, $14.95 USA

The Complete Idiot's Guide
to Works for Windows
ISBN: 1-56761-451-5
Softbound, $14.95 USA

Who cares what you think? WE DO!

We take our customers' opinions very personally. After all, you're the reason we publish these books. If you're not happy, we're doing something wrong.

We'd appreciate it if you would take the time to drop us a note or fax us a fax. A real person—not a computer—reads every letter we get, and makes sure that your comments get relayed to the appropriate people.

Not sure what to say? Here are some details we'd like to know:

- ☞ Who you are (age, occupation, hobbies, etc.)
- ☞ Where you bought the book
- ☞ Why you picked this book instead of a different one
- ☞ What you liked best about the book
- ☞ What could have been done better
- ☞ Your overall opinion of the book
- ☞ What other topics you would purchase a book on

Mail, e-mail, or fax it to:

Faithe Wempen
Product Development Manager
Alpha Books
201 West 103rd Street
Indianapolis, IN 46290

FAX: (317) 581-4669
CIS: 75430,174

Special Offer!

Alpha Books needs people like you to give opinions about new and existing books. Product testers receive free books in exchange for providing their opinions about them. If you would like to be a product tester, please mention it in your letter, and make sure you include your full name, address, and daytime phone.